Mary Buford Hitz

For Love of the Land

A HISTORY OF
THE WINTERGREEN COMMUNITY

For
Love
of the
Land

A HISTORY OF THE WINTERGREEN COMMUNITY

MARY BUFORD HITZ

First Edition

© 2016 The Nature Foundation at Wintergreen

ISBN: 978-1-938205-24-8

Library of Congress Control Number: 2015956069

Portions of *Roar of the Heavens* by Stefan Bechtel reprinted with permission from the author.

Printed in the United States of America

BLACKWELL
PRESS

LYNCHBURG, VIRGINIA
BLACKWELLPRESS.NET

THE NATURE
FOUNDATION
at Wintergreen
NURTURING LOVE FOR THE LAND

3421 Wintergreen Drive, Wintergreen, VA 22967
TWNF.org
434-325-8169

In memory of Carolyn Barkley

"CB"
Whose subtle wit, love of history, and love
of Wintergreen contributed greatly to the
accomplishment of this book.

Contents

Prologue

The legacy of Wintergreen belongs to those who dreamed it, those who sold the dream, and those who turned it into reality. Its natural beauty existed long before its inception, setting the stage for the dream, and, thankfully, is still largely intact today. This book is a tribute to the commitment of all involved including career-long staff members, managers, and the property owners who ultimately made it all work. Without their love, support, and appreciation of Wintergreen's natural beauty, the dream's fulfillment would never have become reality.

It is our hope that what attracted us transcends the generations that follow. While we cannot live in the past, a vision of what it took to create Wintergreen should set a precedent for its future.

The names below honor those who responded to the prologue pledge and made *For Love of the Land* possible. Thank you.

For Love of the Land
$1,000 Level Donors
Pam and Jonathan Ansell
Dr. and Mrs. Eugene M. Bane Jr.
Barbara-lyn Belcher and A. Gordon
    Goodykoontz
Julia and Whitfield Broome
Mary Ellen Condon-Rall and
    Wilfrid Rall
Betty and Ed Dinwiddie
Linda C. Russell
Diana and Kit Smith
Sharan and Ronald Soltau and Mimi
Wintergreen Resort Premier
    Properties

For Love of the Land
$500 Level Donors
Jo Ann and Morgan Armstrong
Kristin and Rob Armstrong
Beverly and John Bates
Jean and Bruce Bertelsen
Nancy and Ben Birindelli
Kathryn Ansell Brennan MD and
    Samuel Brennan
Terri and Art Brooks
Syd and Ed Buynacek
Kathleen and Brennan Carmody

Charlee Channing and Brian Chase
Doug Coleman
Gerald P. Cox
Cindy and John Coy
Judy and Gerry DeWitt
Carter and Brent Douglass
Kathy and Joe Ely
Peter Farley
Mack Faulkner, Cecelia Faulkner
    Soscia, and Jim Faulkner
Mary and Don Faulkner
Barbara Fletcher, Jim Fletcher, and
    Betsy Barnett
Barbara and Ray Floersch
Leigh and Ed Foley
Lynn Fontana and Rob Pritchard
Gary Green
Ellen Hampton
Mary and David Harder
Helen L. Jacobs and
    William T. Hohe
Mr. and Mrs. Crawley Joyner III
Judy and Dave Juergens
Tish and Ernie Keppel (in memory of)
Mary B. and Robert Klein
Lynn and Larry Luessen
Marjolaine and Steve Marianella
Betty-Driver and Jim McCaa

Rita and David McKenzie
Janice L. Miller MD and
    David A. Acton
Mountain Area Realty
Joost and Gunter Muller
Rita and George Nicklas
Beverly and William Garrett Ouzts
Nancy and Doug Pitts
Cicely and Ken Powell
Lydia Pulley and Rodney Willett
Rockfish River Gallery by
    Kathy Bonham
Pat and Charlie Schulte
Sylvia Shenk and Family
Evalane and Bill Slaughter
Joyce and Carl Stargardt
Marti and Joe Szczur
Hon. Anthony F. Troy and Family
Esther Vaughan and
    Lee and Jimmy Beasley
Carolyn and Richard Velletri
Priscilla Wakeman Wampler and
    J. Paul Wampler
Cindy and Stuart Williams
Sylvia and Peter Winik
Carolyn P. Wood

SIGNIFICANT LEGACY GIFTS DONATED TO ENSURE THE FUTURE OF THE NATURE FOUNDATION AT WINTERGREEN

Carolyn Barkley
Yvonne and Earl Behm
Linda and Michael Donovan
Gana and Jim Dunlop
Pam and Christopher Gale

Marj and Desmond Gourley
Betty and Morris Johnson
Ellen and William Kealy
Dahne and Chip Morgan
Elizabeth and Oliver Pollard

Mary Beth and Gordon Smyth
Lisa and Robert Thalhimer
Kappy and Helmut Wakeham

From the Author

Each time I take up a writing project, whether it is self-generated or comes as the result of a contract with others, there is a moment of real exhilaration. Most of this comes from it being a leap into the unknown, whether it is fiction or non-fiction. How long will it take? What research is involved? Who will help when I get stuck? Will the stimulus I feel at the beginning hold up to the finish?

By happenstance it turns out that the development of Wintergreen has spanned my adult life. Its existence has always been of interest to me because I live nearby, love the Blue Ridge Mountains and, like many others, have been alternately admiring and made nervous by the scope of the development.

Taking on the writing of its history has meant depending on the time and patience of my sponsors, the accuracy of the transcripts of interviews done before I was hired, and the willingness of others who are deeply involved in the life of Wintergreen to let me interview them. I needn't have worried about being bored by the work; the history of Wintergreen is flat-out fascinating, with more turns and twists than a who-done-it.

What I wrote often needed the corrections of those who had lived day by day through the events being described, and remembered them vividly. This was done in monthly meetings where, over time, my sponsors, Don Faulkner, George Nicklas, Peter Farley, Gunter Muller, and Doug Coleman became friends, not just editors.

It is Doug Coleman, though, who gets the lion's share of credit for keeping everyone's feet to the fire, and for coming to my rescue when I couldn't see my way forward. He has spent many, many hours making sense out of confusion, and I am deeply indebted to him for it. Our publisher, Nancy Blackwell Marion, has also had a big hand in helping me through the editing process, and I thank her as well.

M. B. H.

x

Acknowledgements

A RECORD OF WINTERGREEN'S HISTORY has been attempted several times previously. Good documentation in the early days by Don Faulkner and others was essential. Later interest and work by property owners Earle Holliday, Jack Manherz, and Vince Fiore helped keep the concept of a written history alive till The Foundation's concerted efforts over the last four years. These latter efforts were started while Don Faulkner was a member of the Nature Foundation Board and with the extraordinary leadership of Carolyn Barkley, our beloved board president who succumbed unexpectedly to cancer on May 12, 2013. Carolyn was a professional librarian, highly skilled as a researcher and published historian. As such, she was expecting to take a leadership role in the project. She and her family provided a significant financial gift to initiate *For Love of the Land*.

The Book Committee was initially comprised of Don Faulkner, Gunter Muller, Peter Farley, Paul Spence , Carolyn Barkley, and myself. Together the Committee interviewed and chose an author and publisher and got under way. Since a number of the early planners, managers, and financial experts were still available to us, we had the benefit of personal interviews with many of them. The Committee evolved as the project took shape into a smaller group made up of Don Faulkner, George Nicklas, Gunter Muller, Peter Farley, and myself. Together this committee represented over 200 years of experience with the Wintergreen story and the book represents to the best of our collective knowledge, an accurate rendition of the events that led to Wintergreen's inception and path to reality. Other traditional sales staff of Wintergreen Real Estate and the original Wintergreen Development team provided a wealth of information and Wintergreen Real Estate gave permission to use many of their photographs. Many of the early construction photographs were also provided by Bar Delk. L. F. Payne, Stuart Sadler, Tim Merrick, Tim Hess, Gary Horvath, and others were enthusiastic about the project and always willing to help.

Interviewed members of the original development team included Gary Green, L. F. Payne, Larry Rutherford, Ed Morrissett, and Frank Louthan, the latter two being part of Jim Wheat's original BLM team. All provided personal interviews with Don Faulkner and other committee members. Members of the early planning and design efforts also came forward for interviews. George Pillorge and Byrd LaPrade come to mind, but there were others as well.

There were many times in the early development days when the failure of Wintergreen seemed imminent and most eastern resorts faced or went through bankruptcy one or more times. Wintergreen survived those trying times during early oil embargos, high interest rates, cost overruns, second home tax issues, and related recessions. During these times L. F. Payne's unique leadership efforts were a major factor in Wintergreen's survival. In many of our Committee discussions of those trying times, it was interesting how our perceptions changed as we realized that some member of the Committee had first-hand knowledge that changed what each of us had sometimes mistakenly assumed we knew as truth.

Doing a book by committee is a frustrating process for participants but especially for the author who suffered through many, many re-writes. Mary Buford Hitz evolved as the perfect author. Being from a prominent Richmond family whose traditional summer home lies within sight of Wintergreen, she knew many of the original investors and advisors that Don Faulkner and Jim Wheat sought out in the beginning. She came to Committee meetings at Wintergreen from Charlottesville on Wednesdays so she could attend choir practice at Emmanuel Church in Greenwood afterwards, but we all suspected that she instead went to prayer meetings after listening to all of us argue the facts that would change her text many times over. As such she earned trust and great admiration from the group.

Mary Buford's laid back leadership role as author was also reflected in our publisher, Nancy Blackwell

Marion of Blackwell Press in Lynchburg. Nancy patiently struggled with low resolution photos ultimately turning the book into the best possible finished product. Without the efforts of these two, we would have all likely needed to go to prayer meetings. Nancy was chosen in part because of her collaborative accomplishment with Paul Saunders in his magnificent book *Heartbeats of Nelson*. Paul, generous as always, allowed us to use the Camille photos from his book.

The reader will note that the book is clearly most focused on Wintergreen's early days and it was assumed that those chapters represented what today's owners and visitors know the least about. As such, well over half the book's chapters focus on the years before and up to 1975 which was the "soft opening" of the first ski season. Major focus is also given to the 1980's as Wintergreen became known as a national example of an environmentally sensitive community with excellent resort amenities.

The legacy of *For Love of the Land* represents one of the most rewarding projects I have worked on in my 40 years at Wintergreen. Despite all the debate that went on in regard to "who did what" or "why things happened in the manner that they did," we all learned from one another's related experiences. There was no other way to get to the "truth" in the book other than by committee, and the entertaining humor of the stories always led us back to our purpose in being together. Following is a tribute to fellow committee members and to all who participated in providing the facts and the "glue of reality" that held all the stories together.

"The Book Committee"
Don Faulkner, 1968. With no dream there would have been no Wintergreen. Don Faulkner's unique ability to paint a picture that Jim Wheat (who was blind) understood, and Don's ability to convince others who were both non-blind and skeptical, was a once in a lifetime accomplishment. This included not only early investors but also an often skeptical Nelson County community. His work to prove the project's feasibility that led to the purchase by Jim Wheat's team was no less celebratory. Don's continued involvement beyond the early development years was an inspiration to many and he remains healthy and inspirational in the current

moment as he tells the stories of what took place. It all started with Don Faulkner's dream.

George Nicklas, 1974. George could perhaps be best described as the "Director of Reality" at Wintergreen for the last 42 years. Readers are encouraged to note the text on page 68 for the compelling description given by Gunter Muller. George remembered the methods followed and in almost all cases knew the underlying truth that drove decisions and understood the mission to succeed. His military discipline and his adherence to disclosure and the truth made him an invaluable member of the Book Committee. He spent weeks chasing down photos that led in most cases to valuable reunions with those who supported him over the years. His years of input on the Committee as well as his tenure in the "dreams to reality" stages of Wintergreen remind us that respect and trust are ultimately earned rather than given.

Gunter Muller, 1980. Gunter, arriving in 1980, brought order and professionalism to a fledgling resort that would become both regionally and nationally known within a few years after his arrival. For over 20 years he led a team of managers and staff whose respect he earned, cherished, and nurtured over the years. Staff and managers who remain at Wintergreen today still hold him and his wife Joost in high esteem as a tribute to the efforts of both of them. He led by example for his staff, knew them all by name, and had the reputation for being everywhere at all times. Staff recognized this as "support effort" rather than "oversight" as he always gave staff creative latitude to do their jobs. The successful, "on the edge" efforts of Mark Glickman in marketing and the "competent independence" of Ski Area Manager Uel Gardner mentioned in the book are some of the best examples of this. Gunter had an innate ability to recognize the unique talent of his staff (sometimes before they did) and they were in turn inspired by his confidence in them. As a result of this he was able to get great participation from former managers and staff that others would not have gotten in helping produce the book.

Peter Farley, 1973. Peter was Wintergreen's earliest sales person of record, who successfully sold the dream when there were no amenities. To our knowledge, as of today he represents the longest continuous serving Wintergreen community employee. As such Peter arrived and worked in the early 70's with Gary Green in the conceptual state of the project. He, along with Tim Merrick, provided some extremely entertaining stories, some of which we could not print. (He may be willing to tell some of these by appointment only, depending on who wants to know.) As a partner in the Wintergreen Real Estate organization, Peter still enjoys and sells "the dream" of living at Wintergreen. His early personal relationships with local people like Marguerite Wade and other local families did much to establish trust within the county. If Peter had not had the ability to sell the "Nature" of Wintergreen when there was nothing else visible, Wintergreen's ability to move forward in those days would have likely not been successful. He served as an example to the sales staff members who followed, and remains fully subscribed to the original concept of Wintergreen.

Special thanks go out as well to the following groups or individuals.

Terri Brooks, board president (2016) of The Nature Foundation at Wintergreen and an experienced editor, who spent many hours assisting with the book's final edits, adding a fresh set of eyes when all of us were weary.

Wintergreen Real Estate's long-term knowledge of the community through senior sales staff/realtors Kyle Lynn, Tim Merrick, Tim Hess, and Gary Horvath; attorney Stuart Sadler; Dick Carroll; and others mentioned in the book. Bo Newell is not forgotten as an important part of this team. He eventually formed Mountain Area Realty which currently has Chastity Morgan at the helm.

Wintergreen Premier Partners with Steve Marianella and Brian Chase (who has a childhood connection with Gary Green) provided financial support and voiced encouragement for the book.

WPOA. Russell Otis, Theresa Harris, Stan Olah, and Curtis Sheets provided interviews and photos.

Wintergreen Resort. Valuable contributions came from long term managers, especially Dan Schablein, Lynn Tyler, and Betsy Dunkerton, among others. General Manager Hank Thiess also deserves credit for recognizing the importance of the book and graciously allowing these senior employees to participate in the project.

Many employees and property owners provided photos from their personal collections. We also celebrate the lives of those valuable employees and early owners we have lost over the time period covered in the book. Many are memorialized by photos or listings in the book.

We are extremely grateful to those who took part in the prologue pledge to make the book financially possible. Their understanding and appreciation for Wintergreen's uniqueness is a most important part of its legacy and its future.

Lastly we are grateful to you, the reader for being interested enough to purchase and read the book. By doing so, Wintergreen's legacy and its future also belong to you. Treasure, protect, and enjoy its natural assets.

Thank you.

Doug Coleman

CHAPTER ONE

The Beauty That Time Built

Maybe, if you had grown up in Jackson Hole, you might not stop as you drove through the Blue Ridge Mountains. The Tetons in your home territory, in all their sky-piercing, angular glory, are relative newcomers on the geological scene. They flaunt their youth, daring photographers, hikers and skiers to record their breath-taking views, scale their heights and ski their virgin snow. Young people are attracted to these young mountains as if a magnet has a hold on them.

On the other hand, if you have grown up in the Blue Ridge Mountains of Central Virginia and find yourself in Jackson Hole, you might feel slightly ill at ease with the scale of the mountains all around you. Awed by their majesty, yes, but also overwhelmed by their size, the severity of their climate and the dangers they pose to the uninitiated. These are active mountains. They spawn avalanches in the winter, and in summer snow and hail catch poorly clad hikers and send them into hypothermia.

Those of us who have come to treasure the solid, rounded mountains that are the Blue Ridge, feel, when we are in them, the tranquility of their age. Yes, they call us to explore their trails, hunt, fish their streams, and swim in the occasional deep pools of those streams. But they also call us to lie in a hammock, peering up through the canopy of oaks as through a leafy kaleidoscope before dropping off to sleep. Most of the time they are quiet mountains.

They are also approachable. If, magically, you were set down on the top of one of them, you could make your way off and down to the valley, scratched up and mosquito-bitten through the rocks, trees, and brush, but in one piece.

The Blue Ridge Mountains are comfortable and comforting, and above all usable mountains. That's not to say that they don't pose their own dangers— venomous snakes and freak storms, such as the backlash from Hurricane Camille, about which you'll hear more later in this story.

Wintergreen is privileged to occupy several of the most beautiful slopes, ridges, and valleys to be found in the Blue Ridge. Its highest peak, Devils Knob, is nearly 4,000 feet high, and views from it are spectacular. According to 2015 figures, there are 2,777 individual properties on two of its mountains that resemble something like a city-state; while in the fields and woods of the Rockfish Valley community of Stoney Creek there are 1,097 properties.

Whether you are up above or down below you are unaware of this density. Both areas were planned and executed with an environmental sensitivity that is expressed in every aspect of the community, which in the 1970s was a radical new concept.

It is a community that might never be built today, as there would be too many lengthy time delays from all the bureaucratic red tape. As it happened there were several times when the difficulties of the terrain,

Catoctin greenstone

Folding and faulting lines visible on a highway cut

the scope of the project and economic and financial upheavals almost brought it to a halt. The tale of Wintergreen's coming to be is a very human story, and we will embark on it, but not before looking at what came before it—way before it.

MAN WAS NOT RESPONSIBLE for the stunning natural beauty of the Blue Ridge. The shape of its landscape developed over the slow march of geologic time. These old mountains, created a few hundred million years ago in the Paleozoic Era, now have a benign appearance that belies their tumultuous birth.

"What we're seeing now are the remains of what was once a majestic range, with altitudes probably comparable to the Rockies," explains Thomas Biggs, an environmental sciences professor at the University of Virginia. "Virginia had an amazingly violent history that included several continental collisions, the most recent of which was with North Africa some 300 million years ago. The Blue Ridge, Virginia's geologic backbone, was the product of an event that moved rocks from Richmond to Afton."

Long before the folding and faulting that pushed up the Blue Ridge, huge lava flows rose through fissures in the earth's crust. They formed a layer of volcanic rock, or basalt, that was thousands of feet thick and ran ribbon-like from Lynchburg to Maryland. Heat and pressure metamorphosed the basalt into a greenstone named for Maryland's Catoctin Mountain. Blasting Afton Mountain to build Interstate 64 exposed that volcanic component, according to Michael Upchurch, geologist with Virginia's Division of Mineral Resources. "The distinctive gray-green rock face is Catoctin greenstone. The green color comes from the minerals chlorite and epidote. Many of the roads and highways in this part of Virginia exhibit that green tint because of the use of Catoctin greenstone in the asphalt."

Despite its color, greenstone weathers into a rust red soil because of its high iron content. Doug Coleman, director of the Nature Foundation at Wintergreen, sees more than beautiful scenery when he surveys the world from the narrow ridge of Rockfish Gap. He sees three of Virginia's five physiographic provinces. "Afton Mountain is on the western edge of the Blue Ridge physiographic province, identified by underlying rock formations that extend 20 miles east to Charlottesville. On a clear day, you can look east beyond Charlottesville and see the Piedmont Province. Just west is the Valley and Ridge Province. Only the Appalachian Plateau in the southwest corner of the state and the Coastal Plain are too far away to see."

The Paleozoic Era ended with a bang; some 320 million years ago Africa collided with the east coast of North America. It collided hard enough to shove rock layers westward several hundred miles during this Alleghany orogeny. All the folds in the Appalachian ridges and valleys west of the Blue Ridge are like a throw rug that has been scooted against a wall. In addition, formations ruptured so that older rock layers could slide over younger ones, in contrast to the natural sequence of "oldest on the bottom layer." This episode of mountain building lasted at least ten million years.

At this point, at the beginning of the Mesozoic Era some 250 million years ago, all the various continents of the world were assembled into one, and were surrounded by one ocean. Since there was no Atlantic Ocean all the drainage was to the west to shallow seas that covered much of today's Great Plains. About 230 million years ago the earth rumbled again as the world began to fragment into our current configuration of continents. As the Atlantic Ocean basin began to open, North America sagged down and began to drain eastward.

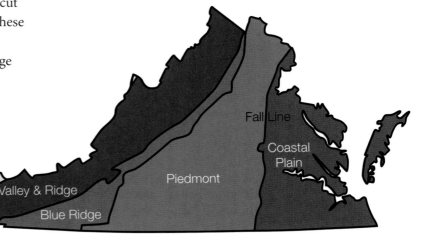

Wisconsin glaciation

At one time, all the Atlantic streams and rivers north of Roanoke had their headwaters west of the Blue Ridge. Their former courses are marked by gaps in the Blue Ridge from Roanoke to Front Royal.

As the three major rivers, the Staunton (Roanoke), the James, and the Potomac eroded downward, they cut sharp gorges through the Blue Ridge. Tributaries to these three big rivers extended their headwaters north and south into the soluble limestone behind the Blue Ridge and decapitated all the smaller streams in a process called stream piracy. Granite, greenstone and meta-sandstone—all are very resistant to rainwater—they stand starkly above more easily eroded rock on either side.

Based on mterial from: web.wm.edu/geology/virginia

3

Pedlar gneiss, a granitic rock

During the peak of the Wisconsinan ice advance south 20,000 years ago, glacial ice reached to present day Pennsylvania and New Jersey. As a result of this colder climate, northern white spruce forests dominated in the Blue Ridge south of the ice sheets. Our currently predominating forests likely existed only in tiny populations on the south-facing mountain slopes and river bluffs, and in greater abundance much farther south. Following the retreat of the ice back into Canada 12,000 years ago, northern forests were out-competed by the more southern (austral) forests as temperatures warmed. The spruce and fir that had formerly predominated could migrate back north or still compete on the highest peaks in search of cooler temperatures. Early man would have seen and lived with these changing forests. Even today, Wintergreen has a few specimens left from the boreal forests at higher, and therefore colder, elevations with northern exposure.

When early colonial explorers from seaport villages crossed from the tidewater region to the piedmont, they saw, from Virginia to North Carolina, a ridge of rock shrouded in a blue haze.

But long before the colonial explorers, this area had been occupied by Native Americans for at least 10,000 years, archeological study has revealed. By the Late Woodland period (900 to 1600 AD), Monocan villages were established in the floodplains of the James and its tributaries between the Blue Ridge and the fall line. What we know as the Shenandoah Valley would have had buffalo roaming its prairie-like grasses. East of the Blue Ridge the Monocan Indians, a Siouan tribe, lived in villages with walls, where they grew "the Three Sisters," corn, beans, and squash. Every year they would leave their villages to visit their hunting campgrounds, where they hunted elk, deer, bear, and smaller game.

Monocan culture was similar to that of the Powhatans, who lived to the east in the coastal plain. The two tribes were frequently at war until a common enemy, the English colonists, made them allies.

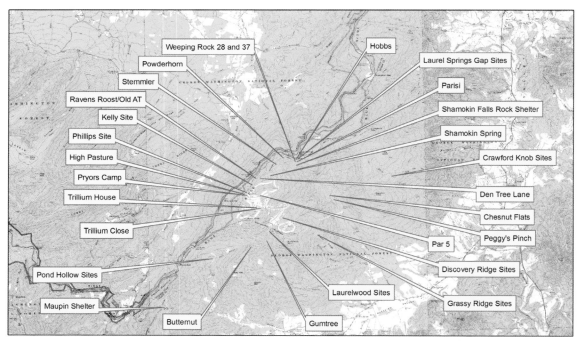

Wintergreen Archaeological Survey, Sites Recorded 2003–2010

RESEARCH BY DR. CAROLE NASH, JAMES MADISON UNIVERSITY, FUNDED BY THE NATURE FOUNDATION AT WINTERGREEN

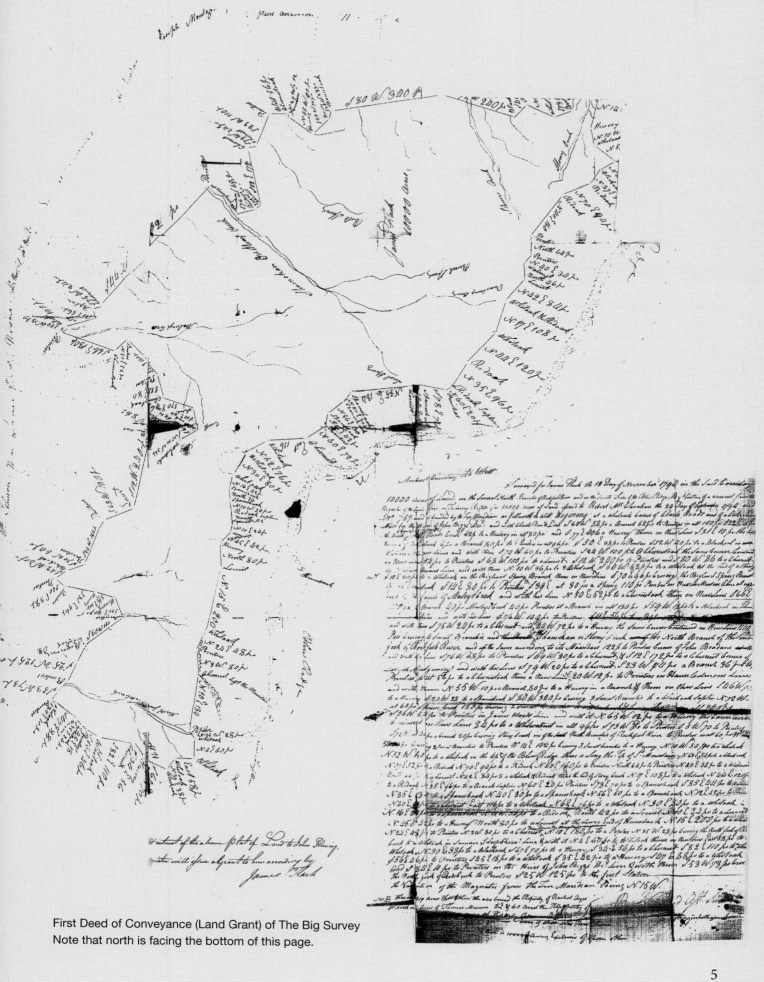

First Deed of Conveyance (Land Grant) of The Big Survey
Note that north is facing the bottom of this page.

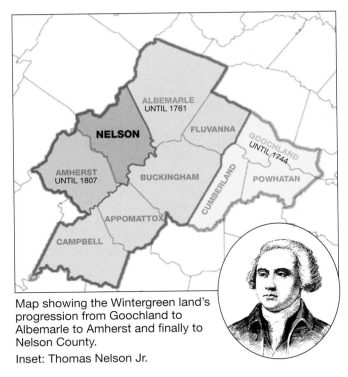

Map showing the Wintergreen land's progression from Goochland to Albemarle to Amherst and finally to Nelson County.

Inset: Thomas Nelson Jr.

Drive, into a terrifying challenge.

The earliest settlers in the Rockfish Valley in the 1730s grew tobacco, wheat, oats, apples, peaches, and hay, as well as vegetables in their kitchen gardens. The first recorded land grant in the Wintergreen area was, surprisingly, to a woman named Rachel Ayers. It was in what is now the Laurel Springs Gap and Pryor's Camp area.

One expression of the history of Virginia's growth is through its creation of counties. If you think of those sets of Russian dolls that have a large outside doll that holds progressively smaller dolls, you will have the process of county division—smaller created out of bigger—correctly in your head.

Until 1744 the land Wintergreen is on was in very large Goochland County. At this point the Russian doll opened up, shed a layer, and big Albemarle County came into existence. Since it included land on both sides of the James River (then called the Fluvanna River) the first county seat and courthouse was at Scottsville.

Allen Howard patented the first land in the future Nelson County in 1728 on the James River, and it soon became known as Howardsville. At that point it was still Goochland County. In the 18th century and well into the 19th, rivers were the main highways of Virginia, and Mr. Howard, as well as the influential Cabell family (James River settlers from 1734), could see future commerce in the area needing access to bigger markets downriver.

There was another Russian doll trick in 1761, at which point there were 100 patentees in the area. Big Amherst County was created which included present-day Nelson. The smallest doll, the present Nelson County, was created in 1807, when there were 400 patentees, grant holders, and other individual plats. Thomas Nelson Jr., for whom the county is named, was a signer of the Declaration of Independence and governor of the commonwealth in 1781, as well as a financer of the American Revolution. When the British chose his home on the York River as headquarters near the end of the war, he was reputed to have offered a reward to any cannoneer who could be the first to put a cannon ball into his home.

Another Virginia county had been named for him, but when Kentucky separated from Virginia in 1792 it

Contact with the English proved fatal. By 1699, the Monocans had largely disappeared, their numbers reduced by war and disease. A century later the buffalo had also vanished.

Almost 100 Native American sites were discovered by archaeologist Dr. Carole Nash from James Madison University in the developed part of Wintergreen, with the majority found around the Black Rock Village Center. Wintergreen artifacts include pottery, projectile points, stone tools, and a necklace piece. It is ironic that the 20th century developers spent a good deal of money to site the Black Rock Center, when man had been choosing the site for thousands of years!

At more than 3,000 feet, Wintergreen can offer those from the tidewater parts of the state or from Washington, DC, significantly cooler, less humid temperatures in the summer. Overnight temperatures that dip even more make for good sleeping weather. Likewise in winter the temperature is low enough to make snow for skiing, bringing not just those who come from afar, but also enthusiastic skiers and college hot shots from nearby towns like Charlottesville, Waynesboro, Lexington, and Staunton.

The weather condition that Wintergreen could do without is the occasional epic, blinding, distorting, low cloud cover. It can settle in for hours or for days, and can make the winding entrance road, Wintergreen

Old church at the bend of the road in the community of Wintergreen.

became part of Kentucky, so in 1807 he was honored again by the Commonwealth of Virginia.

Migration into the county came from two different directions. The English came from the coastal regions to the east, unused to the muddy, rutted roads of Central Virginia, as in the tidewater they had travelled primarily by creeks and rivers. The Scots-Irish and the Germans came from the north, via the Great Wagon Road that continued down from Pennsylvania through the middle of the Shenandoah Valley headed south and west.

Old enmities from the British Isles were so ingrained in the Ulster Scots that they carried over into the New World. The Blue Ridge symbolized a cultural as well as geographic dividing line. The English in eastern Virginia had created a plantation economy dependent on the use of slaves. The Scots-Irish and the Germans tended to be small farmers who worked their own land. Presbyterians and other illegal dissenting religious groups resented that Virginia's Anglican churches were tax-supported.

But wherever they came from, to move into the wilds of Central Virginia they needed to be tough, independent, resourceful people, and so they proved to be. They moved into old-growth forests where making a pasture or space for a kitchen garden required grueling work. The trees needed to be felled and the stumps pulled out years after rotting in place. A house needed to be built from these logs. The settler may have had an ox or a horse to make this work easier, or he may have borrowed one from his neighbor.

Children would be sent out wearing aprons with pockets to spend hours picking up stones to make a field that would sustain an ox, a milk cow, and perhaps a horse. They would gather the stones for the length of the field, and then amuse themselves at the other end by building cairns and stone towers. Even young children were expected to feed the animals and haul the water, which luckily was plentiful in Nelson County.

Meanwhile the doctor was a long horseback ride away. The triple summer scourges of mosquitoes, ticks, and heavy humidity made disease spread as quickly as

Spruce Creek Mill, also called Wintergreen Mill, later called Harris Mill

the onset of a summer thunderstorm. Neighbors who had been around longer and were familiar with local herbal remedies were frequently sought out for their skills, probably learned from the Native Americans.

ALL THAT REMAINS OF THE VILLAGE of Wintergreen, which grew up at the junction of Route 151 and Spruce Creek Lane, is an old store (now a natural history museum) and the deteriorating manor house looking down on the intersection. Construction of the once-handsome clapboard house with a two-story porch was started by Hawes Coleman, in the 1790s, and completed in 1802. For most of the rest of

The old Wintergreen Post Office

the 19th century the house passed down to Coleman sons, and a thriving village of corn, grain, and saw mills, a store, blacksmith shop, foundry and a few residences grew up at the intersection.

Coleman's "Mill Tract" was bought at auction in 1880 by the mercantile partnership of Slaughter and Fitzpatrick, and the village became known as Slaughters; but not for long, as the new postmaster renamed it Wintergreen in 1901.

Slaughter's store, and eventually the mills, were bought in the late 1800s by John Gannaway, a local character who did a land-office business in manufacturing alcohol. Supposedly one year he had four stills running at once, making more than 100 barrels of apple brandy, but only declaring and paying taxes on two. The other 98 barrels he hid around the neighborhood.

The revenuers were tipped off and confiscated the lot, reportedly having to borrow 20 wagons from local farmers to haul the contraband to Rockfish Depot. A railroad conductor later recalled that the train was held up at least an hour loading the barrels, some of which had sprung leaks. The tracks smelled deliciously of apple brandy.

Wintergreen Mill wheel in the lobby of the Mountain Inn

Gannaway went on to distill corn whiskey, which instead of hiding he drank too much of, causing him to be seriously ill. When he recovered his mind was gone.

John W. Harris bought Wintergreen Farm in 1900, and gave acreage across the road to his son, Grover, so that he could build a "store and dwelling place." From 1929 until 1957 the Wintergreen Post Office was in this store. Grover purchased the Wintergreen mill, which he ran until 1953, when he was trapped and killed by the mill wheel while trying to clear an obstruction.

The fledgling Wintergreen Resort bought the store and mill property. It used the store as a sales office,

PHOTO COURTESY OF KEN LAWLESS

Interrupted fern

and took the mill wheel and grinding stones up the mountain to be the centerpiece of the lobby of the Mountain Inn.

Until recent times, much of this mountain land had not been farmed or developed, which means that the original forest floor ecosystems still exist, and both wildflowers and wildlife are a very fragile and narrow link between northeast and southwest along the range here. This is evidenced by the number of bears sighted or killed as they try to cross the highways at Rockfish Gap, and the hawk, monarch butterfly, and green darner dragonfly migrations that occur along this ridge.

As work began to turn The Big Survey into Wintergreen, there were discoveries of unique and rare species such as ancient fern beds. This was before environmental impact statements required developers to recognize and preserve what could be considered historical or natural wonders. Developers did not want to hear about anything living being killed, or anything associated with early man that might hold up progress on the project.

So from the get-go there was a built-in tension between Wintergreen as envisioned and the practical realities on the ground. Those who were passionate about preservation of the botanically unique species that could never be replaced had to work to come up with a rationale to be used with those who were more concerned with the bottom line.

They ended up taking the tack with developers that these unique species added value to the reputation that Wintergreen set out to achieve of being among the foremost environmentally sensitive communities in the nation. This was a smart but perilous tack to take, involving vigilance and battles lost as well as won.

The trick at the time was to tie this unique identity into the marketing of the place, which satisfied those keeping track of the dollars as it seemed to make marketing sense. As the years went by and the community began to win awards and accolades, the tack was justified. We will see in these pages the compromises made on both sides, the battles won and lost, but at forty-five years of age it is significant that Wintergreen can still claim to have—as was its original goal—much more acreage of undisturbed wild than of developed.

Don Faulkner

CHAPTER TWO

The Big Survey and the Man Who Fell in Love with It

In 1961, Earl Hamner's book, *Spencer's Mountain*, came out. It is about a young boy growing up in Nelson County, and it made an impression on Don Faulkner. Don was a Richmonder with a reverence for nature. Horses, farming, and ranching were in his blood, and at that time he was newly employed in farm and ranch management. He was and is a passionate man, an extrovert who will make friends with the fella on the street corner who asks him for a dollar. Quite possibly the two could end up in a diner, talking.

Don, in addition to being a prize-winning talker, is also a good listener and questioner. He catches possible leads in a conversation, follows up those leads, dreams dreams, and has a bullish faith that at least some of them can be brought to fruition. Wintergreen would never have happened if not for Don's dreams. His down home manner is not a disguise, and don't underestimate the mind behind it; it is sharp and remembers everything.

As Ed Morrissett, a Faulkner contemporary and an advisor to Jim Wheat, commented recently, "You can't over-emphasize how much Don Faulkner is the thread through this whole thing, (Wintergreen) from then until now."

Don's exuberant, inquisitive, and idealistic take on life is coupled with constant tension and what he referred to as behindedness. This was caused by his extreme difficulty with left-brain activities such as organizing, ordering, prioritizing, learning, and paper and computer work. This has kept him most of his life in a chronic state of stress, resulting in a roller coaster experience of the ups and the downs of frequent depression.

He has sometimes been led by his idealism and dreams to dead ends; but not in the case of The Big Survey, which, with careful study, research, good contacts, and commitment, became a vision that came true. Everyone who knows Don loves him, but keeping up with him when he is in the throes of an enthusiasm can be confusing and exhausting.

In early 1963 Don had to give up his work in farm and ranch management and the expectation of raising his family on a farm or ranch. His mental difficulties created such havoc that he could barely manage his own life, let alone any farm or ranch. With his dream and passion shattered he was "a lost ball in tall weeds," as a friend of his said.

His good friend Jack McElroy, a young officer in J.C.Wheat & Co., suggested he talk to Jim Wheat, a successful Richmond businessman and entrepreneur with whom Don was acquainted, and who shared a love of land, horseback riding, and hunting. Don did so, and speaking about it all these years later says, "Jim did all he could to help me, sending me out to do evaluations on land and real estate projects of interest to him. He kept saying "you have got to do something with land.""

A Wheat-related real estate group had retained Fred McCall as a consultant. With Wheat's introduction, Don went to work for McCall, a well-respected real estate appraiser, consultant, and broker. Working with him nearly three years for up to 60 or more hours a week, including brokerage in addition to appraisal, Don got his solid foundation in real estate.

In 1965, Joe Stettinius, a good friend, invited Jim Covington and Don to join him in buying out a remainder interest in a small real estate firm with a healthy rental and management business. The plan was that Jim and Joe would concentrate on commercial and residential real estate development and management, and Don on brokerage, primarily of high-value country properties.

It was not long before Don had an opportunity to list as an agent and sell to the Elisabeth Scott Bocock family a large and beautiful property bordering the Skyline Drive above Greenwood Hollow, a stone's throw from property the family owned. This became the catalyst for his listing and selling a number of Blue Ridge mountain properties totaling several thousand acres in Albemarle County over the next few years.

The first time Don heard of The Big Survey was in a book written by a real estate mentor of his, Bill Stevens. The book featured outstanding properties in the Charlottesville area. Stevens' description of this mammoth mountainous property of 10,000+ acres called The Big Survey fascinated Don. An accompanying picture of a 400-pound black bear deepened the allure.

Not only was The Big Survey a physically challenging and spectacularly beautiful part of the landscape, but a century earlier the busy historic Howardsville Turnpike had traversed it. In the first half of the 19th century the livelihood of those living in the

more remote western regions of the commonwealth depended on their ability to get their goods, farm and mineral products, and livestock to eastern markets. For these settlers, the fastest way to Richmond was the James River.

For those in the Shenandoah Valley, this meant crossing the Blue Ridge to get to Howardsville on the James. The first section of the turnpike was authorized by the legislature in 1847, and when completed, it was carrying a daily load of wagons filled with flour, whiskey, corn and other grains, and vegetables. There were also beasts of burden carrying crates of chickens balanced on either side, as well as livestock being driven along on their own steam.

Wagons of iron ore, lime, gypsum, other minerals, and a variety of seeds from the Shenandoah Valley also made their tedious way up and across the face of Humpback Mountain on the Howardsville Turnpike. This was a long and arduous trek for teams of horses and mules, livestock, men, women, girls, and boys.

By 1850 both the Howardsville and Rockfish Gap Turnpikes had a superintendent and crew that saw to the very challenging maintenance of these roads, used all year and subject to blockage by heavy snowfall and washouts. However, the heyday of turnpikes over mountains didn't last long. By the end of the 1850s, trains were using the Crozet Tunnel, going through the Blue Ridge Mountains instead of over them.

Claudius Crozet, who had been an engineer for Napoleon's armies, emigrated to the United States from France. He taught engineering at both West Point and later at Virginia Military Institute, and became chief engineer for the Commonwealth of Virginia. The Crozet Tunnel, at the time it was built, was the longest tunnel in the United States. For those in the Shenandoah Valley it opened up a slew of new markets.

The Howardsville Turnpike has been both a victim and a beneficiary of benign neglect. Trains abruptly ended its commercial life, but even today a hiker can find himself on it, and follow it down the face of Humpback, admiring its gentle grade and the traces left of substantial brick and stone abutments that support the road over swales and creeks.

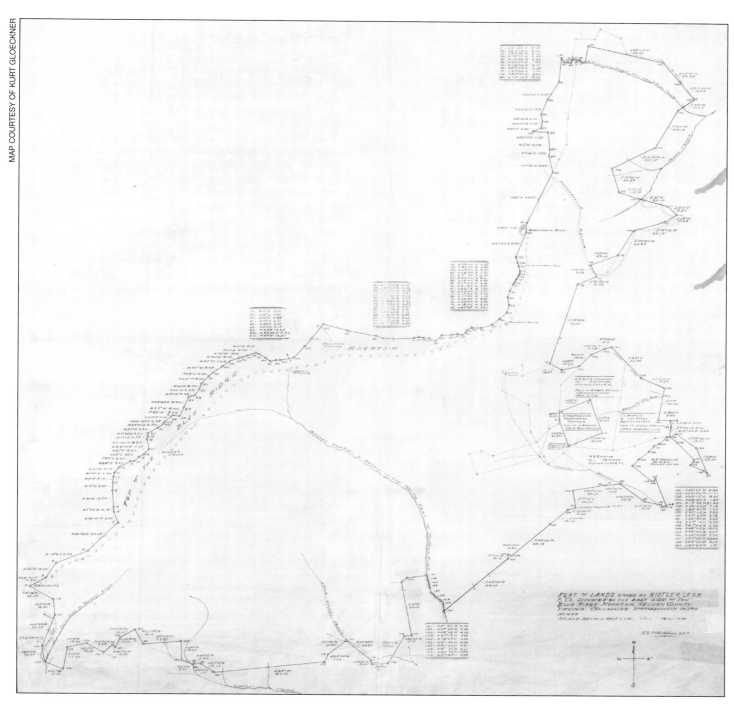

Plat of The Big Survey
by E. E. McCutchaw, S. A. C., 1910–1914

Wintergreen House

THE FOLLOWING HISTORY OF THE BIG SURVEY is taken almost word-for-word from painstaking research of existing records done by Elizabeth Richardson, a Nelson County historian.

By far the largest land patent ever granted near the Wintergreen village area was the 10,000 acres that lay between the 2,460-acre Chiswell/Morrison patent and the crest of the Blue Ridge Mountains, stretching from Reids Gap (sometimes known as Reed's Gap) northwards past Humpback Rocks. This was known as The Big Survey.

It took in Dobie Mountain, separated from Elk Ridge by a small hollow drained by Shropshire Creek, and Humpback Mountain overlooking the northern Rockfish Valley. Turning the corner as the valley begins to run in a more southerly direction is the "Cold Hole" of the Pinnacles, followed by Crawford Knob, Black Rock, and Devils Knob Mountains.

In 1796 this 10,000 acres was granted to John Fleming (see deed and plat, page 5), who may have lived in eastern Virginia. The new grant surrounded several properties of a few hundred acres each, which had previously been granted to several different individuals. At least four of these were owned by Rachel Morrison Ayers, an enterprising woman who appears to have been the only female to patent land in today's Nelson County before the Revolution. (She was the widow of William Morrison, who had patented the 2,460 acres mentioned above.)

The most significant of her properties lay along the top of the Blue Ridge: 129 acres at Laurel Springs Gap and 259 adjoining acres at Pryor's Camp. These were valuable locations, including as they did a pass over the Blue Ridge, and a source of water. There is evidence of a home site, and the land probably was used for small-scale timbering, foraging, and pasturage in its clearings.

The 10,000-acre Big Survey was owned during the first half of the 1800s by a series of out-of-staters, several from Pennsylvania (including a Thomas Morrison who may have been related to William Morrison), and even by an investor from Scotland. The first local owner was John J. Coleman, who in 1853 bought the 10,000 acres, which adjoined his farm and home place, Wintergreen.

In response to lawsuits after Coleman's death in 1869, the court nine years later sold The Big Survey to two men from Albemarle County who split the tract between them, with the dividing line in the vicinity of Stoney Creek. They also purchased the smaller tracts surrounded by The Big Survey along with a few adjacent tracts. In 1882, a Baltimore company leased the rights to "cut down and strip the bark from all chestnut oaks" (they may have meant American chestnuts) on the northern half of The Big Survey, for use in tanning hides. The company was given permission to erect sheds, buildings, and enclosures on the property for its laborers, teams, and wagons. It was to start operations at "Doby's" (Dobie Mountain, just north of Humpback Rocks) and proceed steadily southward.

This was the first indication of how The Big Survey property was being used by absentee-owners and investors. Added Don, "from earliest times, The Big Survey was subsistence farmed and logged on a small scale for many years by quite a few families here and there. It was used as an 'open range' by mountain and valley residents for grazing and foraging cattle and hogs, and, of course, for hunting deer, turkey, bear, and small game. Chestnuts, and plants for eating and healing such as ginseng were also sought after. It was said that the tract 'fairly teemed with bears,' offering some of the best hunting in the county."

In 1902, the entire Big Survey was bought by the Boston enterprise Kistler, Lesh & Company whose five owners lived in Massachusetts, Pennsylvania, and North Carolina. It is said the company intended to log the chestnut trees on the property as a source of tanbark, which contained tannic acid for curing hides.

According to a book on the history of logging in the nearby Tye River Valley of Nelson County, by the 1900s formerly lucrative logging areas in Pennsylvania, New York, and Michigan had been clear-cut, and timber investors were looking for new land to log in states farther south. Adding incentive to the search was the chestnut blight, introduced in New York around 1904, and found in Virginia by 1908. Chestnuts were the most valuable timber trees in the eastern United States, and there was a rush to get them cut before they died and rotted.

In 1917 Kistler Lesh formed the Rockfish Valley Land Corporation, to which it turned over all its holdings in the Rockfish Valley area, including The Big Survey. The new corporation's purpose was said to be buying and selling real estate and timber lands, and developing and dealing in their natural resources.

During the next decade, the Rockfish Valley Land Corporation is said to have done some logging of the most mature and accessible stands of timber (including dead chestnuts) on The Big Survey and nearby properties. From 1902 to 1951 the company reportedly hired local resident Adolphus (Dol) Small to supervise these properties.

Their principal offices were moved from Lynchburg to Lovingston in 1945, though their officers continued to live in other states. But logging became less profitable with the dwindling of both the quantity and the quality of the remaining dead chestnuts, and with the development of man-made chemicals to tan leather, the company eventually sought to sell their extensive land holdings in the area.

In 1950, William R. Mattox of Durham, North Carolina, purchased 10,580 acres of the company's land, including The Big Survey, and subsequently bought several additional tracts in the area.

The new owner carried out logging operations in the 1950s, including most merchantable timber on Black Rock Mountain. Logs were trucked down the mountain to be processed at a sawmill built on the present Black Walnut Lane in Wintergreen Resort's Stoney Creek development.

Logging camps, portable sawmills, and logging roads of unknown age once dotted the mountainsides of The Big Survey, and wagons and trucks removing the cut lumber or whole trees rumbled down area side roads. While in operation, the lumber industry furnished numerous jobs for local residents.

IN ADDITION TO A LARGE BOARD FOOTAGE of red and white oak on dryer soils, poplar in the hollows, and a miscellany of other hardwoods, The Big Survey held a substantial board footage of hickory. The hickory logs of higher quality were sold to Bill Phillips, who had come up from North Carolina as had Mr. Mattox, and had established Phillips Hickory Mill north of Woods Mill on Route 29. Bill sawed most of these logs

into billets exported to Norway to be made into skis, interesting in light of the land's next incarnation as a ski resort.

After ceasing timber operations, Mattox continued to hold the land as an investment. Don pointed out that for a considerable time, Mrs. Mattox had urged her husband to sell in order for her to retire from teaching. Over the years he had indicated to a few real estate people his possible interest in selling "if I can get what it's worth."

Don was just about to head down to Nelson County to find out more about this intriguing piece of real estate when he got a long, rambling letter from Mattox. Don's success selling many large tracts of mountain land in western Albemarle led Mattox to contact him. In addition to the letter there was a single mimeographed sheet containing what Don describes as details about the property that proved to be exaggerated.

Delighted to have been contacted, Don readily accepted Mr. Mattox's invitation to meet him at Margaret Garth's Tuckahoe Tavern near Nellysford in the Rockfish Valley, at 9 a.m. of a morning shortly after mid-January in 1968. Don and Mattox spent all morning at Tuckahoe Tavern, with Mattox giving him a great deal of information about The Big Survey.

Mattox agreed to give Don four to six weeks to do his ground reconnaissance and research. After that time they would meet in Durham for Don to present his firm's appraisal of value, marketing, and sales proposal, and exclusive listing agreement. Mattox had in mind an 'open' or at a maximum a 90-day exclusive arrangement. Don, on the other hand, knew it would take much more time than that. He needed time to come to know it even more thoroughly, and to research and determine its potential, let alone to market it, find and show prospective purchasers, weed out those who were not really interested, and close a sale.

As little as Don knew at this point, he was certain that this exceptionally large, majestic, well-located property, and the potential it represented, deserved careful study and handling to assure that it would be put into good hands, and to good use. He wanted to avoid its sale to those whose purchase would likely result in indiscriminate fragmentation into large

Margaret Garth

Don Faulkner (right) and bear hunters

parcels, as recently had begun to be a trend with large rural holdings.

Literally the day after he met Mattox, Don went back home to Richmond knowing he had to drop a bomb on Martha, his wife, and their plans for a ski vacation. The Big Survey, and the attempt to piece together exactly what it consisted of, had to come first. When he got home, he told Martha that they were going to rent horses and explore The Big Survey on horseback instead. This might have held some attraction if it had been May or June, but it was February!

Don was a horseman and a fox hunter, and was acquainted with Grover Vandevender, renowned and beloved huntsman of the Farmington Hunt Club for many years. In addition he ran a high-end boarding, teaching, and livery stable in the Farmington hunt country west of Charlottesville. Grover loaned him a truck, trailer, and horses for two days, and Don drove Martha and the horses south into Nelson County.

As if the cold weren't enough, it began to rain, and as Don put it, once they set off, "I had us pretty much turned around except as to down and up most of the time. I didn't know the boundaries but that wasn't so critical because they were all on these side slopes you couldn't get to anyway."

They were unable to stay at the Boar's Head Inn as it was booked, and, worse, Don had forgotten to tuck a bottle of bourbon into their bags, a necessity since there were no bars in Virginia in the days before liquor-by-the-drink. Don, who 15 years later was sadly divorced from Martha, added, "That might have been the end of our marriage right there."

For the short term, Don needed a crash course in the geography of The Big Survey and comparable sales data, if any, in order to come up with a purchase price that was fair, achievable, justifiable, and which Mattox, he hoped, would accept.

Don knew in the core of his being that this property, spectacularly rugged and accessible only with difficulty, was his big chance. He needed to acquaint himself intimately with a huge expanse of mountain land.

Using a Jeep rented from Pete Small, Don spent a number of weeks learning as much as possible, driving and walking the length, breadth, and heights of The Big Survey, studying USGS Topo maps and USDA aerial photography, doing research on records in the clerks office, doing his utmost to find sales of comparable properties from which market data he could derive a value of The Big Survey. He learned all he could from George Vest, a prominent local resident, and Margaret Garth, his hostess at her Tuckahoe Tavern, which became his home in Nelson County for the next eight or nine years. She was "Margaret" to all of her many guests who came to stay with her later while working on The Big Survey/Wintergreen.

Margaret, somewhere in her sixties but with the get-up-and-go of thirty-five, was a vast, totally reliable source of information on everything Don needed to know, passed on during breakfast, supper, and early evening conversations.

Margaret knew quite a bit about The Big Survey and most of Nelson County. She had ridden horseback with her father, Montague Coleman, regularly for many of her younger years, and had covered much of The Big

Survey. They rode up to leave salt for the cattle, and to check on both cattle and hogs every one to two weeks in the summer. In the fall the livestock was rounded up and brought down to the valley.

Her father's business and political interests were widespread. For many years he had been the Rockfish District member of the board of supervisors, serving a number of terms as its chairman. Margaret often accompanied him in his travels on horseback and in an auto around the county.

Taking after her father, and all her adult life an avid leader in the county Democratic party, as well as a highly regarded teacher, Margaret knew who was who, both high up and at ground level in the county. Don, speaking in admiration and affection, said, "She knew her way around more than any other woman I have ever known."

Margaret Garth had told Don there were two people he needed to know, both absolutely reliable and trustworthy: Maxie Campbell and George Vest. Maxie ran Campbell's Store and the Nellysford Post Office within it. At that point it was one of only two commercial structures in the community of Nellysford, the other being an automotive garage.

Maxie was a man of impressive stature and presence, obviously of Scottish descent with bushy, reddish-blonde eyebrows and a Scot's highlander's demeanor. He was big-hearted, kind, and strong, and not to be messed with. He was raised on the old Campbell mountain farm up near Reids Gap, between The Big Survey and Love, with the extended Campbell clan owning land southward taking in Campbell Mountain.

As Don put it, "Maxie had grown up there, lived, fished, and hunted there, knew everybody who had lived up in those mountains and everything about that part of the world." Maxie particularly loved bear

Left to right: Bill Whitehead, Hoyt Hatley, Rudolph Small, and Maxie Campbell

Don Faulkner and George Vest

hunting, and had taken for granted all the hunting he enjoyed in the country between Three Ridges (now designated a federal wilderness area) and The Big Survey. Maxie either knew or knew of most everybody, especially hunters, his store being the closest source of ammo.

"Maxie was a big help to me over the years," continued Don, "and maybe saved my life after the only real run in I had in all my time in Nelson County. When Maxie, near a living legend, died, Beech Grove Christian Church was filled literally to overflowing. His coffin was in place, covered by a giant bear skin with the American flag over it."

George Vest was an African American who took care of the property for Mattox for a number of years, hunted it from his days as a young boy with his Dad, Oscar Vest, and knew it as well or better than anyone. It didn't take long for Don to realize that not only was George Vest an incredibly hard worker whom he could trust in every way, but also that he knew the plants, both indigenous and invasive, the trees, wildflowers, bears, foxes, and snakes, and how to handle them all.

George had traveled the world with the military in a parachute supply unit during the Korean War, and it had been his job to push supplies attached to parachutes out the door of the plane. Twice, by accident, he had gone out with the parachutes, and had to hold on tight since he himself had no parachute!

Once he landed so far away from his unit that it took him two weeks to make his way back.

Don commented, "George and I began working together, just on my getting acquainted with the property. From the start, I determined, I didn't want anybody knowing why or what I was doing. I pure and simple wanted to get to know the property and find out what it could be. I had no idea, but I thought it had big potential. I was working night and day when up in Nelson to find answers to never-ceasing questions. I had to take a small number of people into my confidence: obviously Mrs. Garth, George, and a few others as time went on [not sharing all I knew or thought], and to the best of my knowledge that confidence was never shared with others.

"George and I would explore any and every way to get on, up, over and around anywhere and everywhere on the property in a Jeep, and we walked many miles exploring, with George pointing out this and that and what happened where, whenever.

"I had this topo map, a portion of a standard USGS topographic map enlarged from a scale of 1"= 2,000' up to 1"= 1,000' covering all the area in and surrounding The Big Survey or of relevance to it. Bob Atherton, a very good friend and draftsman in the design section of VDOT who moonlighted for me from 1966 to 1989, had, carefully and as accurately as we could pin down, put the boundaries of The Big Survey from the McCutchaw plat on a mylar of the map from which as a base we ultimately made many different maps for multiple purposes. That base map together with stereoscopic aerial photography flown by VDOT was very helpful to me getting around and having a pretty good idea of where I was when I got there.

"George had never seen a topographic map of any kind. One day we were up on the ridgeline above Crawford where the stone wall runs for miles along or near the Nelson/Augusta line. This had been built by Nelson people years ago to keep their cattle and hogs foraging in the mountain from heading down the west slope of the mountains into the Valley of Virginia, never to be seen again by their rightful owners on the east side of the Blue Ridge.

"George had gotten some respect for handy-sized contact aerial photos that I carried because he in time had learned to read them as well as I; but he did not understand, had not figured out, topo maps, and had little or no confidence in their value to me or anyone else until one day when I tripped and fell hard. I got up and said, "George, this is the first time that I know exactly where we are on the ground and on my map." He did not believe it. He had doubts, even when I showed him the USGS benchmark I had tripped over on the ground, which was pinpointed on the map."

What happened in those weeks is that Don got a better feel for The Big Survey, and even at that stage was mulling over what its highest and best use might be. As is said the first rule in real estate is to identify a property's highest and best use. "I was in awe of that property," Don said, "it was the closest I'd ever been to wilderness since my teens up in the Northeast Kingdom of Vermont, and I wanted to put it in good hands."

AT THE END OF THE EXPLORATORY PERIOD in late February, 1968, Don drove to Durham to meet the Mattox's on their own turf. The first trip was unsuccessful. On the second trip they negotiated for three days. Don gave all the reasons why $1,400,000 was a fair price; and why an 18-month listing period was necessary to do justice to the property and its possibilities. Mattox wanted $2,000,000 for the property and was very reluctant to give an exclusive contract let alone one for 18 months.

Maddox was convinced that the value of the timber on The Big Survey was huge. Don could see that the property had been extensively timbered in the 1950s. He felt that Mattox was over-estimating the board footage of the remaining harvestable stand and its value, considering the vast area over which it was scattered, and the myriad difficulties of access. Don realized that for aesthetic reasons the property held more value and sale appeal with the remaining timber intact.

Don commented, "By that time, I'd fallen in love with the property. …I saw it sort of as an adventure of a lifetime. I had then no ideas about what it could be or where it could go or even how I'd sell it. Or even what it was exactly. But I was really up for it. So I was going to get that listing.

"In the end Mrs. Mattox made sure her husband signed the listing contract giving Virginia Landmark Corporation the exclusive right to sell the property for 16 months with a price tag of $1,400,000. There

were two contingencies. First, the adjudication of the existing timber valuation issue, a most challenging task; and second, the possible adjusting of the acreage and listing price if it was determined to be greater or smaller than the old survey indicated.

"The latter needed to be done by some means less expensive than a complete boundary survey, which should be devised as reliable and calculated within reasonable accuracy by a respected and certified Virginia surveyor."

Don also agreed to do his best to obtain from the future purchaser a 15 percent interest in the property for the Mattoxes, although he could not contractually commit to such a provision. Don finally negotiated with him a price of a $1,400,000 plus the value of any timber over and above 14 inches DBH (Diameter Breast Height) that was feasible to log with a value in excess of $100,000 as determined by a certified forester of their joint choosing and engagement, such a cost not to exceed two thousand dollars.

"I figured I could get a thousand dollars together, but I couldn't get any more than that," Don said. "Mr. Mattox agreed to this arrangement. I went to people that I knew I could trust to get the names of foresters who would be qualified, would be totally reliable, and who had credentials sufficient to satisfy Mr. and Mrs. Mattox.

"After I had written letters to several foresters who were recommended, Stuart Keedwell responded that he would be interested in doing it, and could do it for $2,000, which was pretty amazing even back then— that $2,000 could get an estimate of value on 11–12,000 acres. Mr. Mattox agreed on Stuart Keedwell, who came back very shortly with a letter of appraisal in which he estimated, I think, an aggregate of under $80,000 worth of timber, not enough to change the listing/offering price." Keedwell's estimate, according to Don, was based on a recent cruise done in cooperation with the US Forest Service. Keedwell had only to check a sufficient number of the plots to verify accuracy.

Don continued, "So, then I went back to Mr. and Mrs. Mattox and Mr. Mattox said, "no way in hell." He wouldn't sign the listing agreement; it just wasn't enough money. But Mrs. Maddox prevailed and said 'Bill, we've got to sell the property, and Don seems to know what he's doing so you've got to sign that listing.' And he did."

Looking south along the Blue Ridge

THAT TIMBER should have been at the heart of their argument is no surprise. From modern geologic time the Blue Ridge Mountains and their valleys had been graced with valuable timber. It was said that until the early 1900s, one in every three trees was an American chestnut, whose blooms turned the mountains white every spring. Oak, beech, and ash were other hardwoods that flourished as well.

Some of the chestnuts in the virgin forests of the 19th century grew to stupendous sizes upwards of 100 feet, with such massive trunks that it took several men to encircle one mature tree. Chestnut lumber is very durable, resistant to decay, easy to saw or split, light to carry and was prized for houses, barns, rail fences, and furniture. The bark was also valuable for the tanning of leather.

The ultimate loss of the mountain-dominant chestnut forests not only was a major economic loss to all of Appalachia where it reigned as the most valuable tree, but was equally a sociological loss. The multitude

Bee Tree Lumber Co's. Saw Mill
Massies Mill, Va.

of families living in the Blue Ridge, and throughout the mountains of chestnut forests, depended on its chestnuts as a source of nutrition and enjoyment over winter. It was also an essential medium of barter for salt, sugar, coffee, and other staples in Appalachia, and for the little essential cash required in an increasingly cash economy.

As the chestnut disappeared, so increasingly did the mountain people from their homesteads. For several generations they had been independent, except for their reliance on nature and one another. Most faced entirely different lives, dependent on poor-paying jobs in the rapidly emerging timber industry that came to Appalachia. Some were lucky enough to get unionized industrial jobs in nearby Waynesboro and Stuarts Draft.

In areas surrounding The Big Survey, when the lumber barons turned their attention south, options were secured on 50,000 acres on the slopes of Three Ridges and the Priest mountains. Then more acreage was added along the watersheds of the Rockfish, the Piney and the Tye rivers contributing to a very large number of board feet of timber.

The final blow for these isolated mountain families came in the 1930s, when they were evicted to make way for the Skyline Drive, and years later for the Blue Ridge Parkway, projects created to boost employment during the Depression era.

Logging in Massies Mill

Much of the following information comes from the book Sentimental Journey, *by Carl Lathrop.*

These mountains were flush with timber that was so much in demand. The only problem was that these trees were far away from the eastern seaboard market they were supposed to serve, and especially far from the tanning factories along the New York and Pennsylvania borders. At least two band saw–type mills would need to be established, and they would need access to the Southern Railroad stop at the village of Tye River.

The volume involved meant that this access would need to be by a small local railroad connecting the mills to the Southern tracks. Mr. R. G. Leftwich, a Lynchburg businessman, sought financing from among his business acquaintances involved with the New York and Pennsylvania Railroad who had experience with similar short-run railroads. Financing was arranged, and a charter was issued in 1914 for building the Virginia Blue Ridge Railway (VBRR). Construction began on the original two-mile stretch in 1915.

New Industrial Section of Massies Mill, Va.
Bee Tree Lumber Co's.
Mill and Employees' Cottages,
Du Priest Mountain in the distance.

All of the work was done by men with shovels and horse-drawn scoops. The railway was never meant to be permanent, just to serve the 15 years or so that it would take to get the chestnut trees out. The crossties were cut locally, not treated, and were placed directly on graded dirt. Its crude construction was the cause of many derailments over the years. On May 25th, 1915, the engine and tender slid, tracks and all, down an embankment, probably because of a lack of adequate ballast. Amazingly, no one was killed.

The railway reached Woodson, site of one of the band saw mills, in October of 1915, and service was inaugurated. The VBRR also offered passenger service into the Tye River station so the ladies could transfer to the southbound local and travel to Lynchburg for a day of shopping.

The route of the VBRR continued on towards Massies Mill. The repair and maintenance shops for VBRR were built at fast-growing Massies Mill, as was a two-story headquarters that also served as a station. The railroad was complete two and one half years from its start.

Massies Mill was named for a gristmill in town that was sometimes used for extra-legal purposes. Legend has it that the miller always knew when the boys were about to make a run (to distill moonshine) as they would arrive with meal sacks of corn and ask to have it coarse ground.

Massies Mill was also the site of the Bee Tree Lumber Co., a holding company for Tye River Lumber. Bee Tree signed a contract with Kistler, Lesh & Co., although disagreements about rights of way issues persisted. The two companies were to split profits evenly. Both companies joined forces in a race to get the lumber out, although time would prove that the chestnuts' natural immunity to decay would protect them for years after they stopped growing.

The wood mill and lumber storage piles took up 93 acres in Massies Mill. As the lumber was sawn it was loaded onto a transfer car pushed by workers along rails set in the long docks radiating out from the building. It was manually unloaded into piles next to the VBRR rails for the freight cars into which it eventually would be loaded. The bandsaw system was steam powered by water from the Tye River.

There was some employee housing, and also a commissary. Mr. Crowell, known as "the Boss," lived nearby and had a bulldog. Mrs. Crowell would put her list in a basket and give it to the dog. The old bulldog would deliver it to the commissary. Mr. Bernard McGinnis, the storekeeper, would read the list, fill the basket, and send the dog back home!

As the originally secured forests got timbered, Bee Tree Lumber, by arrangement with Tye River Lumber, bought timber rights in the Rockfish River watershed assembled by Kistler, Lesh & Co. This meant that they needed to build a tram road to get over Brent's Gap, with a terrific grade at the headwaters of Hat Creek requiring five switchbacks and a trestle.

The engineering challenges were too great for pushing on over Brent's Gap and into the Rockfish watershed. All building of the railroad came to a halt.

One of the last shipments of lumber out of the Bee Tree mill was in January of 1922. It went to Pennsylvania via the Reading Railroad. The Reading did not get paid, and after a lawsuit the lumber was sold off to pay the freight. All work ceased at the mill and in the mountains.

Bee Tree and the Tye River Lumber Co. were at loggerheads. They finally submitted to arbitration, and settled in May of 1924. Bee Tree kept the mill, the tram road, and all the equipment; Tye River Timber received the rights to all the timberland they had contributed to the venture. After the settlement Bee Tree Lumber was free to continue logging, but closed down instead, as the timber that still had not been cut was not of great value.

VBRR, of course, was hard hit by the closing of operations at Bee Tree. Most of their freight was dependent on the mill, with coal coming in to feed the operation and the milled timber going out to be hauled to larger markets. VBRR limped along, but then revived and was supported by the American Cyanamid Plant. Surprisingly perhaps, VBRR's engines were powered by steam until the 1960s, when American Cyanamid, too, shut down.

Massies Mill was essentially wiped off the map by the backlash to Hurricane Camille in August of 1969. Today, walking around that area, it is hard to imagine the busy, thriving village that existed there for a brief time in the early 20th century.

Jim Wheat

CHAPTER THREE

The Visionary and the Blind Man with Vision

I t is not surprising that the relationship Don Faulkner was to enter into with Jim Wheat was built, for both of them, on deeply rooted memories of the past.

James Clifton Wheat Jr. was a Richmond businessman who had an enormous influence on the city's and Virginia's financial and political life during the mid-twentieth century. Anne Hobson Freeman wrote a book about him titled *A Hand Well Played: the life of Jim Wheat, Jr.* Wheat, who, in his own business career was a real risk taker, was brought up by parents whose experience with the Depression made them wary of risk. His father's investment banking firm had crashed in the '30s, and although they had never been rich, they were, suddenly, poor. As Wheat put it of his family and the friends around them, "We all grew up poor…but we never knew it. Growing up poor you were not destitute. You studied and you went to school, and you were clad perfectly soundly and reasonably and warmly…but you didn't have a lot of extras."

He made his way through Richmond's public schools without distinguishing himself, and enrolled at Virginia Military Institute in 1937. As Freeman points out, "Jim did not easily adapt to the military regimen. He was, in fact, almost constantly in trouble, piling up demerits. 'I was a nonconformist,' Wheat said, 'but not rebellious… There's a distinction.'"

Later, he put to use in his own business the lessons he had learned from the military. "To be successful you have got to have people who understand the linkage between discipline, responsibility, and a sense of duty. I don't suggest for a minute that the military experience is the only way you can get it, but it is a way you can get it."

In the late 1950s and '60s there was a fierce battle in politics and education playing out in Richmond. State lawmakers had shut down public schools under the banner of Massive Resistance rather than follow federal law and integrate schools. Realizing that this policy was not only wrongheaded but also likely to do great damage to Virginia's businesses and its legal reputation, a group of business leaders formed an organization called Richmond Forward, and persuaded Wheat to run for City Council.

This was at a time when Wheat and Company had expanded its employee base by 40%, opening other offices in Virginia and in West Virginia. City Council meetings often degenerated into loud arguments that went on too long. Wheat stuck with it into his third term, finally leaving in 1969.

He served his city out of a sense of duty, which he described this way. "My idea of duty is different from the present day concept of duty…something unpleasant and involuntary, a burden, something negative. To me, duty flows from a sense of gratitude and obligation… It expresses itself as a need to put something back into a world that has given so much to you."

The remarkable thing about this statement is that it was made by a blind man. Wheat had inherited retinitis pigmentosa from his mother, Emma, but he had also inherited her determination not to let blindness define her.

It was during his years at VMI that Wheat began to have real trouble with blindness closing in from the sides. Despite memorizing the eye chart, he was not able to graduate with a commission once the Japanese bombed Pearl Harbor and the United States entered the war. He went home to Richmond and worked for his father for a time, and then returned to VMI to teach civil engineering. When his eyesight completely failed him he returned to Richmond.

It was said about him by everyone who met him, socially or in the course of business, that they either didn't guess or they forgot that he was blind. All of his other senses were heightened to make up for the one that was lacking. He could recognize people by their voices, and even introduce others based on where they stood in the room.

This is what Wheat had to say about his condition. "It's tough going blind. It's no problem at all once you're there and once…you accommodate to the realities of what you need to do. But going blind is tough as hell."

It was about 1946 that Don, who was only 13 years old, first became acquainted with Jim Wheat, who later became his mentor and dear friend and exerted a profound influence on his life. Don had known Wheat's parents, who lived across the street from him. His dad, Jim Wheat Sr., an avid horseman, had given him his first riding coat. Soon after The Deep Run Hunt Club moved west into Goochland County, big Jim Wheat, his brother-in-law, Gen. Edmund Conquest (Jim Wheat Jr.'s uncle) and others kept their horses at nearby Dover Farm.

Commented Don, "It was there and then that I first got to know Jim Wheat Jr., who from childhood and through his years at VMI loved to ride. Because he had recently lost his sight, he had to have someone ride with him as a guide. Usually his dad or General Conquest or his contemporaries rode out with him. On a few occasions I was his guide. He was fearless as he rode into a jump, blind as could be, with a lead from me and some prior warning on what type of jump it was. He always held his crop in front of his face when jumping to ward off branches."

IN THE SPRING OF 1968, when Don had the exclusive right to sell The Big Survey, his first need was for a good, tough vehicle to explore in. At first he borrowed a Jeep from friends, members of the Whitehall Hunt Club in Albemarle, but after slightly damaging a tire and rim realized he needed to buy his own. He bought a used one from the Jeep dealer in Richmond for $2,500 with the caveat that he could have 48 hours to have his trusted mechanic friend examine it.

When he drove over to his friend's shop he found it closed. He had to be in Lovingston, the seat of Nelson County, to research land records, so he drove the Jeep west, wondering where to find a mechanic to evaluate his new purchase. On arrival at the courthouse he figured he would put his predicament to Sheriff Bill Whitehead, to whom he had earlier introduced himself. He told Sheriff Whitehead of his dilemma—how was he to know whether or not to buy this used Jeep?

To this day Don remembers his answer. Whitehead said, "I know just the right person, but unhappily he's in jail." Don responded that he would pay a competent mechanic $100 (a lot in those days) to do an evaluation. "Well," said the sheriff, "maybe we can work something out."

Don looking back on it says, "Sheriff Whitehead was a kind man, and knew the family could use the money. The mechanic had been working at the sheriff's house, and had left his tools there. I drove him from the jail to the Whitehead's house for his tools, and then back to jail. I went to do my work, and about four in the afternoon he was done." Not only did the Jeep more than pass muster, but the mechanic gave Don some tips on how to check out a used vehicle.

This story is a reflection not only of the times, but also of the role of trust in a sparsely populated area like Nelson County in 1968. Sheriff Whitehead knew his man.

"By June I was really loving The Big Survey, and well into thinking of its resort potential," said Don. "I was determined to do all I could to learn as much about it as possible in a short time frame. I wanted to assure that it would be sold by Virginia Landmark into good hands, and for uses in harmony with nature."

He spent much of the summer when not in Nelson County doing some inquisitive traveling. First he visited Sea Pines, Charles Fraser's model of enlightened community development on Hilton Head Island off the coast of South Carolina. He had a considerable leg up on the trip, having been lent a cottage for his family by friends of Martha's mom and dad. Additionally two Richmond friends, George Freeman and Angus McCauley, classmates of Charles Fraser in law school, put in a good word for him with Fraser.

He got a lot from that trip, as did Martha, who was very helpful with his work on the The Big Survey from start to finish. However, Fraser was skeptical of any development potential for The Big Survey.

Said Faulkner, "It came to me a little before mid-summer that the possibility of a resort and surrounding community could be significantly enhanced if it included a ski area, which would make it a four-seasons resort. With Jim Covington, my partner in Virginia Landmark Corporation, and an experienced skier, we had spent two days the summer of 1967 with Peter Bryce at Bryce Ski Resort (now named Bryce Resort) in Bayse, Virginia, on an assignment given us by a Richmond brokerage and investment firm."

Peter Bryce was an adventurer, manager, and with his family, owner and promoter of Bryce Ski Resort. Don reported, "We were impressed with Peter Bryce's knowledge and entrepreneurial spirit, and amazed at the ground he covered with us relative to prerequisites and requirements of successful development of resorts and ski areas and their operation and management."

In late summer of 1968 Don traveled to Banner Elk, North Carolina, to visit Beech Mountain ski area, a resort being developed by two brothers, Harry and Grover Robbins. They were willing to talk about what they were doing, and shared with Don openly the meteorological advantage of their location and how it was responsible for the potential of the resort. This led Don to focus on how to figure out The Big Survey's meteorological potential for skiing.

Don remembered, "Bryce had made the point of telling me that there would never be skiing in the Blue Ridge because the west slopes would be too warm, which made a lot of sense; and the east slopes would have too high a humidity coming off the ocean and up from the Gulf of Mexico. I knew that temperature, humidity, elevation, topography, vertical drop of skiable terrain, and a sufficient source of water were all critical."

The idea of a resort that had begun to take hold in Don's mind was not a resort typical of that era, but one based on his idealism together with what he had taken in from his visit to Sea Pines, and from reading a book by Ian McHarg titled *Design with Nature*. McHarg was a landscape architect of Scottish descent who had moved to the United States. His thinking and teaching pioneered the concept of ecological planning, and encouraged the incorporation of natural systems into regional planning.

The values, principles, and priorities involved in creating an environmentally sensitive development meant making the structures blend into the nature around them, instead of the other way around. It also meant putting in infrastructure of the highest quality and latest scientific design: roads, water treatment plants, and underground electricity. In other words, spending as much on what you couldn't see as on what you could see. The net effect was of a tranquil, harmonious whole.

The more Don explored the more his vision began to define itself. Even though his was a mountain landscape, he used sea imagery to define his vision. As he put it, "I wanted The Big Survey to become a year-round resort of finest quality…a mountaintop island of culture and amenity within a perpetual sea of wildness and nature…an example of excellence of design in working with nature."

Don was acutely aware that the mountain landscape of The Big Survey would make this kind of development an enormous undertaking. He realized, too, that to be profitable it needed to be a four-season resort, which meant it must include skiing.

"BY MID-SUMMER '68," said Don, "George Vest and I had become tight friends. George was working with me in the daytime when I was in Nelson County, and then working nights over at the Morton Pie Factory in Crozet. I don't know how he ever did it." Don was able to help Vest regain his auto insurance when he ran into insurance problems over his car, which was essential to get him to his various jobs. As a result, said Don, "From then on, George would have done anything reasonable I asked him; and I felt the same about him."

In the fall of 1968, with the knowledge Don had gained from his visits to Beech Mountain and Bryce, he knew he had to get a leg up on the meteorological likelihood of making sufficient snow for enough days to make skiing feasible on The Big Survey. Don remembered, "I headed down to Virginia Tech, then named Virginia Polytechnic Institute (VPI) in the fall to consult with Virginia's meteorologist then stationed there. My theories, which I tried out on him, were: one, to obtain past long-term records of stations in Virginia and North Carolina where we knew snowmaking was done, and two, to somehow obtain comparable data for the winter of 1968–69 on the upper north slopes off Black Rock and Devils Knob for comparison."

"We identified the existing long-term stations; I obtained such records and his approval of my approach. Following that, I learned about Joel Myers, a young, already highly respected and recommended meteorologist. I called Myers, told him enough of what I was about, obtained some advice, and was told of the best source of recording thermographs which I could manage to buy. In December I located thermographs on elevations about 3,400' and 2,400', housed within what we hoped were the vertical and horizontal limits of the areas with the most likely ski potential."

Don recognized that if there was to be a ski resort, geology and water would be important factors in snowmaking. To find answers to this question Don knew he needed a geologist. This led him to Dr. Byron Cooper, geology department head at VPI. So while he was there on his meteorological quest, he visited with Dr. Cooper, who right off was intrigued with Don's emerging thoughts on the potential of The Big Survey. He agreed to join Don later in November for a weekend exploring the developable areas of The Big Survey, including what might become the ski area.

Dr. Cooper and Don really hit it off. He consulted on several visits that fall, and, as Don put it, "was of immeasurable help to me then and in the next years, until his very premature death in 1971. As our relationship and our knowledge of The Big Survey progressed, his interest and enthusiasm nearly matched mine."

One day in late December, Cooper and Don were sitting on the rock face above and behind Crawford Knob, having a picnic lunch of Vienna sausages, store bought cheddar cheese cut from a round, saltines, and a bit of bittersweet chocolate, while they looked out over Shamokin Gorge to the south. Bob Atherton was Don's very able moonlighting map man, and they had Atherton's map with them. When they looked up at Devils Knob and looked over at Black Rock and Potato Patch Mountain, everything was laid out before them. That is when Don, for the first time, expressed

Dr. Byron Cooper

his vision to someone else. He laid out his "island of recreation in a sea of mountain wilderness" to Cooper, who responded enthusiastically and came to share Don's vision.

"Cooper was so affirming of the ideas I had," said Don. "Most people would have thought I was crazy. Byron was an idealist, and yet he was a pragmatist too, which was a very helpful balance to my way of thinking. To honor Dr. Cooper, I later named that outcrop Cooper's Whole (on Humpback Mountain, facing south), because from it you could take in the mountain village and the ski slopes of The Big Survey. I put it on an early map, and later Cooper's Vantage was the initial name of the restaurant above the ski rental/administrative building."

The fact that Cooper reacted with such excitement was very important to Don. As he explained it, "All of 1968 I was alone in my emerging vision, until that day in December. This was the first time my vision of what The Big Survey could be came into focus. …It crystallized for both of us."

Later in December Cooper came back for two days

and wrote up a preliminary report dated January 3, 1969. His field studies revealed that a large percentage of The Big Survey was underlain by Catoctin greenstone, and pedlar gneiss. These formations ranged from 450,000,000 to more than a billion years old.

His report on water resources pointed to the many good mountain streams, with the probable availability of good well water near the headwaters of Stoney Creek and of drilling many small wells at higher elevations. He mentioned an alluvial "fan" a mile wide further north and downstream. Cooper pointed to the need to drill a test well, perhaps as deep as 250 feet, to get through the alluvial deposits and discover what he suspected would be a large amount of underflow water.

Speaking of The Big Survey's other natural attributes, Cooper pointed out that Shamokin Gorge is perhaps the deepest gorge in the eastern United States, that the range of altitudes would be the perfect setting

Wild geranium

for a botanical museum "of the first order," and that the rocks, minerals, and wildlife also were abundant and could be studied firsthand.

Note: The original name for Shamokin was spelled Shamokan or Shumokan found on an early hand-drawn plat map. A large cache of shoe soles more recently found in the area points to a possible phonetic spelling of Shoemaking Creek.

Cooper compared The Big Survey to Beech Mountain, and made the following statement, "Beech Mountain has no overwhelming advantage of its own, or any special advantage over The Big Survey tract. However, The Big Survey tract has an overwhelmingly great advantage of ready accessibility to high-speed highways, commercial airports, and can serve as an immediate attraction to a much larger population than Beech Mountain."

Dr. Cooper's conclusion was that "The Big Survey area is a choice block of acreage for construction of a diversified, multipurpose, high-class resort and recreational area."

Incorporating the preliminary views of Dr. Cooper, demographic data from a brief analysis and report done at Don's request by Charles Meiberg, professor at University of Virginia Darden School of Business, and other information he had assembled, Don completed his first write-up. It was titled "The Big Survey, The Property in Brief" in January 1969.

This report is a mixture of statistics and persuasive

Streamside classroom

prose that hammers home the unique quality of beauty that The Big Survey held, and the once-in-a-lifetime opportunity that it represented. The report was a comprehensive attempt to describe the property with its amazing natural landmarks, the variety of people who would be attracted to it, its accessibility to major metropolitan areas, the surrounding historic region, and the character of Nelson County.

One humorous note: the section on accessibility reads, "Within its bounds (The Big Survey) there is an extensive and exceptionally good network of woods roads most of which are of easy grade and reach all but the most inaccessible areas."

In the margins someone later wrote, "no—lousy even for logging!"

Perhaps its most persuasive section was an Atherton map based on a slope analysis done over a 1" = 1000' USGS topo map. Atherton had earlier imposed, as accurately as possible, the boundaries of The Big Survey on this map, and it proved indispensable.

Don was able to make the following statement: "Among these insights are the facts that the greatest majority of the 4,300 acres having slopes of less than 20 percent (i.e. slopes that could be built on) lie on the tops of the mountains at elevations greater than 2,400 feet; and, also, that these areas are largely separated one from the other by considerable areas of more difficult terrain but connected by corridors (ridges) of relatively easy topography."

Don also referred to Cooper's initial two-day reconnaissance of the property and his sense, from the geology he observed, "that the ground water resources were plentiful, accessible, and well-located relative to potentially useable areas."

Don wrote a paper titled "The Opportunity" in late February 1969, in preparation for presenting The Big Survey to prospective purchasers. Don used his real estate savvy to outline the ways in which The Big Survey satisfied the three requirements for successful development of a year-round recreational community: namely location, location, location. It was within two hours of a substantial metropolitan population (Richmond), and within four hours of a population of upwards of 10 million people (Washington DC, Norfolk, Newport News, Hampton Roads, and Richmond). A ski area was another requirement for a four-seasons resort.

All of these requirements, he stressed, were or could be present in the case of The Big Survey.

The meteorology revealed by the thermograph records came up looking essentially like what was going on at Beech Mountain in terms of temperatures and weather. Comparison with long-term data from stations thought comparable to The Big Survey were tight enough to be encouraging so far as the feasibility of a ski area development.

Wanting to learn more about recreational development, Don attended The Urban Land Institute Winter Conference in Florida, the focus of which was "Recreational Community Planning, Development, and Management." It proved to be very valuable as an eye opener, and provided a wealth of information. Don had a chance to see, hear, meet, and get a sense of who was who among land planners, landscape architects, and marketing and economic consultants. He got a feel for who made the most sense and who impressed him. He was especially impressed by presentations given by Sasaki, Dawson, and DeMay; RTKL; and Robert Gladstone and Assoc.; all of whom worked with Sea Pines, as well as several other top-flight competitors. RTKL and Gladstone were invited, came to The Big Survey, and made proposals later in 1969.

Don was at the stage, by year's end 1968, where he had to find someone who could provide an objective and reliable study of and opinion on the practical feasibility of a ski area. Don's sister, Closey, and her husband, Whit Dickey, avid skiers living in Vermont, put Don in touch with Fred Rogers, mountain manager at Big Bromley Ski Resort in Vermont. At that time Bromley was the only resort in New England relying on making snow. Rogers was persuaded to come down to do a very preliminary evaluation of The Big Survey's potential as a ski resort.

Don engaged Sid Trott, an expert pilot and manager of the Eagle's Nest Airport in Waynesboro, to first fly Rogers and him over the length and breadth of The Big Survey to gain a good look at variations in snow cover.

What they observed was persuasive that *if* skiing would prove to be feasible it would only be where the snow lasted longest (where the slopes are today). Don and Rogers soon climbed to Cooper's Whole, from which they could envision the most likely ski area. They focused on all of the areas which Rogers

Sunrise over the Rockfish Valley

thought could possibly be developed for skiing, while they talked, walked and scrambled over the ground and studied aerial photographs and topo maps. In the evenings they reviewed the data that had been collected on weather and meteorology; and Fred sketched possible ski slope and lift scenarios.

Rogers' mindset began to turn from skepticism to enthusiasm, and he got just as excited as Byron Cooper with the possibilities. He and Don stayed up late drinking a little bourbon and discussing all the possibilities. Rogers early recognized that The Big Survey's topography would require an "upside down ski area," with the "base" at the top of the mountain rather than at the bottom. Somewhat offsetting the difficulties this imposed was the advantage that skiing would start at 3,800 feet and descend to 2,600 feet, elevations that would facilitate snow making.

In addition, Fred's traveling to Beech Mountain and meeting with their management gave him a close look at the area and ski operations of that community. Don and Rogers (working separately) also acquainted themselves with the ski operations at The Homestead in Hot Springs, Virginia, and made a repeat trip to Bryce's in the Shenandoah Valley. Beech Mountain's elevation of over 5,500 feet was greater than all of the others, and this superior elevation gave Beech Mountain the edge in terms of making snow.

In every other capacity The Big Survey had the potential to offer better skiing than the others. Rogers was very enthusiastic (as it turned out later, perhaps a bit overly enthusiastic) about the possibility of a ski area on The Big Survey, but at the same time he pointed out the need for more study of its geology, soils, water, temperatures, and general weather conditions.

IN THE YEAR THAT PASSED between Don getting the exclusive contract to sell The Big Survey and going to present it to Wheat, he had done a great deal of research himself and had commissioned the work of others, paying for much of it himself, along with considerable help from his Virginia Landmark Corporation partners.

Commented Don, "I prepared to go to market with maps, weather data, a demographic analysis of the proximate market, the report of Byron Cooper, what I had gleaned from The ULI Conference, and the just-completed report of Fred Rogers. I was full of confidence and conviction in my vision, so where and how to proceed? First and foremost was to take what I had to Jim Wheat, the man with the farthest reaching, clearest vision, and most entrepreneurial mind, outlook, and temperament I knew. I also knew Wheat was unsurpassed as a pragmatic idealist. This was a long shot, and maybe my only shot, with just a few months before my exclusive right to sell expired."

Don remembered that a few years before this, he had had property to sell on Bear Den Mountain, not far from The Big Survey. He had notified Wheat about it, and Wheat had asked him to take his father, Jim Wheat Sr. to see it. They visited it, riding all over on horseback, and the elder Wheat was so impressed by its beauty, with vistas into both the Shenandoah and Rockfish valleys, that he wrote a glowing report of it for his son.

Don was aware of Jim Wheat's emotional response to the beauty his father described, even though he couldn't see it. Knowing this added weight to Don's decision to put Jim Wheat first in line as a prospective purchaser.

"In mid-March I went to see him fully armed with reports, maps and papers. On this first meeting Jim was interested, and as he familiarized himself with all I presented him in person and in writing, he became enthusiastic."

Just as Don hoped, Wheat was intrigued, but before coming up to "see" for himself he appointed Ed Morrissett, from his corporate finance department, to go visit and report back to him. Don left with Wheat all the written materials he had brought with him. Wheat had Jane Brooke, his administrative assistant, as well as several men, who read aloud to him. He frequently took papers home, which his wife, Wiley, would read to him.

Morrissett, as Wheat's point man, and Don did not have a promising start. After walking up to the vicinity of Crawford Knob, both of them feeling the trek, Morrissett remarked: "I don't know why or what I'm doing here on this deal. My only interest and experience with the outdoors and nature has been on a golf course, and I prefer the seashore over mountains." Don added, "We both wondered how this would progress with Morrissett's then little experience working with the land and his level of enthusiasm."

"It was not until we arrived at the Pryor's Camp area and around Devils Knob, some of the higher mountain land, that the possibility of a golf course came to the fore. Suddenly Morrissett became more enamored of the idea. From that point on, it didn't take him long to get interested. Morrissett became deeply involved, and contributed from day one his practicality and powers of observation."

Finally, later in May, Don did "show" Jim Wheat The Big Survey. Five of them crammed into Don's Jeep to drive around the property. Don was driving with Wheat next to him. Also with them were Frank Louthan who was a close business associate of Wheat's; Jack Bryan, a silent partner and major investor with Wheat who had the deep pockets necessary for a project of this scope; and Morrissett, point man for the project.

During their tour Frank Louthan got boiling angry at Don over the detailed descriptions he was giving Wheat about what he envisioned. Don commented, "We had had lunch at Pryor's Camp, and I had been explaining to Jim Wheat, who of course couldn't see, how you could tell that Pryor's Camp at one time had been farmed and was opened because of its grassed areas and its type of woodland regrowth. And Frank listened to all this stuff I had been saying for three or four hours as we travelled over the mountain, and he had gotten to the point where he didn't believe any of it. When we were at Cooper's Whole, I was pointing out that here would be this, and here would be that, and here would be the other, based primarily on my dreaming. I referred to Byron Cooper's findings, and Fred Rogers' feasibility report on skiing. Frank had had it, and he blew up."

"'God damnit,' said Louthan, 'you've got to stop misleading Jim Wheat. He can't see the stuff that you're telling him, and it ain't so.'" Don continued,

"He was essentially accusing me of lying. I got hotter than he was. But for once in my life, though, my better judgment prevailed."

"That was on the weekend, and the next Monday, I called up Frank and said I needed to come down and see him. So, I came down (he was president of Everett Waddey, Inc.) and sat across the desk from him. I was a little nervous—this gentleman was quite my senior and a tough guy. I'd known about him for some time. He was one of Jim Wheat's men to get out and take charge of difficult situations."

"I explained to him that I had really been offended and hurt by essentially being called a liar, and I was quite gratified when Frank immediately apologized. He said he was sorry. And he didn't say any more than that."

In Anne Freeman's book, Don spoke of Wheat's tremendous vision. "He could see things that you and I couldn't see. I would point out to Jim…aspects of

Frank Louthan, Ed Morrissett, and Don Faulkner circa 2009

the land that I thought were significant. Someone else riding in the Jeep with us…would say, 'Let's not waste time on that.' And Jim Wheat would say, 'No, that's real important…the fact that you have trees growing and also grass growing up under them would indicate much better soil.'"

"So he had this vision that was not only broad and conceptually big, but also acute. He could get right to the critical element that you and I would see without really seeing it…. That impressed me. He could see

the dream, he could see the big picture, but he could also see the critical path of feasibility that had to be followed to find out if, in fact, you could get there."

After this crucial showing of the property, as Don put it, "Wheat was more than interested and as time telescoped it all became condensed." Don noted, "Ed Morrissett's and my work the spring of 1969 involved his digging in and doing his homework on all the information I could provide him, researching state requirements for development and with anything else he or I thought was related to the potential of The Big Survey."

"During this time we invited to visit three highly regarded firms with whom I had become minimally acquainted and very much impressed at the ULI Conference…:Sasaki, Dawson, and DeMay out of Boston; McDonnell & Co out of Denver; and RTKL headquartered in Baltimore. We asked them to make proposals on land planning and design of a community encompassing a four-season resort community. Firm principals, key management figures from Vermont ski areas, marketing and other consultants, all very informing and impressive came."

"To a man they were impressed with The Big Survey and its potential. The reports and proposals they submitted were comprehensive and convincing of their enthusiasm, including that of Dan Kiley who had a hand in the original design of 'Mad River Glen, Ski It If You Can,' and Carl Norcross, a highly regarded marketing consultant."

Their reports, all very favorable (though clearly with the bias of seeking a role as planners) clinched the confidence to proceed to purchase.

THE EXPIRATION DATE of Virginia Landmark's exclusive listing was very close; and Don knew Mr. Mattox would not extend except at a much higher price, probably with another agent, and at a later date.

Said Don, "This culminated in our coming up with the difficult design of a contract drawn up by Waller Horsley and George Sadler of the Hunton, Williams law firm. The contract would be finalized, signed by the purchasing entity, and delivered to Mr. and Mrs. Mattox and their attorneys. I continued to do work on searching titles, learning as much as I could about owners of adjoining properties, and developing strategies for approaching owners when the purchase of land would be on behalf of a named nominee i.e. a 'straw man.'"

"By summer I had begun identifying surrounding properties I thought were important enough to warrant consideration for acquisition, and had them sequenced in the following order of priority:

ESSENTIAL: development would not be feasible without it.
CRITICAL: development would be compromised without it.
IMPORTANT: potential for development would be heightened if owned.
DESIRABLE: would allow for expanded residential development.

"These were busy times. We had a lot to figure out before presenting a contract to Mr. and Mrs. Mattox, and time was not on our side. I had every reason to fear if that, if we failed to meet the deadline, all of our work and our vision for The Big Survey would be down the creek.

"As was true of all the first people who became involved in the long and tenuous process whereby Wintergreen came to be and many, many people after," commented Don, "The Big Survey gets a hold of you and your heart. It certainly did me; and as a result I could have easily missed living up to my responsibility to Mr. and Mrs. Mattox and to my and my partners' fledgling firm, Virginia Landmark Corporation. I spent more than the first half of the term of my exclusive listing learning the land in every way I could think of. As I explored, I tried to determine its 'highest and best use,' as it is put in real estate appraisal valuation.

"Most realtors in my shoes would have put it openly on the market soon after receiving the listing so as to miss no opportunity of selling it. Or, considering that skiing in the south and resort-based community development had become hot topics, they might have come up with the idea of The Big Survey's becoming a four-season mountain resort much sooner than I.

"But with all my shortcomings, I have been unwavering in my reverence for land and nature. So, as unknowing as I was and feeling as I did, I was committed to making every effort to sell The Big Survey into good hands and good use, as much as

possible in harmony with nature. Unquestionably this spirit has been shared by many others connected to Wintergreen, whose nurturing and stewardship governed their actions as they helped build its unique character and history."

Wheat appointed Bryan, Louthan, and Morrissett (who became BLM Corporation), and Don to, first, review the issues that could most likely kill potential development as envisioned; and, second, to make sure that the contract as drafted would allow time to deal with these issues, as well as limit the purchaser's future liability.

Those issues were as follows:

1] Access to the areas of Black Rock and Devils Knob suitable for development, including the potential ski area.
2] Studies by a respected meteorologist showing that, from his standpoint, the potential ski area site had conditions that were favorable for snowmaking.
3] Determining the adequacy of water for residential development on the mountain; and the means, through acquisition, of developing an impounded source of water sufficient for snowmaking December through March.
4] Identification and acquisition of high priority surrounding properties.
5] Land planning and engineering consults having to do with roads, utilities, sewer and waste treatment, extension of electric service, and economic analysis.
6] Reasonable assurances from VDOT, the Virginia Department of Health, and other state agencies of approvals for development as planned.
7] VDOT agreement to bring Route 664 up to the standard necessary to serve a resort community of a substantial population.

It was decided that a minimum of two years would be required to do the necessary feasibility studies and land acquisition.

"In late May and June of 1969," remembered Don, "Ed Morrissett, Waller Horsley, and I made several trips down to Durham before getting the contract of purchase agreed to by all parties. This contract provided for deferred settlement and the passage of title in June of 1971, agreed to by Mr. and Mrs.

Mattox as amended by our and their lawyers. These negotiations seemed unending, were very trying, and several times nearly fell apart."

They were finalized in early June with a locked tight contract of purchase and sale between Mr. and Mrs. Mattox and BLM Corporation [Bryan, Louthan, Morrissett]. In this contract there was an added provision whereby the Mattoxes retained a 15 percent interest in the property, as Don had promised that he would try to secure for them. If, in 1971, BLM declined to close on the purchase, it would forfeit the $100,000 down payment.

The selling price was $1,400,000, with settlement deferred for two years while feasibility studies, economic analysis, planning, engineering, and land acquisition were to take place. The property would not be surveyed, but a best estimate determined by a certified land surveyor would be provided . If there were five hundred acres less or five hundred acres more, the price would be adjusted upward or downward by three hundred dollars an acre, which worked for everybody, and was helpful in getting Mr. Mattox to agree to sign.

Even with all of this preparation, the actual signing was lengthy, difficult, and almost did not happen. In June of 1969, Mr. and Mrs. Mattox were invited to Richmond for the sealing of the deal and a cocktail party that Jim and Wiley Wheat were giving to celebrate the occasion. The Mattoxes did indeed show up at Don's Virginia Landmark office at noon of the appointed day, but things went downhill from there. Mr. Mattox had had the whole car trip up from Durham to think about what he was about to do, and announced on arrival, "I'm not going to sign anything." Mrs. Mattox, whom Don describes as "solid as a rock," was in tears. The money they were about to make would allow her to stop teaching school, an agreement she had had with her husband that was long overdue.

According to Don, Joe Stettinius, his partner, managed to soothe the situation, and finally Mrs. Mattox declared, "Bill, you've got to do it." Sign he did, but as soon as the deed was done they took off for Durham. Mr. Mattox wanted no part of a celebration.

As Don described it, "I've never been in as tough a situation as when negotiating with Mattox. He was a good man with good intentions as far as Nelson County was concerned, but he was a difficult man to negotiate with."

Don's take on Maddox's foot dragging was that he truly loved the property, and loved the importance granted him as owner, and really didn't want to give it up. Ultimately, Don's partner, Joe Stettinius, and Mr. Mattox's clear-headed wife, Eunice, were responsible for pushing him to sign.

This ended Don's direct communication with Mattox. As Don put it, "That was the last time I saw or directly communicated with Mr. Mattox, I being the cause of his being pushed through a long process that resulted in the sale of The Big Survey, which was a great loss and blow to him. I felt for him and Mrs. Mattox. Communications after that day were by letter only, and were between Mrs. Mattox and me…a very disappointing end of my difficult and challenged relationship with him. Henceforth all necessary communication between the Mattoxes or their attorneys was handled either by Morrissett or a legal representative."

On the other hand, the mood at the Wheat's house was ebullient. Champagne reigned and there was much toasting. Jim Wheat made the toast that everyone present remembers. "Gentlemen," he said, making reference to the assumption that all eyes would be watching what kind of development job they did, "our hides are on the wall." He would put up with no other approach than one of doing it right.

This major hurdle cleared, Don's first priority now was to acquire up to 3,000 acres in the valley secretly, using straw men so as not to give away the ultimate purpose of development, which would have resulted in prices rising dramatically at the least, and likely killing development.

Red barn at Rodes Farm

CHAPTER FOUR

1969–1971:
Can We Make it Work?

According to Don, "That next June morning in 1969, I came up to Nelson County to do the research I needed to do to start acquiring some land, and I already had a head start, having identified a number of pieces of land that we probably needed to acquire. Of course the Boy Scout property, which is where Lake Monocan is, was essential. And, we didn't have any idea *how* we could get that.

"I was in the Nelson County courthouse looking up deeds and Sam Eggleston, the Commonwealth's Attorney, whom I'd only just met, came down and said, 'I wonder if I can speak with you just a minute.' I went up to his office. He said, 'Don, a man just called me from Norfolk this morning. He's an old friend of mine and a partner with Jim Wheat. He wanted me to know that Wheat just bought The Big Survey.' I'm sure I turned ghastly white.

"He said, 'I want to know if that's true or not.' So I thought for a minute and I decided the only shot I had was to tell him the truth, and to enlist his confidence— which I did. And Sam Eggleston kept that confidence.

"I explained to him what we were up to, and that we planned to build to the highest standards, so that the result would be a real asset for Virginia. We wanted to create a resort not like The Homestead, but of a quality equal to it, a really good family resort. I assured him that, if there was any doubt about value, it would be decided in favor of the land owner.

"Sam kept the confidence because he trusted what I said, and I'm sure because of Jim Wheat's involvement. Wheat was a tough, very savvy bargainer, but honest to a fault, and well respected. His reputation and his exceptional business sense were a tremendous asset from the beginning."

That summer the real business of due diligence began: land acquisition and development, ski area planning, geological, meteorological, engineering, and economic studies. The clock was running, and there were only two years before either being confident the project could be profitably developed and putting up the remaining $1,300,000, or losing $100,000.

"By this time," continued Don, "Byron Cooper was nearly as excited as I, and made the following suggestion, 'I've got this excellent graduate student, Jerry Bartholomew, who's needing a project for his doctoral thesis. He's a passionate geologist and a real outdoorsman. Mapping The Big Survey would be a natural for him. I'm going to talk to him about doing his doctoral thesis on it.'"

Bartholomew decided to accept Dr. Cooper's recommendation and undertake work on the geology of The Big Survey. He worked long and hard, camping out in the mountains in all kinds of weather, and sometimes catching a few 'brookies' for dinner. The result was a well-written and documented geological study and detailed map of the geology of The Big Survey and surrounding area, a valuable resource in planning and, on occasion, construction throughout development. Dr. Jerry Bartholomew has enjoyed a notable career as a professor and sought-after consultant in geology.

Don sought out an expert, Bob Giles, professor of forestry and wildlife, [photo of him, leftmost Boy Scout at Camp Monocan, next page] who could advise on

the ecology of The Big Survey and its watershed to help guide potential development. Despite the information that Mattox had given about lake sites on the property, few of them were there. Don knew he had to get help in determining existing or potential impoundment sites which could be capable of meeting the water needs of a ski area, resort, and residential development.

Fortunately he had a very good friend and long-term mentor, Joe Scales, district conservationist of the Monocan District of the Soil and Water Conservation Service, with whom he had previously worked on a number of real estate projects. Scales probably knew as much about soils and watersheds as anybody in Virginia. He came up on his own time, and spent several days with Don, combing the property. They found that the best lake sites were on property outside The Big Survey.

So early on it became apparent that in addition to all else required for development to be feasible, additional properties would have to be acquired, Camp Monocan, the Boy Scout's property for certain, and, if possible,

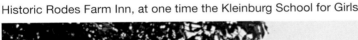

Historic Rodes Farm Inn, at one time the Kleinburg School for Girls

the Rodes Farm. Engineering studies later made essential the acquisition of three acres on Stoney Creek belonging to Phyliss McGann. This acreage would allow a dam to be built to divert more water into Lake Monocan.

Don also contracted with Joel N. Myers, who had been such a help the fall and winter of 1968–69, to come up with a plan for monitoring the weather for the coming winters to determine the feasibility of making snow. Myers later went on to found AccuWeather, which he still heads.

Even while on vacation, Don's obsession with The Big Survey kept him visiting every New England ski area of note, including visits with key people. He was able to meet Bob Dufresne, a principal of Dufresne-Henry, Engineers. Rogers had told him that this was the foremost ski area and mountain engineering firm in New England. Dufresne was generous with his time and promised to keep their information confidential. On leaving, Don was convinced that they could do no better than to have Dufresne and his firm as initial engineers.

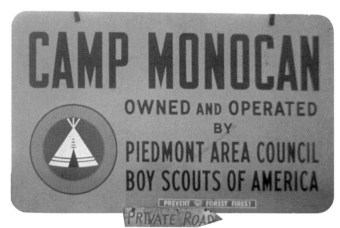

In the summer of 1969 the decision was made to engage RTKL, Inc., as land planners for The Big Survey. "Morrissett and I," said Don, "after carefully weighing the pros/cons of each of the firms who had made proposals, agreed on RTKL—Morrissett because he felt they were more disciplined and less dreamers, and I, because I had high regard for the lead principal, George Pillorge, who shared my admiration for the environmental writings of Ian McHarg."

AND THEN, OUT OF NOWHERE, came an event that dramatically changed the course of Nelson County history. In August of 1969 Camille, a category 5 hurricane, slammed into the Gulf Coast, inflicting unimaginable damage that was not exceeded until Hurricane Katrina thirty-six years later. In the larger scheme of things, this should have meant little to Nelson County, Virginia, but meteorological fate intervened.

Once Camille came inland, heading up the spine of the Appalachians, its winds dropped and it was downgraded to a tropical storm. However, because the area that Camille had covered traversing the Gulf of Mexico was so huge, it was carrying billions of tons of water along with it.

On the evening of August 19, 1969, two cold fronts coming from the Great Lakes intercepted the northern path of Camille, and sent its remnants directly east, into Virginia. When it reached Nelson County it had two towering peaks to get over, mountains called The Priest and Three Ridges.

Each person's perception of Hurricane Camille was unique, and Don's was no different. He remembered, "Early afternoon of a sunny August 19, I started home, and as usual began my journey exploring by leaving Nelson County on a road new to me, this time beginning on a woods road off Route 151 at Brent's Gap which connected with the upper reaches of Davis Creek Road, and relished a slow, easy drive down it to Route 29 at Woods Mill and then home on Route 6 and Route 250, I-64 being under construction at the time.

"The view driving slowly down Davis Creek was remindful of a century before, a creek valley community of modest homes on small farms, most made smaller as divided among family over generations. Almost all were well kept… an idealized

The Southern RR trestle
across the Tye River

Hurricane Camille

Stefan Bechtel described what happened next in his gripping book, *Roar of the Heavens*:

The Priest is beautiful, but looked at in a more ominous way it is also a great broad blade that is almost a mile high that rakes water out of the sky. In scientific terms, its steepness and height create an "orographic effect," lifting moisture-laden air masses up into higher elevations, where they cool, condense, and fall as rain—sometimes not gentle rain but fierce, relentless, murderous rain.

Almost completely without warning, and within the space of eight hours, one of the heaviest rainfalls ever recorded on earth…cascaded down these mountainsides, turning these lovely crags and streambeds into a terrifyingly effective drowning machine for all life below. Humans, animals, trees, boulders, houses, cars, barns, and everything else were swept away in a fast-moving slurry, a kind of deadly earth-lava that buried everything in its path.

The rainfall was so cataclysmic, the Office of Hydrology of the Weather Bureau (now the National Weather Service) later estimated that it approached "the probable maximum rainfall which meteorologists compute to be theoretically possible."

People had to cover their mouths even to breathe. Birds perched in trees simply drowned.…[A] researcher at the University of Virginia pointed out that such catastrophic events were so rare that one had to look beyond

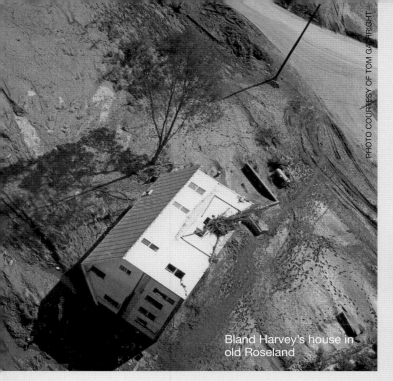

Bland Harvey's house in old Roseland

The Southern RR trestle across the Tye River

Sheriff Bill Whitehead leading flood victims to the helicopter

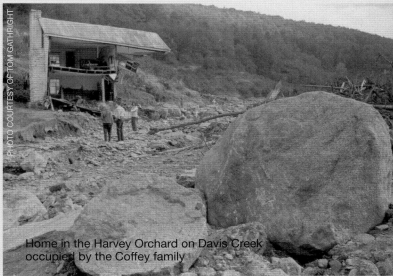

Home in the Harvey Orchard on Davis Creek occupied by the Coffey family

human history and instead study the geologic record of ancient 'paleofloods' imprinted in the rocks and soil. Using radiocarbon dating of these ancient sediments, he calculated that the hardest-hit area (the Davis Creek basin) had probably not seen such an event in the previous three to six thousand years—since before the building of the pyramids at Giza.

After it was over, when the mountainsides collapsed in a deafening, continuous roar, people marveled at the smell that hung in the air—a pungent, earthy smell, the smell of rock and soil that may not have been exposed to air and light for thousands of years. It was the smell of deep time.

Landslides west of Route 29 at Myndus

41

picture of a small valley community such as we see on calendars, with even a few homes having a Jersey cow tethered on grass close to the house or small barn, a rare sight even then." *This scene would be nonexistent by morning.*

"I got up the next morning around 5 a.m., dressed and went down to cook up some breakfast, accompanied by the familiar voice of Alden Aaroe on WRVA radio. His usual broadcast was taken over by the news of Hurricane Camille. It was all very chaotic and confusing to Mr. Aaroe as well as to me, as communication was sporadic. Those communicating were in a state of shock, with contradictions as frequent as clear messages.

"The valley I had driven through the evening before was totally destroyed, and 29 of its inhabitants were dead.

"I called the State Police to get reliable information, and was told by the telephone receptionist that all roads to Nelson County, the epicenter of destruction, were blocked. I made a second call. The sergeant I spoke to, who was irritated and obviously under stress, right off asked, 'Do you know where Woods Mill is?' In response to my 'yes,' he continued, 'There are two tractor trailers trapped in fast-rising flood waters, and the drivers are on the roofs of their trailers. If we can't get a helicopter to them in the next few minutes they will drown.'

"I got the message! And took off up Route 33 to and then down I-81, calling Sid Trott at Eagle's Nest Airport in Waynesboro en route to engage him to fly us over Nelson County north to south, west to east.

"What we saw from the air in over two hours of flight over the hardest hit areas was beyond belief, or adequate description,…sickening destruction of houses and roads, with every stream, even the smallest brook, not only well out of its banks but moving at breakneck speed and force, covering hundreds of acres of valley lands. The soils of many forested mountain slopes had given way, more than saturated by rain that seemed to come down in sheets as opposed to drops. Clogged streams piled up, forming high dams that backed up water, and then at some point the increasing force and height of water caused the dams to break up, creating yet another surge over land downstream.

"We saw this over much of the County. The hamlet of Massies Mill was under water and most of it had disappeared. The Davis Creek valley I had driven the afternoon before was almost totally destroyed. The extended family of the Huffmans had very few left to tell of what had happened. The older houses, sited on hill tops, survived the flood, but the majority of newer houses were right along the usually-lazy stream of Davis Creek, and they were wiped out."

IN THOSE DAYS NELSON COUNTY WAS SO ISOLATED, and communication so basic by today's standards, that for days both citizens and public safety officials had trouble understanding the extent of the devastation. If you were in Massies Mill or Piney River or Davis Creek you thought your area was the only one hit. It took days before the rescue operation was in full swing, and when the helicopters arrived they ferried many more bodies to the morgue in Lovingston than they took injured to the hospital in Lynchburg. One hundred twenty-five people died in the floods and 30 more were never found.

Although in some areas of the county 29 inches of rain fell in five hours, mainly after dark, the Upper Rockfish Valley, and particularly The Big Survey, were much less hard hit. Luckily for BLM, they were still in the stage of discerning, describing, and planning, not of construction. Had construction been underway they might have lost much in the way of equipment and materials. The Big Survey, miraculously, had emerged relatively unscathed, except for major erosion damage to the jeep trails that crisscrossed the property. Naturalist Doug Coleman later found two minor debris avalanches, but they were not on developable land.

It is hard to overestimate the effect of Hurricane Camille on Nelson County. Its two biggest industries, Alberene Soapstone and American Cyanamid, which were already in decline, closed, while more and more people left, looking for work. Farmers' rich alluvial soil washed downstream and left them with land not fit for agriculture. The tax base shrank dramatically.

We will see, down the road, how all of this affected the attitude of county officials when plans for The Big Survey were finally revealed to them.

AFTER CAMILLE, Don was concerned with the mounting risk of forest fires with no access road to get to them. The highest risk was in the fall, so he quickly set out to get roads built that would provide access into the interior of The Big Survey. This also provided access for continuing geological and meteorological research, and exploratory well drilling. In the aftermath of Camille, something as simple as finding a bulldozer and its operator required a herculean effort. Retired district conservationist Jim Prophet was invaluable as a consultant to Don during this time.

While Don was still in the process of road repair, meteorologist Joel Myers came down from Pennsylvania to look at spots that had been identified as a possibility for locating meteorological instrumentation. This involved some mighty rough rides in Don's Jeep, particularly up the steep, deeply rutted pitches of Pond Hollow. While Don negotiated the treacherous road, it was obvious that his passenger, dressed in a black suit and pointed black shoes, was terrified.

Whatever concerns Don had, none compared to the following ten days during which a crew installed the meteorological stations after all the leaves had fallen. Despite the fact that Myers may have been terrified during Don's ride, he nonetheless provided rigorously detailed instructions in regard to the installation of meteorological stations.

As if all of this were not enough, the Rodes Farm property, deemed critical to the entire project, came on the market. Interestingly enough, the risk of purchase had to be taken, even before the purchase contract for the The Big Survey was signed. This seemed premature, but the price was favorable and the purchase was essential.

Don adds, "What this revealed to me was Morrissett's and Wheat's confidence in me. In December of 1969, the Rodes Farm title was deeded over to my partner, Joe Stettinius. It included the beautiful farm with its two-over-two farmhouse and bank barn, which still stand today. I felt as good as if it were mine!"

Myers' initial study included specifications and requirements for the installation of two anemometers, which measure wind speed and direction, with the intent of covering the potential ski area. Don

Red barn at Rodes Farm

shuddered when recalling these installations on Far Knob and Devils Knob.

"The anemometer installation saga began with a van loaded with the necessary equipment meeting me at the bottom of Pond Hollow where the road up the mountain met Route 664 [near the present entrance of Wintergreen]. We hooked a chain securely between my Jeep and the van, and barely made it up to Fortune's Ridge. After this, the grade allowed the van to proceed on its own behind me and "Blue," my Jeep."

"When we got about halfway up the ascent to Devils Knob, along the old narrow and precipitous road, we had a view of the magnificent space below. This ascent had been too much for the van driver, which led to his exit from the van deathly white and shaking. We left him smoking on a stump. With the equipment unloaded, it was up to George Vest and me to install the anemometers."

Myers had insisted that these be mounted on an 8- to 10-foot length of two-inch pipe. This required selecting the tallest tree on Devils Knob and Far Knob and trimming and topping to create a pole on which would be mounted the anemometers to monitor wind direction and speeds. Each unwieldy unit weighed about 50 pounds, and had a propeller and rudder which protruded about 6 and 8 feet above the treetop. It was up to Don to go up the tree to do the trimming and installing.

"So anyway," said Don, "I'm up there on the ladder with all these ropes, pulleys, and everything, but something got to shaking, and I yelled down to George, who was up on the other ladder, asking where the other end of the rope that was shaking was attached. He says,

'Lord God, it's tied to the ladder I'm on!' We avoided a *big* wreck and likely George and me getting badly injured. A narrow escape, which had us laughing the rest of the day!"

MEANWHILE, MYERS' STUDIES led to a surprisingly detailed map of the possible ski area, showing microclimatological variations in slope and aspect.

The answer his initial studies came up with was "Yes, weather conditions were favorable for skiing." The second stage of his studies was to help decide where on the mountain the ski slopes should be located.

His conclusion, in his final report dated 4/13/70, was that, "A properly designed ski area between 2,400 and 3,850 feet could be at least as successful a venture…as any ski area now operating in the south."

Myers found that neither strong winds, fog nor freezing rain, although present, happened enough to be a hazard. Also, his research found that most of the big winter storms that hit The Big Survey had "a strong easterly component," which meant that the wind flow was upslope. This effect was very favorable to high rates of snowfall. The other ski areas in Virginia were further away from the Atlantic Ocean and did not have the advantage of this effect.

Don and Vest continued to monitor these stations on the three sites under Myers' directions. Don remembered how cold the winter was when they were helping with the drilling of wells in different geological areas. "It was so cold," Don said, "that when George and I got back to the Jeep we were just two grown men hugging each other, both shaking so hard the Jeep was rattling!"

The snow really piled up that winter. To make the monitoring easier after a *big* snowfall, Don ordered two pair of snowshoes to help them get up and around the mountain three times a week. Pat Vest, George's wife, also monitored the weather from her own front yard. Four times a day she went outdoors and filled out a form that she had been asked to follow. Said Don, "She did a wonderful job, and she had a laugh that was just contagious; if she started laughing, business was over."

Myers recommended orienting the ski slopes as close to north as possible to minimize snow melt, and keeping as much vegetation as possible for shade, which would also help to preserve snow. Areas of low humidity were sought, which can keep snow from melting even when the temperature is in the 40s.

Myers ended his report by pointing out that they were at the end of a decade of higher than normal levels of snowfall, but that often there are three-year periods of poor conditions in the ski industry. Investors should expect to look at ski area revenues in terms of an average return over several years.

"In the winter of 1969–70," continued Don, "exploratory wells were dug into varying geologic areas per Dr. Cooper's directions. They were to determine the water-yielding capabilities in the different geologic formations. The weather was miserable. All of us would be just covered with ice and snow, particularly the driller. George and I had the greatest respect for his knowhow, diligence, and stick-to-it-ness, either dripping wet and/or ice covered. I think we drilled six wells. Meantime, all winter with all this weather going on, George made the trek by Jeep and, on occasion, some distance by foot two times a week without exception, with me accompanying him when necessary."

With meteorological and weather monitoring continuing into March, Myers' final report in April of 1970 supported the feasibility of sufficient snow-making and retention for ski area development. He made further recommendations and suggestions based on meteorology having to do with the design and construction of the ski slopes. Myers echoed Rogers' and Dufresne's recommendation that Sel Hannah of Sno-Engineering be engaged.

In April Sel Hannah made his initial visit for reconnaissance of the potential ski area. Hannah pointed out to Don what he saw as initial errors and potential problems in Rogers' feasibility report. On May 5th Hannah had his first meeting with Bob Dufresne and John Layman, who was associated with Stratton Mountain.

On May 6, 1970, Wheat, Bryan, Louthan, Morrissett, and Don flew in a private plane to Vermont, through a violent thunderstorm that Don remembers too well, as most everyone but he was airsick. They were there to hear the first reports of the firms hired to plan the initial phases of development, including the ski area.

Bob Dufresne hosted the meeting, which was also

attended by ski consultants Sel Hannah, Fred Rogers, and John Layman. George Pillorge of RTKL was also present along with others.

The issues discussed were:

FIRST, the challenges in design, engineering, and construction of the ski slopes, as well as snowmaking.
SECOND, getting VDOT to upgrade Route 664 to handle significantly increased traffic.
THIRD, the challenges of gaining access up to Black Rock by a road meeting VDOT standards for public access.

Don reported that they returned to Virginia feeling buoyed by what they considered a strong start, only to be pulled up short by a huge drop in the stock market.

Once BLM came into the picture, they started paying Don a monthly stipend of $1,000. Up until that time, his livelihood had been dependent on commissions. So, for the first time in a long while, he felt relatively flush.

Don, Martha, and the children needed a bigger house, and about this time a house on Roselawn Road that Don described as ugly but bigger came on the market. In addition to the house they were currently in, they had kept as an investment a small apartment they'd lived in when they were first married. Ideally he would rather have sold these two properties before buying a new house, but when the market calls you've got to jump. Jump they did, and got the house.

Unfortunately the stock market jumped too, and fell way downwards. BLM put The Big Survey project on hold and cancelled Don's monthly stipend. A friend in the neighborhood of their new house saw him one day looking at the house, perplexed, and asked him what he was doing in the neighborhood. Don replied, "I have two houses to sell and this one to buy and no money!"

Luckily the dip didn't last long, and the Faulkners were able to get rid of their overabundance of housing.

ANOTHER MEETING WAS HELD at RTKL's DC offices on June 23rd, at which most of the principals and professionals involved were in attendance. It was a good meeting and a positive turning point, but there were issues. Most of the problems involved the Rogers

report and Sel Hannah's skepticism as to some of the feasibility conclusions of his report. Sel Hannah had only visited one time, but he spoke of the problems he foresaw, and stated his inability to further describe them without a thorough cruise (physical observation) of the proposed area. A cruise to gather his expertise was authorized.

Following the meeting Don was also authorized to pursue acquiring high priority properties. (The reader will remember that Rodes Farm had already been acquired.) The delicacy involved in pulling off these acquisitions is hard to overestimate, because the whole project had to be kept secret from the public. One slip could have jeopardized the entire effort, with a resultant spike in real estate prices at the least, and possibly failure to acquire properties critical to development. With each landowner that he dealt with, Don made sure that they got a fair price. If there was a question of value it was decided in favor of the landowner, as he had promised Sam Eggleston.

Ed Morrissett recalls, "Everything was very hush hush, and Don's intensive, energetic way of verbal

Sel Hannah

communication was a key to lining up something like seven or eight properties comprising some 1,400 acres of land in the valley. Sometimes even I could not understand what he was driving at. I concluded that the 'fog' that he created made it possible to acquire the land at a reasonable price."

No attempt yet had been made to buy Lake Monocan, thought it had been obvious early on that its acquisition was essential to making snow on the mountain.

Byron Cooper, who had initially been so thrilled by the beauty and possibilities of The Big Survey while with Don, had come back to do additional studies in great detail. This was based on field research begun in the summer of 1969 directed by him, and assisted by the detailed geological mapping done by his graduate student, Jerry Bartholomew.

In the summary of Cooper's report dated 2/11/70, he "tended to back up" the projection that The Big Survey could support a year-round resort development. Among his conclusions, he pointed out that the topography of the Catoctin greenstone forms "extensive gentle slopes flanking the prominence of Devils Knob." These slopes were favorable for both a large golf course and a ski area, as the ski runs could all face north. They could also support an inn or hotel.

Cooper estimated that there were 700 acres of upland that would make a prime area for recreational and resort development. This area also had the advantage of thicker soil layers, which would mean a lower cost for installing water lines well below the frost line.

He noted the abundance of building material in the rocky landscape, and pointed out his suspicion that the alluvial soil deposits at the foot of Stoney Creek would be found to harbor a great deal of underground water. If this were true, there could be a separate community of homes in the valley.

On the all-important water issue, he said that the greenstone made it preferable to dig many small wells, "isolated water supplies for localized areas," instead of a few big wells that would require an extensive waterline system to carry the water where it was needed. He was encouraged by the test-well data, and urged that the sewage system drain away from Stoney Creek.

Cooper also had studied the possibilities for the access road, and determined that a 10–15 percent grade should be the maximum allowed. He also pointed out the importance of installing cross-drains all along its length, as runoff from storms would be huge. Building materials for the road were abundant, and Cooper recommended using a portable quarry that could move as the construction site moved.

Humpback Mountain and its surroundings, he felt, should be left for hiking trails and camping areas, perhaps in partnership with the Blue Ridge Parkway.

As of this presentation, they had finished geological maps of one-third of the land in The Big Survey, and expected to finish the mapping by April. This, in conjunction with the land-use plans being developed, would give them more information about where to drill wells. He saw the need for cooperation between the geological and ecological divisions of the project in the production of a land-use capability map.

Cooper's report ended with his own version of the strong sentiment brought to the project by the vision of Don Faulkner, first, and Jim Wheat, second. "All of us recognize that preservation of the natural environment of the mountainous interior of The Big Survey is an absolute requirement and represents an inescapable restraint on its use," wrote Cooper.

Ed Morrissett, as point man for BLM, felt all along that it was his responsibility to be the hard-nosed realist in order to balance the visionaries with whom he was dealing, which included not just Don, but Jim Wheat as well. He had his worries. As he put it, "As we continued to explore how to proceed, I became increasingly concerned about how different this enormous real estate undertaking was compared to the securities business of Wheat and Company."

Huge amount of money to build the infrastructure, roads, water, sewer, etc. would be required before any revenue would come in. Morrissett was also worried by the total lack of liquidity of the project. As he put it, "Unlike the securities industry in which you can change your mind about whether to own a particular stock or bond and sell it the next day, real estate doesn't work that way. Once or twice Wheat said 'Why don't we run a road in here or there and sell a few lots to generate some cash?' I told him we ran the risk of spoiling the whole project if something such as that were done."

Don, deeply influenced by environmental writers like Ian McHarg and Lewis Munford, wrote many presentations in this period. They always pointed to the developers' ultimate responsibility to protect the unique beauty of The Big Survey. Beyond this, they varied from factual to downright fanciful. In a presentation in the spring of 1971, Don used the striking statistics that the property's boundary was 40 miles long, that the interior

MASTER PLAN

JANUARY 1975

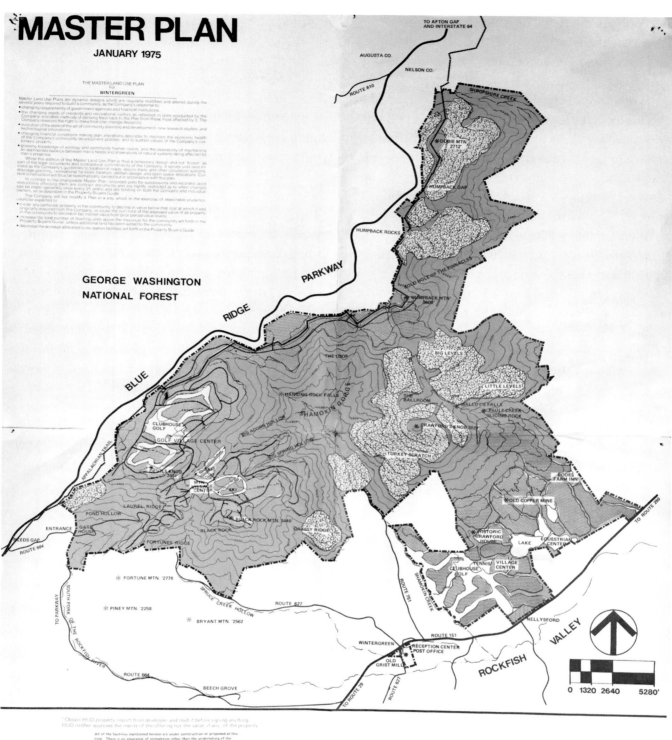

THE MASTER LAND USE PLAN
For
WINTERGREEN

Wintergreen's original Master Plan

Wintergreen

A CABOT, CABOT & FORBES / SEA PINES COMMUNITY
WINTERGREEN, VIRGINIA 22938   (804) 263-4851

COMMERCIAL

BACK COUNTRY PARCELS

CLUSTER/MULTI-FAMILY HOUSING

HOMESITES

NATURAL AREAS

* WINTERGREEN COUNTRY STORE
- - - Property Line
— Roads
—— Appalachian Trail
- - Streams

occupied almost 20 square miles, that it contained 60 miles of streams and creeks, that it had 30 miles of roads for four-wheel drive vehicles and a 9-mile border along the Blue Ridge Parkway.

In an earlier presentation, Don went to the opposite extreme. Describing The Big Survey as "Big, rugged, inviting, diverse and beautiful…. It's easy to get to and hard to leave." Then he turned fanciful. "It is someplace else, a different world; but just as real as Christmas, birds on the rise, ducks decoying, night hounds sounding, a starlit night; Pete Seeger, John Denver or the Rolling Stones doing their thing…"

At one point, in a presentation on environmental opportunity, Don referred to the potential for a majority owner with deep pockets to work in tandem with a minority owner with a deep knowledge of the terrain, able to direct a resource team. He was leaving no stone unturned to convince his Wheat and Company investors, real estate agents, and anyone he came across, that this was a unique property with the potential to become a national model if developed with environmental sensitivity.

During mid-winter of 1971, Bob Dufresne came down for a three-day visit with Don when there was deep snow on the ground. He came to study all possible routes of access up to Black Rock/Devils Knob mountains and up to Big and Little Levels and Crawford Knob. He and Don also studied the developable land, both from the air and on the ground. At one point, as they were going up Crawford Knob in the late afternoon, the Jeep's gas line froze, and they had to walk off the mountain in the dark.

Of the several alternative routes up to Black Rock and Devils Knob reviewed by the engineers, only one qualified as practical and economically feasible. This was the route up Pond Hollow from Route 664. Although it was categorized as doable, to build it to state standards for a semi-private development with public access presented huge problems and challenges. On top of that, Route 664, Reids Gap Road, remained a dirt road that did not meet VDOT criteria.

It had been apparent from day one that access to the top of Black Rock was going to be a bear, and in fact in earlier planning discussions serious and enthusiastic

View of Three Ridges from Devils Knob

consideration had been given to getting visitors up the mountain by gondola. Pillorge was a big promoter of the gondola. As he envisioned it, "We thought that if there was a dense center at the bottom and a dense center at the top, the gondola could connect them. It would be a great ride." But as it turned out, that development as planned was not just dense at the center, but also spread out with single family homes along the ridges. This spelled the end of the gondola concept.

In the spring of 1971, initial planning, engineering, and economic analysis were nearing completion, as was a draft form of the Master Plan. This included the ski area layout and Black Rock and Devils Knob Villages. This was paired with a great deal of quantitative and economic analysis supporting the feasibility of development.

Even though land acquisition work was proceeding slowly, Don was encouraged, particularly in respect to Camp Monocan and its lake. The Boy Scouts of America was moving in the direction of acquiring 4000 acres in Goshen, Virginia, in order to offer a greater

camping experience to Boy Scouts than could be afforded by much smaller camps all over the country like Camp Monocan.

To Don's relief and delight, by June of 1971, Wheat and BLM had made the decision to go ahead with the transfer of deed of The Big Survey. Both parties had agreed that it would be too expensive to do a new survey of the property, so they had agreed to get surveyors to examine the plat for soundness, and to search for possible errors. If the adjustment was at least 500 acres more or less, then the purchase price would be adjusted up or down. This turned out to be unnecessary.

The challenge required locating the corners of The Big Survey. This was a challenge that would have been much more difficult except for the excellent monumentation of The Big Survey's corners by McCutchaw the 1936 surveyor, with near-identical, pyramid-like stones. Don, Hal Bush, a retired George Washington National Forest surveyor, and Vest were able to find most of these corners.

View of Three Ridges from Devils Knob

CHAPTER FIVE

From Dreams to Reality

Over a period of months after BLM had finally bought The Big Survey, the consultants' reports were fleshed out, and it became clearer and clearer that just the infrastructure of road, sewer, water, and electricity, was going to be an enormous—and expensive—job.

At one point, Jim Wheat, Ed Morrissett, Frank Louthan, and Jake Bryan were sitting around after work, looking at the computer modeling. As Louthan reported it somebody said, "We're gonna have 10 million laid out on this project before the cash flow turns around and any money comes in." Louthan's reaction to this was, "You've passed my choking point. Count me out." Wheat's response, "Don't worry boys, 10 million is it."

But then when Gladstone's financial feasibility study came in stating that $50 million worth of investment would be required just for the infrastructure, Wheat declared, "Now I'm choking!" Don remembers being tearful coming out of the meeting, as the way ahead seemed out of range because of the expense of dealing with the rugged mountain landscape.

Wheat's most trusted advisor in Wheat First

Securities was his right-hand-man, Carlyle Tiller. Wheat knew that Tiller's conservative outlook went a long way towards balancing his own enthusiasm. When he had asked Tiller whether BLM should buy The Big Survey, Tiller's reaction was "only if you get a developer." He had reminded Wheat that his expertise was in finance, not in real estate and resort development. Both Tiller's advice and the report from Gladstone pushed Wheat into the realization that what they needed was a partner with experience in development, one with a reputation for excellence and for environmental sensitivity.

Their aim was to bring the project to fulfillment, return its capital investment to BLM, retain a 15% interest in the project, and, they hoped, to ensure that RTKL, Gladstone, and Virginia Landmark Corporation would have ongoing roles long term.

Don joined Wheat, Morrissett, and Louthan on a scouting trip to New York City to meet Robert Simon, the developer of the planned community of Reston, Virginia, also known for his enlightened approach to development. Don had enjoyed a dish with too much garlic in it the night before, and it wasn't long, in the confines of a small private plane, before the others began to complain about his smell. Instantly he was the butt of all jokes, and was sent to the back of the plane. When they reached New York City he was made to walk a ways behind the others!

THE NAME OF CABOT, CABOT AND FORBES surfaced from many directions. CC&F was a big, well-known Boston-based development company with projects all over the United States. RTKL had worked with them, as had Gladstone. George Pillorge of RTKL contacted Brooks Dodge at CC&F, and Dodge, a former Olympic skier, was interested. It was Dodge who tapped Gary Green to look into The Big Survey with him. Green was a recent hire at CC&F and also an avid skier, having gone to boarding school at Lake Placid, New York.

During their visit south they were put up in the very-Virginian, understated elegance of the Boar's Head Inn in Charlottesville. When they saw The Big Survey, Green says, "We were very, very impressed. It looked to me like Vermont must have looked many years before."

At that point Don was the only person who knew enough about the property to show Green and Dodge its extraordinary features. He lit their imaginations by outlining his vision for it, and being willing to track down the answers to their questions about feasibility. Don was uniquely able to convince them to recommend the project to their superiors at CC&F, which they did.

Like BLM before them, CC&F wanted to do their due diligence before irrevocably committing themselves, and so a two-page letter of agreement with BLM was written that would give them a period of roughly a year to study the project.

Commented Don, "A letter of intent to purchase negotiated with CC&F by Ed Morrissett [with Jim Wheat very much involved] was written in late fall of 1971. This letter of intent provided for a year's due diligence period. Gary Green took the lead for CC&F, and Ed Morrissett and Frank Louthan for BLM, with us all doing whatever was necessary to resolve the contingencies.

"Among the contingencies were: consultation with a licensed Virginia engineering firm and VDOT as to right of way design requirements up Pond Hollow (Wintergreen Drive); commitment by VDOT and the Commonwealth of Virginia to improve Route 664 to necessary standards prior to commitment by CC&F; and acquisition of Camp Monocan from the Boy Scouts. Many other engineering issues stood out, among them the feasibility, physically and economically, of getting water to the mountaintop for snow making etc.; meetings and negotiations with the Nelson County Planning Commission and Board of Supervisors regarding the Master Plan and all related county approvals; proof positive that an entrance road could be designed, surveyed, engineered, and safely constructed.

"We were already aware of pending legislation whereby Virginia's counties and municipalities would have the local option of the sale "of liquor by the drink" in qualifying local establishments. Passage of this legislation and an ordinance by Nelson County was of major importance to the resort operation's success! This involved a lot of effort on the part of all of us, especially Morrissett, Louthan, and Wheat, together with Gary Green…. Much time was spent, even into the late night. We lobbied the governor, the legislature, VDOT, Richard Sperry (the Nelson County administrator), Sam Eggleston (Nelson County commonwealth's attorney), and its planning commission and board of supervisors.

"RTKL and engineering planning continued on many levels, especially that of Dufresne-Henry and Sel Hannah on the ski area and the design and location of roads. Wiley & Wilson, engineers from Lynchburg

Ellis Maples

52

Don Charles walks the course with Ellis Maples

worked on sewage and waste treatment, Route 664, and roads within The Big Survey meeting state requirements."

CC&F took the early, important, and expensive step of hiring Air Survey Corp. from Northern Virginia to do topographic mapping sufficient for more detailed study, planning, and engineering of the most probable areas to be developed. This involved doing a ground survey to locate and place targets that would provide measured spot elevations viewable with aerial photography done later that fall when no leaves were on the trees.

Green admitted, "We probably were over-interested in the skiing. We talked to Sel Hannah, the founder of Sno-Engineering; to Bob Kinney, the lift expert; Bob Dufresne at Dufresne-Henry Construction Engineers,…and worked on what was and was not developable."

Green also busied himself learning about golf courses, talking to Ellis Maples, and going to see the course Maples had designed at Grandfather Mountain in Georgia. This course was similar in its topography, and in the challenges created by that topography, to what was planned at The Big Survey.

CC&F's due diligence stretched out until the announcement in local newspapers, on March 16th 1973, that they had purchased The Big Survey from BLM the day before. They stressed that they had been working closely with the county planning commission.

Under the terms of the sale, BLM, Mr. Mattox, and Virginia Landmark Corporation collectively had a 15% interest going forward.

Gary Green was now the Wintergreen project manager for CC&F. What follows is a heartfelt explanation of the importance of Green in getting such a momentous project underway, written by Peter Farley, the very first salesman at Wintergreen:

"It is agreed that Wintergreen is a marvel of vision, commitment, and planning. But when Gary Green arrived 'the rubber hit the road.' To paraphrase author Tom Wolfe 'when the dynamite starts—the BS stops.'

"Gary had the enormous responsibility of taking 13,000 acres, mostly untouched and mostly inaccessible mountain land, and converting this challenging terrain to a mountain utopia. Simultaneously, he had to sell property "lot by lot" to pay the bills. This was unbelievably complicated. This was not a government project but a private enterprise and one that involved great risk. Gary was in charge. On my first visit in 1972, there were very few signs of man on the rugged mountains and debilitated farms in the valley, and yet it was very beautiful, very quiet, a sleeping giant for millions of years. How does one go forward?

"Gary Green, at that time, was the perfect general to fight this war. Engineer, Wharton MBA, seasoned skier, ice hockey background, winter sports guy, and a lover of life. He also had a full appreciation for the history and heritage of Nelson County. There was a softer side that appreciated fine woodwork, antiques, and early American style and ingenuity. Who else would have a collection of antique wood molding hand planes? He possessed all the best attributes of a fighter from New England—a man who showed no fear. He was resolved to do it. But…How? One-step at a time, one explosion at a time, one loader at a time, one road at a time. He was a prime mover and proponent of the original pledge to protect the "open space" (approximately 50 percent). It is ironic that now we refer to the protected land as "green space" or "greenbelts." To Gary Green and to the rest of us this was not a job, this was a life's mission.

"As one of the lucky initial crew at the development's start (I started officially in 1973) I was amazed at the magnitude and scope of what Gary was tackling. True, he had an abundance of consultants, but he still commanded the show, grasped the responsibility, and took all the heat. A man of few words, Gary kept his eye on the many incoming balls and grenades and somehow "moved the mountain" from a state of absolute silence to the major momentum needed to have it take shape. He was a force when there was no easy way to do this.

"The early 1970s were not a good economic time. I often worried about how tough and lonely it was to be straddled with such responsibility to produce final marketable results. To me, Gary had excellent "cool." Karl Malden could play his part. Quiet, authoritative, taskmaster, little expression but always thinking,

Gary Green, recent photo   L. F. Payne

evaluating and moving forward. On the outside, calm, and on the inside, I believe, there was a war going on.

"There had to have been many opportunities and pressures to short cut, compromise, and accommodate, but Gary knew that he had only one opportunity to get it right from the start. To this day we should all appreciate the man who took little credit for himself, but won the initial battles and set Wintergreen's tone forever. We take it for granted now. It was a "war zone" then. We are all here with smiles on our faces because Gary Green took the ball and ran with it. He scored big time for all of us."

WITH THE TRANSFER OF OWNERSHIP, Green needed an assistant project manager, and went looking for one at UVa's Darden Business School. L. F. Payne, scheduled to graduate late that spring, was very interested. He had been raised in Amherst County, and

knew neighboring Nelson County well, having gone to camp at Lake Monocan.

He had gone to VMI, left as an engineer, and had served in the military in Korea. Once he was released he decided he'd prefer a career in the building and developing world. He was influenced by the work of a famous economics advisor named Pierre Renfray, who predicted a boom in the leisure home business in the southeast because of aging demographics and an increase in disposable income. When offered the position by Green, Payne jumped at the chance, and began work that spring, even before he graduated from UVa.

When the project formally came before the planning commission, Lewis Gantt, one of the three commissioners, declared, "This is the greatest thing that's ever happened to Nelson County. My mind still has trouble taking it all in."

Don and BLM had made a point of wooing the planning commissioners early on, inviting them to dinner at the Boar's Head Inn to unveil their plans. The commissioners, in their turn, had taken time to do their due diligence. Hughes Swain and Sam Mawyer took a class on resort development. They also studied FluCo, a big development in nearby Fluvanna County that had run into trouble. Swain contacted a former teacher of his who assured him that CC&F had done work all over the United States and was a class act. Hughes Swain made the motion that they adopt the plan, and the vote was unanimous. A few days later it came before the board of supervisors.

Following the disaster of Hurricane Camille and the shuttering of two major industries in the county, the

Pipeline installation

-Virginian
Tuesday, May 21, 1974
Waynesboro 942-6211   Staunton 886-3400
Price 1

WINTERGREEN'S 13,000 acres are outlined on this drawing. L. F. Payne, assistant project manager, points to the Mountain Village, where work now is in progress. Va. 664, the access road, is at bottom right. The Valley Village, which will be developed later, is at lower right.
(N-V Photo by Berlin)

'Artistic Success' Said Wintergreen's Top Aim

By ED BERLIN
N-V Staff Writer
NELLYSFORD — "We intend to make this an artistic success first, an economic success second."

These are the words of L. F. Payne, assistant project manager at "Wintergreen," the 13,000-acre recreation community now rapidly taking shape in the Blue Ridge Mountains just west of here.

If the comment sounds like so much propaganda from the developer, which happens to be a prominent Boston firm, then please hear out the spokesman.

"Our company (Cabot Cabot and Forbes) is well known in the area of commercial development — things like industrial parks and business structures — but this is our first venture into the recreation field. If we perform the right kind of job here, we'll gain a favorable reputation that will enable us to do the same thing elsewhere. But if we do not make Wintergreen an artistic success, well..."

Mr. Payne, an Amherst County native who holds an engineering degree from VMI and a master's degree in business from the University of Virginia, makes no effort to hide his enthusiasm for the project as he describes the technique of building an expansive all-season resort without ravishing the environment.

"By no stretch of the imagination," he said, "are we tearing up the mountain. What we are doing is opening it up for people to enjoy. It would be very easy to go in and indiscriminately clear out roads and other facilities. But it is our aim to minimize the effects of

these things on the surroundings and to create the most visually pleasing atmosphere possible."

Right now the mountain is astir with the rumble of road-building equipment, the hum of ditch-digging machinery and the activity of landscaping people. From this busy construction scene will emerge, if all continues to go well, one of the finest leisure-time areas in the East.

Thanks to disruptions born of the energy crisis, timetables remain a bit hazy. But it now appears that land sales will begin about Labor Day, that some of the sports facilities and a few rental units will be ready next summer, and that the magnificent ski slopes will be in use by December 1975.

Wintergreen — formerly known as Big Survey — eventually will have within its borders some 6,000 housing units, including individual homes, condominiums and so-called cluster dwellings. Also in the plans are a half-dozen or so ski runs with modern lifts, a couple of golf courses, indoor and outdoor tennis, swimming, overnight facilities, restaurants and shops, all modern in every respect, but all designed to blend harmoniously with the environment.

The development is divided roughly into two major parts, the Mountain Village where work now is concentrated, and a
(Turn to Page 2, Col. 4)

ENVIRONMENTAL FACTORS are playing a big role in the development of Wintergreen in Nelson County. Note the seeding and landscaping of bank and the naturalistone gathering along entrance roadway. First land sales are expected about Labor Day.
(N-V Photo by Berlin)

SKI SLOPES offering magnificent scenery have been cleared and seeded at Wintergreen's Mountain Village. Water for snowmaking equipment will be piped from the valley below. Humpback Mountain looms in background. Ski operations will begin in 1975.
(N-V Photo by Berlin)

announcement by Gary Green that "Economic projections indicated that development will more than double the present county revenue," was greeted with great enthusiasm by the supervisors.

Green also estimated that in the mountain village most of the owners would be weekenders and vacationers, meaning that the county most probably would not need to pay for educating their children. Best of all, Green reported that the project would employ some 400 people, most of whom would be from Nelson County, and construction would be done by area contractors as much as possible.

George Pillorge of RTKL was present, and assured those in authority that if the motion passed work would begin immediately. "There will be two villages, one in the mountains and one in the valley at the location of the old Boy Scout Camp. The mountain village will get first priority. There will be about 100 acres of total skiing area. The village at the top will have one of the most unusual golf courses in the country.

"A 12- to 16-inch water line will be laid from the lake at the Boy Scout Camp to the top of the mountain to provide water (about a million gallons a day) for the ski slopes. Distance: four and one-half miles with a graduated elevation from 800 to 3,000 feet. A sewage system of enormous proportions will be built…there'll be no septic tanks at the resort."

Payne, who was present at the time, described an exchange that evening between Green and Supervisor Odie Carter, a very small man whose head could barely be seen above his desk. "Mr. Green," he said, "I got just one question for you: are you going to put a merry-go-round up there? My grandchildren like them." Green didn't hesitate to reply, "Mr. Carter, if you want a merry-go-round we'll put a merry-go-round up there!" Looking back at this, Payne said, "If you look at what's there today, it's all happened (according to the plans submitted) except for the merry-go-round."

CC&F had left no stone unturned in preparing

Wintergreen plant *Gaultheria procumbens*

their case before they went to the county for approval. A news report points out that "In anticipation of the project, last fall the county's board of supervisors added an article to its zoning ordinance that permits the planned development." In any case, the supervisors, like the planning commission, were unanimous in acceptance of this project that would take Nelson County in radically new directions.

Various people had been batting around for some time what to formally name The Big Survey. Morrissett

joked that it should be called "Last Resort." Finally, Reeves Louthan, son of Frank Louthan, sent a memo saying it should be called "Wintergreen," since the small community of Wintergreen, that had survived for most of the 20th century, was nearby, and its name had long appeared on the official Virginia State map. Apparently this memo sat in a drawer for a few months, until Green discovered that it was also the name of a wildflower common to the Blue Ridge, and that the Indians used its leaves to make tea. That decided it; out came the memo. Morrissett reports, "It (the name Wintergreen) was such a natural that there was never any more discussion."

Green, anxious to see skiing at Wintergreen as soon as possible, put Hannah and Nils Ericksen, a young, savvy project engineer from Dufresne-Henry, in charge of laying out the ski slopes. They sat on a rock at Cooper's Whole with a topo map in hand and laid out where they thought the first slopes should be. They loaded a truck with bailing twine, and walked down either side of Eagle's Swoop, yelling back and forth at each other, confining the width to two hundred feet, which was as wide as snow makers could cover. They laid out six slopes in this fashion, very concerned about saving the beautiful trees. Those to be saved were marked with paint over fifty-three acres of what were to become ski slopes.

County officials may have welcomed Wintergreen, but it met with a significant amount of fierce resistance as well. Among those opposing it were men living in the area who were used to treating The Big Survey as their own bear hunting and fishing grounds, as well as those who just plain didn't like change.

Nelson County, after all, had seen a peak of population in the early 20th century when industry and the American chestnut logging effort reigned, but in the last fifty years had lost a couple thousand of that population. It had become an exceptionally beautiful backwater.

The parallel ridges separating the two main corridors of Nelson County (Route 29, through the county seat of Lovingston, and Route 151 through the town of Nellysford) made Nelson's western inhabitants feel a long way from Lovingston. Some degree of lawlessness likely prevailed, left over from Prohibition and earlier times in these mountains. There was the

DON FAULKNER'S

SURVIVING

↗ LOVE

FIRST WHOLE EARTH CAMP-OUT

SINGING ↗ B.O.F. ↗

PUG ALLEN and

ROCKFISH BOYS!

DANCING ↑

Rockfish Valley, Nelson County, Virginia

SOCIALIZING ↑

Saturday June 2

Nellysford Stew

Sunday June 3 1973

← mountain dew ↓

GREATEST EVER!

THANK YOU BOTH

HSTR + WTR III

Sheriff's department headquartered in Lovingston, but its limited staff and state police had much other territory to cover.

Lester Hibbs, who began work at Wintergreen in 1974 and is one of its longest-term employees, told the following story about Maxie Campbell and B. C. Small. As it happened, Hibbs was engaged to marry Kristy Ward. Kristy's grandmother was B. C. Small's sister. One day Hibbs was in Maxie's store in Nellysford; B. C. Small's house was right across the street.

This particular morning when Hibbs showed up, Maxie grabbed him and said he shouldn't be marrying into the Small family. When Hibbs asked why, he said it was "because B. C. is a nosey old man." To prove it, Maxie went and got his 25 automatic and pumped some shots into B. C.'s chimney across the street. Sure as shootin' B. C. pulled the curtains back and looked out. Said Maxie, "See, I *told* you he was nosey!"

This wasn't much different from the feud between the Harris brothers, who, in the early 20th century, lived on either side of the road in the little town of Wintergreen. One lived on the hill on the northwestern corner of the intersection, the other owned the store and mill across the street. Their disagreements led them to shoot at each other so frequently that it's said there was probably more lead in those buildings than wood!

Don celebrated his 40th birthday by inviting many friends from Richmond up for "Don Faulkner's *First Whole Earth Campout for Sports Only*." It was a celebration of good eating, drinking, singing, and square dancing with his Nelson County and Richmond friends, most of whom slept out under the pines on the shore of Lake Monocan the night of June 2–3, 1973.

Don signed up Pug Allen and the Rockfish Boys to make music. Bill Clark was the guitarist (with such a big belly as to have to play his guitar laid horizontally on it). The music and liquor flowed well past midnight. A hat had been passed more than once to keep the music and dancing going, when the band just had to quit. Several of the Richmond girls asked Don the best way to give them extra thanks. "Just give 'em a hug," he said.

They did! The smallest of the 'Richmonders' went up to try to hug the biggest musician, Bill Clark, when seemingly out of nowhere came a fist that knocked her

Long-term Wintergreen surveyor Steve Key planning his next move

unconscious! What passed in Richmond for thanks didn't pass muster in Nelson County, certainly not with Bill's lady friend. It took quite a hustle by Maxie Campbell, Don, and others to prevent a melee.

After the big breakfast next morning, those who were sufficiently recovered formed a caravan for a perilous ride up the nearly washed out Pond Hollow Road. Fortified with a libation at Devils Knob, they hiked back down the Shamokin Creek Road to Camp Monocan…as Don put it, "the first marketing of Wintergreen to bleary eyes!"

ANYONE INVOLVED IN PLANNING thus far could see one issue that was a sticking point, and needed to be handled delicately. Route 664, which would have to bring all traffic from Route 151 up to the entrance of Wintergreen, or further up to Reids Gap on the Blue Ridge Parkway, was a sub par state road that would have to be improved. Where the money would come from to improve it, and when it would happen, became big questions.

CC&F was smart enough to know that on issues like this, where politics entered in, they had best stay away, and turn matters over to the big hitters in Richmond. By now there was a "VMI mafia" associated with Wintergreen, as Wheat, Louthan and Payne had all gone there; what's more, they knew Doug Fugate, head of the Virginia Department of Transportation, who had also gone there.

Louthan put the VMI arm on Fugate and others, particularly legislators, and Don managed to bring the Nelson County officials down to Richmond to lobby for the project. The full-court press worked, and the state agreed to fund the project in three phases over three years. State officials would have liked to have seen more progress in the development first, but they were assured that it would happen fast.

Steve Key, from the engineering firm Gloeckner, Lincoln and Osbourne, was a young surveyor working with George Vest and Dave Gilbert doing early work to plat the sub-divisions at Wintergreen. Once they had finished a surveying assignment they sent it on to George Pillorge at RTKL, who signed off on it and used it in creating his Master Plan.

Kurt Gloeckner, early surveyor and land planner

George Vest in his element

Key and Vest were the front chainmen; Vest cut the lines and set the foresights. Gilbert was the brains of the survey team, and kept up with all the mathematical calculations needed in the days before electronic instruments. The fourth man was the rear chainman and pack carrier, commonly called "the donkey."

They would meet early in the morning at the construction trailer at the foot of the mountain, where Vest would have a pot of coffee brewing. He would also have fueled the truck and loaded the equipment they needed for the day. Once they had gotten as far up the mountain as they could go, they were on foot all day. Says Key, "We had to carry everything we needed—chainsaw, gasoline, oil, machetes, hammer, chain, survey instruments, lunches, and water. The donkey carried most of this at the end of the line."

George cut the stakes that were used to set each point; it would have added too much to the load to have hand-carried all the stakes they would need in a day. When a stake was difficult to put in, they would build a pyramid of rocks around it. Some are still there today, but the stakes have rotted away.

Often Vest and Key had time to talk, while they waited for the brains and the donkey to show up.

"George Vest," said Key, "was one of the finest men I've ever had the pleasure of working with. I tried to imagine it as he told me stories about being alone on the mountain in all kinds of weather and storms."

Vest had an old Jeep that was usually parked where the guardhouse is today. It was loaded with charged batteries to replace the ones in the weather stations that he monitored. In the winter he had to make at least two trips a week up the rutted trails to visit the stations at Devils Knob and Black Rock. Often the trails would be impassable, and then the batteries had to be carried by hand. In the summer he only had to make one trip a week."

One day the four of them had finished their work and were eating sandwiches before starting down the mountain. They were sitting on a log when one of them looked up in a nearby tree and spotted an owl putting that penetrating owl stare on them while perched, eerily still. Idly, they began pitching stones from around them at the owl, missing it by yards. Vest asked them if they wanted to hit the owl, and they said they did. Vest picked out his stone and on the first try hit the owl, which then fell from the limb and lay, out stone cold, on the ground.

Early road building

Early ski slope clearing

Bar Delk

Shocked that they had done this they began to feel badly, and decided to take it with them down the mountain. That day they had two Jeeps, so Vest and Gilbert got in his Jeep, and put the owl under a wooden apple crate that was in the back seat. Key and the donkey got in the second vehicle and started following Vest slowly down the bumpy road.

As Key described it, suddenly Vest's Jeep sped up and weaved erratically from side to side of the road. As they watched, horrified, it veered straight into a ditch and turned over! The owl had had the last laugh—it had come back to consciousness, not liked where it found itself, and had managed to fly, with the apple crate still over it, into the back of Vest's head! As Key and the donkey hurried down the hill to help them, Vest and Gilbert climbed out of the door. The owl had managed to ditch the crate, and escaped through the window.

Bar Delk was another young man hired early on. He had grown up in the county and knew it well. He had had to grow up fast, because when Hurricane Camille hit, he, like many young men his age, volunteered to go with the rescue helicopter pilots to show them where to look for the missing and the dead. Death was something he learned a lot about quickly.

He'd also gone to VMI and knew Payne, who had graduated two years ahead of him. He was planning on getting married in the spring of 1973, and was anxious to have a job. He applied to work at Wintergreen, but didn't hear anything back. He persevered, and proved his usefulness by shuttling Green, Payne, and various visiting engineers back and forth to the airport in Charlottesville in his Bronco.

Delk was formally hired in April of 1973, got married in May, and commuted to work from where they lived in Waynesboro. He remembered that once he arrived at the bottom of the mountain, it took forty-five minutes in four-wheel drive to get up the rutted track, which was sometimes in a streambed, to where work was beginning, clearing way for the ski slopes.

Once the hurdles of both the sale to CC&F and the approvals from the county were accomplished, everything started to happen at once. Road building, clearing for the ski slopes, work on the sewer system, work on the water pipeline from Lake Monocan in the valley up to the ski slopes, planning for the golf course—all went into high gear.

The "chicken before the egg" syndrome went instantly into effect: it was hard to sell lots without a road, it was hard to ski unless snow could be made, snow could be made only if the piping system up from the valley was finished, it was hard to flush the toilet if the sewer system wasn't complete, but the sewer pipes were going to go in the roadway…etc., etc.

Management also suffered from its own "chicken and egg" problem. Without investment nothing could happen. Everyone could see the potential, but the challenges were as great, or greater. When money waxed and waned so did construction, as we will see in the next chapters. Residential development needed amenities to attract buyers, and the amenities needed skiers and golfers to use them to make them profitable. In the spring of 1973 the light turned green, and the rush to construction was on!

CHAPTER SIX

No Turning Back

The amount of money being spent, particularly on the portion of Wintergreen Drive between Fortune's Ridge and Route 664, scared CC&F. Because of the vast amount of rock, grading was done on a time and materials basis with no cost guarantee. Plans that got laid out on a drafting table sometimes underwent drastic changes in the field due to unforeseen site conditions. When this happened, which was typically several times a day, rapid command decisions were made to keep the job moving. If a job came to a halt, the hourly cost of all that "yellow equipment" sitting, waiting for a decision, kept right on mounting. So decisions were made, right, wrong, or indifferent, irreversible or not.

The Catoctin greenstone proved to be difficult to dynamite and excavate, and costs for Wintergreen Drive far exceeded the engineers' estimates. If this type of cost overrun was to be expected throughout the life of the project, was it an unsound financial decision to proceed?

Early construction blast photo showing difficulties dealing with greenstone, blurred by the moment of blast.

As if there weren't enough problems already, the whole world developed a problem. The Arab-Israeli War broke out in the fall of 1973, and OPEC, the Organization of Petroleum Exporting Countries, declared an oil embargo aimed at nations, like the United States, that were aiding Israel. Not only did they ban sales to these countries, but they also cut production. The world teetered on the brink of recession when the price of a barrel of oil first doubled, and then quadrupled.

Anyone who lived through that fall and the winter of 1974 remembers the long gas lines and prices that continually rose. President Nixon announced Project Independence to promote domestic energy production and lessen our dependence on imported oil. This was the era of Secretary of State Henry Kissinger, and through his diplomacy, the United States gave the Middle East the prospect of negotiating an end to hostilities. As a result the embargo was lifted in March of 1974.

Interestingly, the fuel crisis did not have as negative an effect on Wintergreen property sales as might have been expected. This is because those from Northern

Drilling Wintergreen Drive to dynamite for the water line

Early construction field office

Virginia and the Tidewater area interested in looking at property could generally get to Wintergreen (and sometimes back home) on one tank of gas. That could not be said for resorts like The Homestead and The Greenbrier, which were farther away from big population centers.

The devaluation of the dollar happened at the same time as the embargo, and the United States' economy was one of many that suffered as a result. CC&F in the fall of 1973 decided to put on the skids. Work at Wintergreen was brought to a halt to try to staunch the outflow of money.

During this period a *Richmond Times Dispatch* reporter heard rumors about Wintergreen's financial woes and decided to come up and investigate. At that point, Bar Delk and Dave Garwood, "two very hard working, bright college guys," according to Payne, were still working operating dump trucks.

Payne prearranged with them where he would bring the reporter, and sure enough, there they would be, yelling back and forth at each other, positioning the dump trucks and working hard. While Payne would drive around, Delk and Garwood would reposition themselves up the road in another cul-de-sac, and be working away when Payne again arrived with the reporter. This hoodwinking went on several times, with the reporter not noticing that it was the same crew. She finally exclaimed, "Oh my gosh, there IS a lot going on

here, isn't there!"

At this early stage, said Payne, "There were so many hurdles to overcome that had anyone understood going in what was involved probably it would never have been attempted."

When work stopped in '73, there was a collective holding of breath; everyone was afraid, not knowing if there was even going to be a 1974, as far as their jobs and the future of Wintergreen were concerned. But the realization must have set in at CC&F that they had gone too far to call it quits. With the embargo called off, work started again in the spring of 1974, and not in a half-hearted manner.

To start again was a monumental linchpin decision, to go forward not just with Wintergreen Drive, but with the Sports Center Complex, Eagle's Court Condominiums, the golf course, the ski area, Laurel Ridge Subdivision, the Black Rock Subdivision, the wastewater treatment plant, the raw water system bringing water over four and one-half miles from the valley, the electric transmission system, telephone systems, potable water distribution, sewage collection, the Rodes Farm Houses and restaurant, the upgrade of Route 664, and other projects too numerous to mention here. All this required total commitment. Now there was no turning back.

Command Center for coordination of all of these critical early projects was a small field office trailer located in a parking lot across from where the Black Rock Market is today. There was no electricity, no telephone, and limited two-way radio communication. In order to make a telephone call to order material, contact a contractor, or deal with any of the countless day-to-day challenges, it was necessary to use a ship-to-shore radio in the field office trailer, and call an operator in Lynchburg who would patch the call through by telephone to the requested party. Often there was a line of men outside the trailer waiting to use the phone.

Green and Payne proved to make a good team. Payne, who was very fond of Green, described him as "very able and well schooled. He loved the out-of-doors, skiing, and hiking, and was always working on constructing something." At first Green divided his time between Boston and Virginia, finally moving his family to Virginia after several months.

He bought a small house on Rodes Farm and spent hours there reconstructing it. His role was very important, because he was the link between the needs at Wintergreen and the resources of CC&F. They were operating under an unsecured line of credit of $10,000,000, and at the time CC&F was simultaneously building another resort, Sailfish Point, in Florida.

Payne describes Green "As a very colorful guy, but he was somewhat tone deaf to local politics." First of all he was a "Yankee," whereas Payne was a local from nearby Amherst County with an uncanny ability to read people correctly and to put them at ease. Payne often found himself in the position of cultural interpreter, the point of connection between Green and the locals.

Green understood and appreciated the role Payne played. He said, "You can't imagine how important it was for us to hire Payne. L. F. went to VMI. L. F. grew up down the road. L. F. was very smart. L. F. went to Virginia Business School and he was a professional engineer. So he hit all our categories as my right-hand man, and there were many times when I was much more comfortable putting him out front."

Green and Payne used to have long discussions about what they called the soul of Wintergreen. As Payne put it, "I felt very strongly that while there were lots of things we could add, i.e. golf courses and ski slopes, that the real value was in what was already

there." He was speaking of both the natural beauty and the people.

Green felt just as strongly that natural beauty was Wintergreen's strongest asset, and agreed with Payne on the importance of involving and employing the local people of Nelson County.

As Payne put it, "We could either keep them (the locals) at bay, or we could try to incorporate them. So we started hiring lots of local people, and working on our relationship with the board of supervisors." He estimated that between the two of them they probably went before the board around a hundred times.

Continued Payne, "We'd been given this opportunity and we had a special responsibility. We invited the supervisors to come up and let them know what we were doing…so there'd never be a time when they would feel we were doing secret things." This was important, because rumors flew around the valley and on the mountain. Supervisors had the ability to quash misinformation.

Remarkably, according to Payne, "Over fifteen years there was never a single thing we ever took to that board that we didn't get approved by unanimous vote. We're very proud of that." Whether locals approved or disapproved of the Wintergreen project, or couldn't have cared less, they all knew that it was going to cause radical change, and change, for many people, is scary.

At that time, Nelson County was one of the ten poorest counties in a state with 95 counties, so, as far as the supervisors were concerned, Wintergreen was their best hope in years to improve the tax base. Also it would mean increased employment, which would help lift Nelson out of poverty.

At the time there was no requirement of an environmental impact statement, nevertheless Green and Payne put in place an erosion plan, adapted from one like it at Sea Pines. They bent over backwards to make contact with organizations like the Soil Conservation Service and Trout Unlimited, which initially had a negative reaction, assuming that Wintergreen would muck up all the streams. Payne commented, "So we said, let's get together and have a monitoring process.… We wanted to be part of the community…and we were trying hard to do the right thing."

For many years there had been two ways to reach Devils Knob from the valley: one a rough Jeep trail on the north side, coming up from Stoney Creek, the other was an equally poor road, sometimes in a streambed, on the southern end of the mountain, angling upwards from Route 664. Both roads were a challenge to drive, and in the rain quickly became impassible.

Wintergreen Drive was to start at Route 664. Because of the difficulties in finding a possible route up the steepest part of the slope, the road was built from the top downwards; from Black Rock down to Fortune's Ridge being the first, and easiest, part. Next came Fortune's Ridge down to Route 664, by far the most difficult part. The leg from Black Rock to Devils Knob at the top of the mountain was the last to be completed.

Dufresne-Henry had the contract for the design and engineering of Wintergreen Drive, and Bob Dufresne quickly established that there was only one viable route for road access to the mountain, and that was up Pond Hollow from Route 664.

The first order of business was to clear land, not just

D-8 Cat at work clearing

for the road, but also for the ski area, the golf course, and the first houses and condos that were to be built. L. F. Payne, reminisced about the early days of clearing and construction, "Torrance Construction Company from near Harrisonburg was there for years, charging by the hour for every piece of equipment. They must have made a fortune!"

Nils Ericksen, George Vest, and Reeves Louthan tried hard to establish a route for the drive based on in-office design, but the bedrock, cliffs, and the steepness of the slope were nearly impossible to work with. According to Faulkner, "Bob Dufresne called me one morning, informing me of their difficulties and his concern about getting a route established up Pond Hollow. I suggested to Bob that he hire Byrd LaPrade, originally from Virginia, then a civil engineer in Vermont with his own firm doing similar work to that of Dufresne-Henry." LaPrade was contacted, and came down from Vermont at a pivotal time to join the effort to survey a centerline for the road.

In previous studies, using aerial photogrammatic topographic contour mapping of the area, the difficulties were found to be unresolvable. The only way forward was to have an on-ground survey done. As LaPrade described it, "The four of us (Ericksen, Green, LaPrade and a burly, powerful football player named Carroll Jarvis) started at the likeliest location of an entrance at the base of what was known as Pond Hollow from state Route 664, then a rough gravel road going from route 151 in the Rockfish Valley in a western direction over Reids Gap in the Blue Ridge to the Shenandoah Valley.

"We then proceeded through the woods, up the hollow for what was anticipated to be between 3 to 4 miles of access road. We began at the ground level at route 664 and ran a 10% grade up the mountain. In doing so, I simply used a hand level, which is known as a Locke level. It is simply a small scope, ten inches long, with a cross hair and a level vial. By looking through the scope you can see in a straight horizontal line. We went through the woods, mostly hardwood forests, some dense brush, up the hollow with a cloth tape and the Locke level.

"As soon as we approached what we considered a good turn around or reverse travel, we swung a large arc with over 60 to 80 foot radius to start the backstretch of what became a serpentine road up to the top. Now this was picked at random also using topographic maps which might lighten up as we meandered through the woods and forest.

"The football player from Virginia was the best instrument we had. We measured 50 feet horizontally from station to station, the Locke level at my shoulder being one station and Carroll's feet positioned at zero elevation the next station. It was more useful to have him there with all his strength and youth than to have a bulldozer. He crashed through the woods at a fairly rapid walking pace. I would put him up or down the slope to give us the 10% grade. Following me was Nils, with a compass, to take notes on the direction of travel as we went along. Green was along as an observer, to see how this part of his project was developing."

"We began the first day at the highway and started in the direction of the property all the way to the top of the hollow, and proceeded in this awkward way, probably, at plus or minus a mile a day, making the switchback and flagging at 50 foot intervals as we proceeded up. The climbing and bush-whacking were quite difficult and strenuous, which took a toll on Green. So we had to discontinue for the day and start again the next. We made it easier for him on the 2nd, 3rd and 4th day by slowing our pace down and keeping the football player at a slower pace. We reached the top of the hollow where there was a crown in the mountains (Fortune's Ridge) with much gentler topography, and left it at that."

Ericksen remembered, "As the final access road location took shape and had been flagged on the ground, a timely opportunity developed. On our planned day of walking the road again, we learned that we were going to receive heavy rain all day. So we headed out anyway, and with patience and persistence we walked the full length of the planned centerline, and located every active stream crossing and drainage way. These were all marked with red flagging and noted on our plans. Also the amount of water flowing was estimated as to the size of the pipe that would be required to take it under the road. This information became the backstay of all drainage design work on the road."

LaPrade summed it up, "Sometime later, after our four days and over three miles marking out this road, they decided to put a bulldozer to work carving out a single center line for the road. This was done but in so doing, the cross slope coming across the roadway was so steep that the bulldozer itself rolled over. The bulldozer operator was able to jump during the rollover and was not hurt.

"They had to employ a tank retriever to go up and set the bulldozer right and continue the work. The bulldozer was a D-8 Caterpillar which was one of the the largest they manufactured, and was the model the Corps of Engineers used continuously to built airport runways and roads throughout the world. This news

was given to me perhaps a year after the work was completed. We returned to Vermont and I was told that the access road was built almost exactly as it was flagged in this early preliminary survey."

The entrance road was yet another make-or-break operation for Wintergreen. After reaching an impasse, those who had responsibility for designing it worked their way through to a solution. In only a few days, using one of the simplest and oldest methods of road layout, the impasse no longer existed and the most difficult section of Wintergreen Drive had been dealt with. Challenge met.

Faulkner commented, "If it hadn't been for Jarvis, it wouldn't have gotten done. He was the only person strong enough to cut out the line of sight essential to the initial routing of the right of way alignment of Wintergreen Drive." LaPrade added, "Jarvis could literally move trees. Without him I would have quit." Sadly, Carroll Jarvis died in a car accident not long afterwards.

D-8 Cat clearing Wintergreen Drive

Nils Ericksen, looking back on his Wintergreen experience, recently reminisced, "After the basic opening package of the Wintergreen project, we returned at least 42 times to provide planning, surveying, engineering and inspection services between 1988 and 2008."

Payne referred frequently to the difficulty he had in passing on to workers his vision of what they were after. Said Payne, "It really matters that the people in the field understand, and everybody's buying in and saying O.K. here is what we are trying to do. We aren't trying to build the widest or fastest road; we're trying to build the one that looks like it belongs there. In many places we didn't have a set of plans. People were kind of making this up as they went along."

Payne told a story that shows how hard it was to instill the Wintergreen vision. There was a young man who was still in high school, and in the afternoons he would come to do landscape cleanup. Payne's office was then in an old farmhouse in the valley called Goodwin House, which had become the administration building for Wintergreen. For several weeks after the young man started work, Payne would give him specific orders as to what to do. One day when he came, Payne said to him, "You know what to do around here by now, just

make it look like your house."

The young man's immediate reply was, "That won't work." When asked why, he explained that where he lived didn't look anything like the setting of Goodwin House, and so he couldn't imagine what needed to be done next.

At one point the top executives of the Roanoke construction firm that expected to get the contract to build the sewer plant, were in a meeting with Morrissett, Brooks Dodge, and Jarvis, who was accompanying Morrissett. The Roanoke firm argued that they should also build Wintergreen Drive. Frustrated that their prospective client was not enthusiastic about that idea, having already signed on Dufresne-Henry to build the

When you look at the total development of Wintgreen, there is very little that does not carry George's "Stamp of Approval." It started with the construction of the Devils Knob Golf Course in 1974 and from there his responsibilities increased exponentially every year after he was promoted to director of planning and development in 1976. What most people don't know is, that in addition to his development responsibilities, he played a key role in the start-up or operation of a number of departments or organizations that are now a vital part of Wintergreen. Always up for a new challenge, he assumed responsibilities for the ski operation snowmaking, lifts, grooming, and ski patrol in the winter of 1976–77 prior to the arrival of Uel Gardner in June of 1977. Calling upon his past experience with volunteer fire departments, he organized and trained Wintergreen's Fire Department and served as fire chief for a number of years and then continued to serve on the board of directors. He organized the first maintenance department and hired the first manager, Henry Nowak, who reported to him until 1984. He was responsible for all road and property maintenance as well as a number of other areas now under the Wintergreen Property Owners Association until 1989 when Russell Otis was hired. He hired the first police chief, Bill Taylor. He was responsible for the operation of the Wintergreen Utility Company from 1976 until the water and sewer system was sold to the Nelson County Service Authority in July, 1988. He continued to manage the utility company under contract to NCSA until 1991 when the first

George Nicklas

director, Stuart Taylor, was hired. He managed and operated Wintergreen's Raw Water System from 1976 until 1984, and then, under contract as MeadowBrooke Associates, until the present. He managed and operated the Wintergreen Valley Utility Company, providing water and sewer to Stoney Creek, from it's beginning in 1986 until 1995, and then, under contract as MeadowBrooke Associate, until July, 2015, when it was sold to Aqua Virginia. During his tenure he was responsible for the development of over 1,500 mountain lots, 1,000 valley lots, and 1,200 condominiums, townhomes and single family homes. He oversaw the planning, engineering and construction of nearly all the infrastructure (roads, water, sewer, electric, telephone, CATV) serving Wintergreen, interfacing with numerous government agencies, contractors, consultants, and engineers.

George is quick to point out that Wintergreen has come to be, not because of any one individual, but as the result of many people, over time, working together, sharing the same vision. The leadership of Gary, in the beginning, and then L. F. in the "long haul," gave good, solid direction and commitment needed to succeed with a project of this size and intricacies. George is also quick to point out that L. F., with his engineering background, was responsible for the initial, and probably the most important master planning and engineering of Wintergreen. He gives credit to L. F. for being a vital part of his transition into his new responsibilities, and more important, being a good friend and being there when needed. George is very mindful of the important part that his employees played in the success of Wintergreen. Andy Yowell, Bar Delk, David Garwood, Dave Gilbert, Fred Nowak, John Taggert, Robert Duncan, T. L. Baldwin, Emma Fitzgerald, Gordon Bormann, Tommy Johnson, as well as so many others, who came together, rose to the occasion, to contribute to the creation of Wintergreen.

—Gunter Muller

road, the head of the firm burst out with, "I don't think you know who we are!" Just as quickly Brooks Dodge replied, "No, who *are* you?"

George Nicklas, who later became a key player in Wintergreen management, first came to visit in November of 1974. He had been responsible for construction of the 18-hole Groundhog Mountain Golf Course designed by Ellis Maples, and came to see Wintergreen with his wife, Rita, and their two infant daughters. George and Rita remembered being impressed, as they drove up Wintergreen Drive, that there was no clearing debris visible, and all the trees left standing by the road had been pruned and wounds "black coated."

This attention to detail was an early indication that this project was going to be "first class." Nicklas walked the proposed route of the Devils Knob Golf Course, and remembered being interviewed very informally by Green and Payne, sitting on the ground under a maple tree in the front yard of the Goodwin House Office, eating Nabs and drinking Coke.

Says Nicklas, "I came to Wintergreen for one reason and one reason only, that was to build the Devils Knob Golf Course." He was hired, and spent from fall 1974 until the spring of 1976 working at the top of the mountain on this project. He often joked that he had the highest position at Wintergreen!

Nicklas was promoted to director of development and later served as vice president of planning and development, responsible for all aspects of planning, engineering, and construction at Wintergreen. Forty years later he is still involved.

Said Nicklas, "Maybe everyone didn't share the same vision, but the vision was that something that was bigger than all of us was happening here."

Everyone working at Wintergreen knew that the naysayers were convinced that such ambitious plans would founder, and certain Richmond skeptics were calling Wintergreen "Faulkner's Folly."

Nicklas put his finger on what did make it possible, against all odds. "We were all young and inexperienced, but we had energy that created synergy. We were up to the challenge and were committed to proving the naysayers wrong. It was fun to come to work. It was a good and special time in the history of Wintergreen. Workers knew they would be proud of what they were

creating." When he took the job, Nicklas told Rita he'd be gone before the sun came up, and wouldn't be home in daylight, and then lived up to his prophecy.

DESPITE ALL THIS EMPHASIS on doing it right, Green and Payne had money troubles almost from the start. As Payne put it, "CC&F never got any permanent financing, which was the reason it never had a lien, so we were always sort of operating on a line of credit. You'd go a certain way and then Gary and I would go to Boston and we'd talk about how we were doing. And they'd give us a little more money…It was really a hand-to-mouth thing. There were a number of times along the way that you never knew where the money was going to come from, even to meet payroll on Friday."

For Payne this posed an ethical question. "How can you ask people to come here and do something not knowing how they are going to get paid?" He had to

Encountering one of Wintergreen's prehistoric inhabitants

talk to workers and explain that, despite not being paid that week, they should trust him that they eventually would be paid.

Payne remembered, "Son Small came to me once with tears in his eyes and said, 'I've used all my savings and the money I was going to use to build a porch on my trailer…That's real important to my wife.' And I had to look Son in the eye and say, 'Don't worry about it. You just keep doing what you are doing and this is all going to work out.'"

Payne, asked about this period, says, "All of us had a

great deal of faith that it *would* work out. I had been a company commander in a construction unit in Korea. I was used to accomplishing the mission with limited resources."

Green and Payne had one particularly difficult assignment: convincing Walter Tucker, head of the Central Virginia Electric Co-Op, that it would be worth their while to invest in running an electric line up the mountain, and when it reached the top taking it underground to serve the resort. Up until this request, the company had not built any underground lines. Payne remembers, "They struggled to make it from house to house, and we were asking them to spend well over a million dollars."

"Tucker was about as tough a guy as you could imagine on every front. His wife had lived with my family when I was growing up and baked my first birthday cake," which may have been the only reason Payne was able to persuade Tucker to go to Boston to meet the CC&F big guns.

Tucker was unimpressed by all the projects CC&F was involved in, but when he found that they were working on a building at 8th and Main Streets in Richmond, he brightened up! Payne continued, "He eventually decided he would go on and put the line up there, but he wanted the lien on the building at 8th and Main Streets as collateral."

"I don't think CC&F would have ever been able to get a line up the mountain on its own because they didn't have a million dollars and weren't going to pay for it. It's been the best investment that Central Virginia Electric has ever made; they have done very, very well with it."

Rights-of-way had to be obtained to bring the line eleven miles across country from the Miller School substation, despite significant opposition from some influential landowners. This source of power was added to that supplied by the substation at Martin's Store at the intersection of Routes 151 and 6. Once it got to Wintergreen the electric line went along Stoney Creek, moving in towards the mountain, and then up the face of Black Rock Mountain to the base of the ski area, where it went underground. Although it and the water line that was to follow joined in several places in the valley, they took separate routes up the mountain.

Bar Delk was in charge of the men working to clear the ski slopes. The very first day they killed three rattlesnakes, and the second day they killed another. Said Delk, "It was amazing that nobody was ever bitten."

Jerry Terry, hired a short while after Delk, was a big man from Texas who was in charge of the first water and sewer pipelines in Laurel Ridge and Black Rock, as well as the construction of the sewage treatment plant. He had grown up with enormous diamondback rattlers. He was amused that the workers at Wintergreen were so afraid of four-foot and smaller timber rattlers.

Wintergreen had bought a new work truck for him, and the day he picked it up he spied a three-foot rattler coming up Wintergreen Drive. He used a stick to put it in the bed of the truck, and rode around the rest of the day with the snake rattling away in the back, scaring the life out of those curious workers who looked in the truck bed!

The men were cavalier about what trees they cut as they cleared the ski slopes, sometimes ignoring the blue ribbons left on trees that Sel Hannah and Nils Erickson had wanted left uncut. Delk complained to Green about the workers' attitude, telling Green they were lazy and slow. Green advised him, "If you're hired to manage, don't get too close to the workers, just make sure they get the job done."

When big equipment came up the mountain on the as-yet-unimproved road, Delk said, "I would have to put two guys on the gravel shield of each dump truck to cut overhead limbs so the tractor trailers could get up the mountain."

One of Delk's most important jobs was as a photographer. He bought a camera and a telescopic lens and, according to him, "took pictures of rattlesnakes, burnt up dump trucks, overturned bulldozers, and early progress." When there was nothing going on except clearing, Delk was counted on every few weeks to go over to the Waynesboro Airport, and with a rented plane and pilot, fly over Wintergreen taking pictures.

These were important, as they were used to prove to the initial investors that progress was being made. In April Wintergreen had an unexpected snowfall. At that point there was no lodge, nor was there a completed road, but Green okayed another flyover to get pictures of the white ski slopes of the future set off against the gray of the still-leafless branches of the trees.

The infrastructure of roads, water, sewer, electricity, etc. really drove the construction sequence more than any other aspect of development of the Wintergreen project. Because roads would generally follow the top of ridgelines and houses would be built below the road, a difficult challenge was how to get sewage up to the road where the sewage main lines would connect to the sewage treatment plant.

Grinder pumps were brand new; they had come out of the research and development department of General Electric. They appeared to be the best solution, but they had not been approved for use in Virginia. After much investigation and research, the Virginia Department of Health approved their use, and Wintergreen became the first place in the commonwealth to use the individual sewage grinder pump. There would be no septic tanks

Of course, neither skiing nor golf were going to happen until high volumes of water appeared on the mountain. It is easy to overlook the importance of water in the creation of Wintergreen. Luckily, the planners in 1973 realized its importance, and put a great deal of thought into engineering an innovative infrastructure to serve a community of Wintergreen's size and location, with its many unique features.

As early as 1972, Dufresne-Henry had used results from a limited number of wells drilled on the mountain to come to the conclusion that there was not enough from these sources to supply a requirement of one million gallons a day. This led to further studies by both Dufresne-Henry and Wiley & Wilson, a well-known Lynchburg firm. Ultimately Dufresne-Henry ended up in charge of ski area engineering, and Wiley & Wilson were engineers for the potable and raw water systems.

Road cut through Catoctin greenstone

Raising of the Lake Monocan dam

on the mountain.

Workers in the field had already learned the lesson that in the mountains you cannot build exactly as planned. Daily they had to make adjustments—to miss rock outcroppings, save important vegetation, or avoid water. Steve Key constantly had to work his way around the very hard rock of Catoctin greenstone, the single biggest factor in driving up costs. Says Nicklas, "We were a bunch of cowboys out there every day making hundreds of field decisions on the spot in order to keep a job on track."

As it turned out, Wiley & Wilson had engineered the dam, built in the 1940s, that created Lake Monocan for the Boy Scout Camp in the valley. Wiley & Wilson decided that Lake Monocan would have to be the primary source of water for snowmaking and golf course irrigation as well as the raw water supply for a water treatment plant. Faulkner had realized its importance early on and purchased it to add to The Big Survey. The design challenge: how to get water from the lake elevation at 680 feet up to the ski snow-making building at 2,830 feet of elevation over four and a half miles away, the last mile-and-a-half going almost straight up the exposed Catoctin greenstone face of Black Rock Mountain at a slope of almost 100%!

Because constructing and operating an intermediate pumping station on such a sheer rock face was impractical if not impossible, a very high pressure pumping station was needed at the base of Black Rock. The so called Peggy's Pinch pumping station and the mountain pipeline were designed and constructed to standards so rigorous that they were more in keeping with the American Petroleum Institute's regulations.

The snowmaking pumps would then be used as another booster station to deliver water to the highest point of Devils Knob Golf Course at 3,851 feet elevation. At the top of Devils Knob, water would have been pumped almost six miles and lifted almost 3,200 vertical feet.

Estimated water requirements along with growth predictions led to the decision to build the raw water

Pipeline construction

system to deliver 2,000,000 gallons per day (GPD) initially, but provide for future expansion to 3,500,000 GPD. Wiley & Wilson recommended a future, much larger additional lake, as well as expanding the recharge area to both lakes. This led to the design of the "Diversion Channel," which would connect Stoney Creek with Lake Monocan, adding 7.58 square miles of drainage area.

The senior engineer for the project was Steve Shenk. Several articles have been written for professional journals featuring this unusual and efficient water

system, and the firm has received awards for its design. The contractor for the project was H & F Construction Company from Mobile, Alabama, which began work in the spring of 1974.

T. L. Baldwin was hired as the owners' representative. The extremely high operating pressure at the Peggy's Pinch Pump Station required an expensive, long lead-time, and in some instances custom-built pumps, motors, valves, electrical equipment, and controls. Redundant safety devices, to prepare for water hammer and surges as the result of power failure or malfunctions, were a necessity to protect both people and equipment.

Lester Hibbs graduated from high school on a Sunday in June of 1974 and went to work Monday on the water line. Except for thirteen years when he ran his own company, Hibbs has worked for Wintergreen ever since.

Where they were working, constructing the pipeline up Black Rock face, was too far to carry water, so thirsty men drank from the creek. They quickly learned to watch where they put their face and feet, as copperhead snakes like the water. No one was bitten, but there were close calls.

Tons of dynamite were used to blast into the sheer rock for benches for equipment and the trench for the pipeline. It was dangerous, hard work. Hibbs remembered a blasting expert who had a drinking problem.

They were supposed to use two sticks of dynamite, each 18 inches long, to blast out a hole. As Hibbs described it, "Somebody had the bright idea of filling in the hole with sticks of dynamite." It set off a blast that sent a two-hundred-ton rock the size of a house down the hill, taking out huge trees as it went. Hibbs remembered thinking that a fast-running man could have run under the airborne rock when it came up out of the earth. That was the expert's last day on the mountain.

Unless you were there, it is hard to imagine the degree of difficulty of working with steel track machines on loose rock on so steep an incline. It was easier to weld the 20-foot pipes on the ground instead of in the ditch, so a dozer with a side boom was used to lift the welded pipe into the ditch.

One day, the cable holding a hundred feet of pipe in place broke. Hibbs said it "looked like a giant blacksnake slithering down the mountain" as it barreled towards them. Another worker was standing next to T. L. Baldwin. Baldwin asked him, "Which way you gonna jump?" He replied, "I think I'll stay right here 'til I see which way that thing is going!"

Baldwin was a colorful man, handy and inventive, so he was sent all over the mountain to deal with one crisis after another. When a crisis arose, as he put it, "I'm no expert, but I can handle it until the expert gets here." At one point Payne asked all the workers to write job descriptions for themselves. Payne reported that Baldwin refused, saying, "If I tell you what I do, you won't need me anymore!"

There was a need for massive amounts of fill dirt to go in the ditches on which to set the pipe, so dump truck after dump truck was pulled up the steep slope by dozers until they had gotten to where they could dump their load. These were 12-ton trucks with 15-ton loads being pulled up the mountain! Halfway up they discovered a dump of old tires, and used them instead of fill dirt for a stretch, to lay the pipe on in the bottom of the rocky trench.

There was constant pressure to complete the raw water pipeline and pumping stations in order to be ready for the opening of the '75–'76 ski season. Often the men worked overtime, taking advantage of the daylight hours, and sometimes even worked 24 hours straight. Without the raw water system up and running, there could be no water to make snow and so no skiing.

Initially the raw water storage was at Lake Monocan, which at that time would have been approximately 30,000,000 gallons. Raw water was pumped through the system Wiley & Wilson had designed to a 250,000-gallon storage tank located near the ski compressor building. Potable water storage was in a 250,000-gallon storage tank above White Oak Drive built in 1975 and a 250,000-gallon storage tank on Devils Knob built in 1977. There are also four wells on the mountain adding to the potable water supply.

Distribution of potable water is by gravity feed; there are approximately 30 miles of PVC, AC, and steel pipelines taking water where it needs to go on the mountain. Rodes Farm and Stoney Creek have separate community water systems. All potable water in the valley is supplied by both individual and communal wells.

In 1973 Len LaSala was a construction manager at Massanutten Mountain Ski Resort farther north in the Shenandoah Valley. He was hired away by Wintergreen because he had dealt with many of the same challenges that Wintergreen was facing. He was apparently over-zealous with his criticism. One day in a meeting, LaSala was going around the room chewing out his foremen for one thing after another. When he got around to Baldwin, T. L. stood up, turned his backside to LaSala, and said "go ahead, start chewin!' Just another day of "Building the Dream."

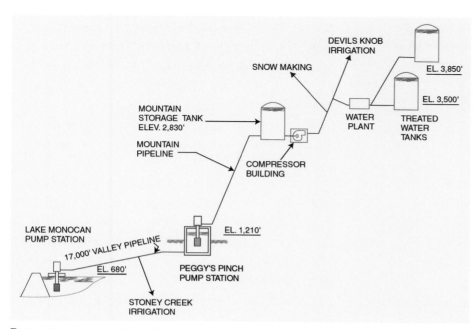

Raw water system schematic

CHAPTER SEVEN

Into High Gear

Payne and Green could see, as Payne says, "that CC&F had this notion that they had these two people that were going to run this. They had no idea that you were going to have to have a whole community of people running restaurants and ski slopes, maintaining roads and selling real estate, doing marketing and all the things they ended up having to do. This was not anything they knew about."

And to the credit of both Green and Payne, they tackled this head on and said, 'O.K., who can we find that really understands this?'" Again they turned to Sea Pines. Charles Fraser, head of the company, was considered one of the most promising young people in America, and had been noted for his accomplishments in *Time* magazine in 1973. With his innovative idea of clustering housing, says Payne, "He transformed real estate as we knew it." Faulkner reminisced, "With his commitment to conserving the natural backdrop of existing trees and shrubs behind the ocean beaches and between every house site, he pioneered a new approach to development." Prior to that, the architectural rule of thumb had been one acre for one family.

Continues Payne, "Sea Pines, when I graduated from the Darden School in 1973, hired more MBAs from major schools than any other corporation in the US." Fraser's head of marketing was a young man named Jim Chaffin, who was from South Boston, Virginia, and had gone to the University of Virginia. He had made his reputation as a persuasive salesman selling Bibles, as had several of the salesmen at Sea Pines.

During this time period, CC&F, through Green and Payne, tried to hire Chaffin away from Sea Pines. Despite his strong Virginia ties, Chaffin refused to budge, but suggested that they contact Sea Pines and try to get Fraser and Gerry Blakeley, president of CC&F, together. This was arranged, and these iconic businessmen from the north and south each came halfway and met at Wintergreen.

Speculating about why Fraser came, Payne says, "He was a big name, but he also saw that CC&F was a big name, and here was an opportunity for them to take no risks but to establish a relationship." Taking him on a tour of Wintergreen, Payne felt he could see his mind working, how this community was going to function and what people were going to do here. Fraser, like Don

Faulkner and Jim Wheat before him, was a visionary—not overly concerned with the details.

When they met at the Rodes Farm Inn, Blakely and Fraser sat at either end of a long table with their subordinates on the sides. "It was like a ping pong match," said Payne, "lots of stories were told, and they said it was an historic event because it was north and south, two well-respected companies, getting together in ways that were going to be productive.

"So we ended up working with the Sea Pines Company. Their responsibilities were sales, marketing and operations, once we got the buildings up. They were going to run food and beverage operations and all that sort of thing. CC&F [would take care of] planning, development, and accounting, plus the ski area," because Sea Pines, being in the south, had no experience with ski resorts. Gary Green had first hand experience and loved to ski, and various scouts and consultants from the

Peter Farley   Charles Fraser

northeast were also contacted for advice.

In 1973 Peter Farley was a young man with an unpretentious good nature living in Gordonsville, Virginia, trying to sell real estate in economically tough times. He had never been anywhere in Nelson County other than driving through it to get to Lynchburg, but he was intrigued by the very thought of an intact parcel of 13,000 acres of mountain land. He and his paint contractor friend, Michaux Grant, took a joy ride one day to find out more about it.

They ran into Gary Green, who must

have sensed in Farley the qualities that make a good salesman. Green also established that Farley was a Virginian through and through, and would understand the culture of clients from Richmond and farther south. After talking to them in the office, Green took them on a three-hour tour to the top of the mountain, pointing out to Farley where everything would be.

Farley says, "It looked pretty far-fetched to me, but I was mesmerized by the outrageous beauty." It wasn't long before Green persuaded Farley to come to Wintergreen to help set up the sales office, which he did in 1973.

"I was determined to be positive," Farley says, "but it was a different world. There were race riots in Washington, DC, and in Richmond, a war everyone was tired of, an iron curtain, and threats of nuclear war.

First of all, to take a client up the mountain was a five-hour adventure. A four-wheel-drive vehicle was required once you left route 664. Wintergreen Drive in the early seventies Farley describes as "a goat path with heavy equipment." Toyota Land Cruisers and Jeeps were the vehicles of choice. You put them in monkey low and shuddered slowly up the mountain, trying at the same time to reassure your clients, who would be wondering why they had signed on for this. These vehicles didn't last much beyond 35,000 miles; tires flattened, motors burnt out, and gears stripped.

Sea Pines Company
Hilton Head Island, S. C. 29928, 803 785-3333
Hilton Head Island

January 7, 1975

Mr. Peter V. Farley
Wintergreen
Wintergreen, Virginia 22938

Dear Peter,

On behalf of the Sea Pines Company, I would like to congratulate you on your outstanding sales performance at Wintergreen. Your performance stands as an example for all of the company's sales executives.

It is especially noteworthy that although all of the other Wintergreen salesmen missed their goals for the quarter, you surpassed yours. We are proud of your performance and know that we can count on your continued success.

I look forward hopefully to thanking you personally for your outstanding contribution to our company when you are next at Sea Pines.

Congratulations again.

Sincerely,

Charles

CHARLES E. FRASER
President

CEF:fjw

76

The salesmen got a transportation allowance of $300 monthly, but they often used this to live on when there were no sales.

There were no restrooms once you set off, as there was not yet either electricity or running water on the mountain. Laying in supplies for a picnic lunch you had a choice of Maxie Campbell's, where the bear hunters hung out and strangers were eyed suspiciously, or Graves Grocery, where you could stock up on Coke, Vienna sausages, Saltine crackers, and a slice off the big wheel of cheddar wrapped up in wax paper.

Farley remembers that it was a huge challenge once he got his clients up to the lots he wanted to show them, as his attempts to point out the wildflowers or get them to listen to the birdsong would be drowned out by giant earthmovers eating into the mountain. However, when his clients talked to just about anybody working on the mountain, they were impressed

properties early on, as Faulkner went about quietly amassing land to be added to The Big Survey to make both the mountain and valley communities of Wintergreen possible.

Faulkner suggested that Wintergreen hire young Stuart Sadler, George's son. Stuart accepted with alacrity, for an extremely practical reason. He loathed wearing ties, and in his new job they wouldn't be necessary! Stuart has been in that job ever since, and remains the go-to person when anyone needs to unravel a confusion or be reminded of a date, a number or a title. He is the keeper of Wintergreen's historical and legal records.

It became clear early on that there was no place nearby for potential buyers to stay and feel welcomed when they came to visit, or to eat a decent "sit down" meal. The Rodes Farm had already been purchased by BLM. Green decided that the old farmhouse, set on

Stuart Sadler, still on the job (in a tie!)

Old tobacco barns at Rodes Farm

because, as Farley put it, "Everyone believed so hard and so deep."

Clients he thought he would never see again would come back, and when they did the situation would have improved. They would go home after another visit and spread the word about the exciting developments at Wintergreen. The first real estate sales were not until 1975.

Even before there were sales of lots there was need for a lawyer. George Sadler of the Hunton Williams law firm in Richmond had handled the purchase of

rolling pastureland with the mountains as a backdrop, should be turned into such a place.

Green was captivated by the two picturesque tobacco barns in the fields, so he got an architect to take their measurements and design simple structures that could each house a family. Soon there were eleven of these, and a swimming pool, forming its own little "village." Farley said, "We did Jeep rides up the mountain. That's how we started sales, long before there was ever a road up the mountain. People were saying, "Hey I like this and I want to be part of selling this property.""

The farmhouse was an obvious spot for a restaurant but the big question was, who would cook and run the place? The perfect answer to this question dawned on Peter Farley as he was sitting on Marguerite Wade's porch, passing the time of day with her one afternoon.

She was a colorful, extremely friendly local woman of ample girth who was also known as a terrific cook. Unasked, she took it upon herself to march into the development office every now and then with meals of fried chicken, butter beans, and potatoes, just to keep the boys' spirits up. Farley was on her porch because he had come to thank her for these missions of mercy, and for the pleasure of talking and soaking up local lore.

In the course of their conversation, Peter was stunned by a statement Marguerite made, "Son, I'd be in heaven if someone would love me for myself and for my cooking."

Then it hit him. Who better than Marguerite to

Marguerite Wade

wow guests with her instinctively welcoming personality, followed up by producing meals that would make certain the guests would return?

Peter hustled back to Green, whose reaction was, "Hire her." When presented with this idea, according to Farley, "Marguerite freaked out. She couldn't see doing the hiring and firing, the ordering, overseeing the

reservations, managing the employees, etc." So Farley went back to Green and described her reaction. Green said, "Tell her we'll do all that for her. She'll get the joy and we'll get the worry. All she'll have to do is greet and cook."

This suited Marguerite perfectly, so Farley suggested they take a trip to Big Canoe, a resort development in the Georgia mountains, to see how a first-class resort "down home" food service operation like that was run. Marguerite considered this a very forward suggestion, exclaiming, "I am not getting on a plane with you and going overnight….I am married to Jack!" So Jack came too. When travel day arrived, Peter picked them up, Marguerite in her pillbox hat and shawl. Sitting between Peter and her husband on the airplane, a new form of transportation for them both, she nearly squeezed Peter's hand off his wrist on takeoff.

But the visit paid off, and quickly she settled into a job that was literally made for her. She loved all the salesmen, and enjoyed being in cahoots with them, talking them up to their clients staying at the Rodes Farm Inn. Her interest in people was genuine, and guests could feel that instinctively. She meant it when she said, "I want you as a neighbor." There was so much synergy between the sales force and Marguerite that she might as well have been an honorary saleswoman.

Farley says, "I remember some wonderful evenings there. Marguerite weighed a good deal, and if she started laughing she wouldn't be able to stop, so she'd get everyone else laughing and tears in their eyes!"

Charlie Peake, the first marketing manager at Wintergreen, remembered, "As we gained early homesite owners, we would host barn dances on a Saturday night in the old barn to create a sense of community and to attract new property owners." Pug Allen and the Blue Ridge Mountain Boys provided authentic country music, with Pug leading on fiddle backed by mandolin, banjo, guitars, and stand-up bass.

Saylor Allen, Pug's cousin, had years before been a sawyer on the Mattox timber harvest in the early 1950s. He would do a forward and back shuffle dance to the music. Continued Peake, "Saylor had keen eyesight and was happiest when dancing with some of our comely staff and guests! Besides good food, there was always a supply of moonshine and apple cider to improve everyone's dancing. Don Faulkner was instrumental in

Bill Peacher

organizing these Nelson County celebrations."

Payne speaks about the goal they had of being part of the community. "We wanted to work with others in the county who had an interest in what we were doing. Our stakeholders were not just us and people who were going to buy property from us…we wanted to get [locals] engaged and involved. The people who came later as property owners appreciated that. They wanted to be part of that environment because Wintergreen was a special place, not just because they wanted to go somewhere that had a big golf course or ski slopes."

As the displays and renovations of the sales office were materializing, Bill Peacher arrived. Peacher was sent to Wintergreen by the Sea Pines Company to oversee the contractual agreement with CC&F. He was vice president for sales and marketing from1975 until 1979. For him, the excitement came from being in on the early stage of development and buying into the dream. "In this case," Peacher says, "the reality was better than the dream!"

Don Faulkner was in transition from being the visionary to working in sales as Wintergreen's real estate broker, in tandem with his partner, Harvie Fitzgerald. He and Harvie had started a new real estate company called Virginia Country. Commented Faulkner, "Harvie and I worked together to provide on-site brokerage supervision seven days a week, as was then required by the state real estate regulations. We were in fact almost entirely engaged in sales activity working with the salesmen.

Harvie and I were spoken of as "Virginia Country," and worked as hard as mules plowing rocky ground. Despite having the advantage of being born and raised in Virginia, the two of us were seldom as productive

Ads by Bozell Jacobs that were consistent with Bob Evans' view of the importance of nature.

as most of the rest of the salesmen. Harvie was an all-round capable man, and highly regarded by all who knew him. He continued to work at Wintergreen several years after I left in 1978."

In the fall of 1975 Gary Horvath came to Wintergreen, having formerly been a licensed real estate broker in West Virginia. He purchased a lot in the valley, and shortly thereafter built one of the first houses in the Stoney Creek development. He is still both working and living at Wintergreen today.

Horvath described three different small, private airplane crashes that he knew of at Wintergreen in which nobody had been killed. The first was at Laurel Springs Gap. In that instance the pilot and one passenger were critically injured. However they were able to walk down off the mountain in a ferocious thunderstorm to Peggy's Pinch Pump Station, use the emergency phone on the outside of the building and call for help.

The second was a twin-engine private plane piloted by two Navy officers. It had engine problems after taking off from a grass strip in the Rockfish Valley. They crash landed near the top of Shamokin Gorge when the aircraft could not gain enough altitude to clear the mountain.

The third, according to Horvath, took off from Waynesboro Airport headed for Nelson County. It missed the top of the mountain by a few feet and ended up on the deck of a Wintergreen house!

Bob Evans arrived to work in marketing and advertising for Wintergreen after having handled accounts for both Sea Pines and CC&F as executive VP of the Martin Agency in Richmond.

He knew Jim Wheat, and when Faulkner and Farley took him for a ride at Wintergreen he remembers wondering if they would ever make it to the top. "I'd never seen road construction in this kind of terrain," he says. "On reaching what would become the mountain village, I recognized immediately that I loved this place, the vision of the developers, the beauty of the vistas, the people I was meeting—and I never lost that love in the ten years or so that I worked there."

At first his involvement with Wintergreen was through the Martin Agency, working on a logo and a marketing "look" for the project. Judging from examples that still dot the walls in the Wintergreen sales office, those ads emphasized families, the outdoors, and views that varied from quietly beautiful to spectacular. Some had no people in them at all, but they were very effective in inviting people to come and be a part of this fledgling community.

Evans' work was vital at this point because it established an image for Wintergreen long before there was a product, such as the ski area or the golf course. In fact there was little more than a road.

What there was, explained Peter Farley, was a generation of potential buyers, many of whom had fought in WWII and had matured into the years of their highest purchasing power. "They had an esprit de corps, a fervor, and a dedication to a shared goal," said Farley. "Many of them were in the military, coming from the navel base at Norfolk and from Washington, DC."

There was also an element of fear in the idea of escape. They were living through the seemingly endless years of the cold war. These were the years of nuclear threat and Russian territorial expansion. If we were bombed, Washington and Norfolk would both be targets. Of greatest concern to these men were their families; they were heartened by the family-centric image of Wintergreen as a peaceful haven, and a wholesome place to which they could bring their children and grandchildren in safety.

"They had a need for a physical and mental escape from all the bad news in the newspapers," continued Farley. "We sold them the dream." Evans made sure that his ads emphasized the peace to be found in the beauty of Wintergreen. The ads didn't say "The world is a dangerous place," but the visual appeal of his ads positioned Wintergreen as the place to get away from it all.

After direct mail contacts had resulted in successful initial sales, both Evans and his boss, David Martin, bought lots at Wintergreen. Evans kicks himself now for having sold his lot at Crow's Nest for $14,000 when he built a house in the valley.

In 1978 Payne offered him the position of VP of marketing, and even though he had just moved to Virginia Beach he took the job. As he put it, "I just couldn't resist. I moved to Wintergreen and lived in one of the Rodes Farm houses, ate at Marguerite Wade's, and began to pursue a dream of positioning Wintergreen not just as a ski resort, but for the year-round beauty of the Blue Ridge.

"Don Faulkner, Peter Farley and Doug Coleman were an incredible inspiration to me. Following in their footsteps, we combed the ridges, streams, and overlooks and began to envision a network of trails that would open much of the 13,000 acres of property to urbanites who had never ventured out into the mountains. I remember one of the first things we did was introduce these natural wonders to our own employees, and through them, to visitors, in an internal campaign based around lapel pins with invitations to 'Ask Me About Shamokin Falls' and other natural attractions, and we produced the first resort guides to an expanding trail system.

"We began to offer off-season special events like barn dances and cookouts in the Rodes Valley; guided nature walks with Doug Coleman; the first Wintergreen Wildflower Festivals; concerts (including Peter, Paul & Mary) and fireworks on the ski slopes. All fledging attempts to introduce this unique outdoor world in all its year-round glory."

Two celebrities that stopped for dinner at the Rodes Farm Inn were John Lennon and Mick Jagger. They left their names in the guest book. Next to their names Marguerite Wade had written "Beatle" and "Rolling Stone," but she called them hippies!

The Hook, a Charlottesville weekly newspaper no longer in existence, described a visit to Central Virginia in an article May 9, 2007. "When a delusional fan shot and killed John Lennon outside his home in New York in 1980, his family lost a father and husband; the world lost a visionary. But what has never been confirmed until now is that Charlottesville lost its chance to be Lennon and Yoko's summer home.

"In an interview with *The Hook* this week to promote the upcoming show of Lennon's art, the avante garde artist and Beatle widow Yoko Ono reminisced about driving through Charlottesville looking for real estate. Ono says she didn't remember the Charlottesville trip until very recently, a lapse she attributes to the timing of the trip, which occurred shortly before her husband's murder.

"If the details of their Virginia visit remain hazy, Ono, now 74, says she now recalls that she and Lennon came away from the area with a positive impression.

"'We were looking for a nice summer house,' she says.…The spirit of the area affected the artistic couple. 'It was almost like being in touch with the true history [of America],' Ono says."

EVANS REMEMBERED THE PUSH to make the message an all-season one. "Our marketing efforts focused on establishing the resort and second-home community as a significant step above competing properties on the East Coast, both in quality and beauty. We brought in some of the region's finest photographers to record both the natural and man-made features of the property. We partnered with well-known area retailers like Woodward and Lothrop to furnish condominium models, and Eddie Bauer to photograph their seasonal clothing at Wintergreen."

"We enhanced on-site signage and real estate displays to emphasize quality and beauty. And our advertising campaigns always sought to establish this special marketing position, even when the goal was to sell ski tickets or condominium units."

Evans summed up his time at Wintergreen sounding a theme that comes from so many that work or have worked there. "I developed a deep affection for many of the people I worked with and some of the property owners who were part of my early years there. We were a family of sorts. I watched the development grow for ten years (and hopefully helped it) but I confess that it outgrew my vision of it. I'm proud to have been part of its growth but I hope there are still those who remember it at the beginning."

As the sales force expanded, from Sea Pines came Richard Buckingham, Steve Kaiser, and Gene Angle, and Kyle Lynn, and Phil Patterson from Big Canoe. They joined Farley, Faulkner, and Fitzgerald in the sales office. They quickly came to appreciate Marguerite Wade's cooking as well as her talent for spoiling both them and their clients.

Some joined Faulkner and Fitzgerald at Margaret Garth's Tuckahoe Tavern, as her cooking also seemed to be a big draw. They enjoyed her company, and learned a lot that was useful to them about Nelson County matters, all for $6.00 a night room and board!

These pioneer salesmen had accepted a monstrous challenge—how to sell lots when there was no resort activity to speak of. They worked seven days a week. On weekdays they made phone calls, first using old Sea

Vernon and Clora Truslow

of those visits resulted in sales in 1977 and '78, when we had the ski area and the golf course." On the weekends they showed lots starting at $7,000 and rising to $35,000.

The renown of Marguerite Wade's fried chicken and biscuits reached to Richmond and Raleigh. After a while word got around about how much fun was to be had at Wintergreen on the weekends, and more famous people started coming. Among these were Mohammed Ali and Jerry Falwell.

One particularly enthusiastic visitor was Jim Miln, the executive VP of General Electric. Jim Wheat and his wife had built a house at Wintergreen, which they had turned over to Miln who had organized a corporate conference at Wintergreen. During a break in their work, a salesman took Miln and his family to see Shamokin Gorge, and they walked up to the lower part of the waterfalls.

Miln was so excited by the beauty of the place he stripped down to his skivvies and jumped into the pool at the bottom of the waterfalls! Not to be outdone, his children stripped to their underclothes and jumped in too. Then they all got out, and with no towels put on their clothes and got back in the Jeep for the rest of the ride up the gorge.

So beauty and Wintergreen's wilderness became the product that they were selling in the early days, before there were any amenities. The visual stimulus was incredibly powerful, which Evans realized and used in his image marketing.

Visitors were also impressed by the care that was being taken to preserve the beauty that was everywhere they looked. Farley pointed out, "The conservation and environmental sensitivity piece was a unique part of the sales presentation from day one until today. It's not a theme, it's a religion, a commitment."

Even today, with amenities everywhere you look, Farley says that, as a salesman before an appointment, he takes time to school himself, and rehearse how to sell the experience, not the real estate. He sells the trails and the sunsets, the bears and the birdsong, as well as the work of the planners and the architects.

Pines lists, and then later referrals from clients. They confessed to beating to death any name they got.

Farley remembered, "We had a boiler room in the old sales office where we made calls from 6:00 to 9:00 p.m. Those calls that we made in 1975 and '76 were to talk people into coming to visit." They were selling a vision as well as a visit. "At that point," commented Farley, "we had no product."

"Those we called were interested, but were waiting to see some completed resort construction. But many

IN JANUARY OF 1975 the Wintergreen office at Goodwin House burned down, and it was clearly an act of arson. The board of supervisors were all in favor of Wintergreen coming to the county, but there were also deep pockets of resentment in the community. Those who just didn't like change, those who feared that the county would lose its identity through the influx of so many people, and those who were used to treating The Big Survey as their hunting preserve; all of these groups kept the pot stirred. As Payne put it, "For some people in that culture, if you didn't agree with somebody you didn't sue them, you burned down their barn."

Perhaps the biggest sticking point had erupted when the bear hunters, used to treating The Big Survey as their hunting preserve for generations back, learned that for liability reasons Wintergreen had said that there would no longer be hunting on the property.

Following the burning of Goodwin House, Green and Payne realized that all eyes would be watching Wintergreen's reaction. It could have been "to hell with these people," but as Payne said, "It just showed us we had to try harder." So management allocated land where bear hunting would be allowed, and Payne

got together with the hunters to talk about where they could hunt.

Payne described what happened one night about 10:00 p.m. when their doorbell rang. It was Bo Zerkel, whom Payne knew from growing up with him in Amherst County, and a friend of his in hunting camouflage. According to Payne, "Susan, my wife, was scared to death. I came to the door, and they had this brown paper bag. It was the prime piece of meat from the bear, the best piece they could possibly give, because they wanted to say thanks."

But there were also times when Payne must have been worried about his own safety and that of his family. The Virginia Department of Transportation had agreed to the widening of Route 664, the connector between route 151 and Wintergreen Drive. However it had no money to buy the rights of way on each side necessary to allow for the widening, so CC&F had paid for the rights of way.

The residents along 664 were opposed to the change, and to show their displeasure hung Payne in effigy. Payne remembers thinking, "This is pretty serious stuff…but you have got to find a way to work through

The Goodwin House fire

Wintergreen's first sales office

[these issues] knowing we are all going to be here for a very long time."

After Goodwin House burned down, some offices were set up on site in trailers, some were above Graves Grocery, and some were in a couple of the "tobacco barn houses" at Rodes Farm. The Country Store was renovated for the salesmen, and opened in what had been the little hamlet of Wintergreen, the valley community that died out in the 1950s on route 151.

Every effort was made to turn this into a charming spot to meet a client. Bill Tyler, a talented woodworker from Crozet, lovingly restored the building and turned the space behind it into a park-like setting with a bridge over the creek.

Green and Payne redoubled their efforts to hire locals in the face of community unrest. Don Martin started working for the Wintergreen maintenance department in August of 1975. One of his first assignments was installing guardrails along Wintergreen Drive. Today, forty years later, Don is road maintenance supervisor. In the early days Don was also involved with the difficult construction of Raven's Roost observation deck overlooking the Shenandoah Valley, one of the most spectacular spots at Wintergreen.

Tim Hess, who was working in the food and beverage area running a tavern near Sea Pines, heard about Wintergreen. Because he was a skier anxious to get a job in a ski facility, he flew up to visit and soon was working at Wintergreen himself.

Hess was hired as food and beverage director in 1975, and was immediately put to work hiring staff for the first ski season. Hess says, "I came up to open up the hotel side of the operation, the restaurant and bar. We ordered all the furniture for the Sports Center and the front desk, and interviewed for the winter season. We must have interviewed everybody in the county!

"Interviewing we kind of worked as a team. A couple friends of mine, Randy Banks, the first ski school director and Ken Grover, the first ski area manager, we were all interviewing long lines of people. We probably hired between 350 and 400 people: all the maids, waitresses, cooks, housekeepers, lift attendants, snow makers, and those that ran the ski rental operation. It was three or four full days of interviewing, and most of those hired were from Nelson and Augusta County."

Once all the people sent from Sea Pines had made the move, Faulkner evidently felt he needed to introduce them to Nelson County culture. They

Doug Coleman teaching at Lower Shamokin Falls

remember Faulkner, with a jug of peach brandy in the back of his Jeep, leading a caravan into Napier Hollow.

They found Cash Napier, an old-timer and traditionalist, skinning out some animal. Said one salesman, "It was not even close to hunting season." Frank Napier, Cash's son, remembered his father sending him at about age seven to deliver shelled corn to Grover Harris' mill. As Frank put it, "I wasn't hardly big enough to lift the bag!"

So his family gave him a little red wagon for Christmas. Continued Frank, "I'd put the sack of corn in that and pull it across the ridge over to Stoney Creek. It had a footbridge that I couldn't pull the wagon across. I'd stop and carry the corn across, set it down, and then come back and get the wagon, carry that across, put the corn back in it and go on."

Frank also remembered when much of The Big Survey was open range, where locals summered their cows, sheep, and pigs. There were no fences, just the occasional rock wall to keep hogs in. At the top of the ridge there was a rock wall that originally went all the way from Shropshire Creek drainage on Dobie Mountain to Reids Gap, following the dividing line between Nelson and Augusta counties. Evidence of it

can be seen behind the houses on Laurel Springs Drive.

When Frank's maternal grandfather had twin sons he had gone to Mr. John Coleman, who was an educated man, to ask him what to name them. Mr. Coleman came up with, of all things, the Roman names, Cassius and Liddicius. Their father did what Mr. Coleman suggested, but the twins were fortunate to get nicknames. Cassius, for instance, had two nicknames. North of Stoney Creek he was known as Cash; south of the creek he was known as Zook!

Salesmen remember the first sales meeting, held in Faulkner's small cabin at the end of Fortune's Ridge. Peter Farley described it as "A one-room cabin with a little pond, very remote, very private. He invited us all up, introduced everyone to moonshine and bear meat for dinner…and we all got a little looped."

It was a very cold November night, and it was late before they finished. Most were in no shape to drive down the mountain, so the next morning there were bodies everywhere. The cabin was built to be comfortable with many fewer people in it, but that night there were thirteen people sleeping there! Phil Patterson was the only one to manage a night in his own bed at Tuckahoe Tavern.

CHAPTER 8

Growing Pains

A staple of "the Wintergreen approach" and Peter Farley's beliefs about selling real estate was the importance of creating, first, anticipation, and second, memories. Helping both of these to develop was particularly vital before many of the amenities at Wintergreen were completed. The weekend that a family spent at Wintergreen passed in a flash, but it was very important that family members looked forward to what they loved doing, and relished the memories until their next visit.

The young daughter of a Wintergreen family might be dreaming all week in her Richmond schoolroom of the horseback lesson at Rodes Farm, where she would finally learn to post to the trot. Her teenage brother couldn't wait to strut his stuff at the tennis tournament. Their father was looking forward to an exciting Jeep expedition, and their mother to the spread-a-blanket picnic and concert on the lawn of Rodes Farm on Sunday. These events stacked up, building season after season, and acting on the whole family to bring them back to Wintergreen soon, sooner, soonest.

In a couple of years, both anticipation and memories would be built on a different foundation. A particularly brilliant drive on the long hole of the golf course might be anticipated or remembered in 1977, or a run down Dobie in the sun on new snow. But in 1975 everyone was working overtime to show new buyers and visitors alike all that nature had to offer on the mountain, and all the fun planned for them in the valley since skiing and golf weren't yet possible.

The October 1975 newsletter crowed that "71 new families have joined you in the last 90 days at Wintergreen." These families had bought single-family home sites, a backcountry parcel, and condos in Eagle's Court.

The backcountry parcels were larger parcels in hard to reach places which were meant for hardier souls who did not want electricity or running water, and who might build either a rustic cabin or camp on their land. Chestnut Flats held 11 large parcels located in a secluded area near the base of Lower Shamokin Falls.

This pristine land was accessible only by Jeep trail and required fording Stoney Creek, which could present a real challenge during periods of high water. The Mt. Horeb Tract, off of Adial Road, was also meant

for backcountry, but was sold to Augusta Lumber Company after the backcountry parcel concept was abandoned for lack of interest.

Even the earliest newsletters confirm that each season had its own highlights. In the winter, social events like card parties, classes in handcrafts, field trips to historic sites, and lectures on wildlife were offered. Spring meant moving out of doors, and brought wildflower hikes, tennis, and the special activities of Memorial Day weekend.

In summer there was no end of activities for all ages, from regular square dances to concerts on the lawn of the Rodes Farm Inn, and the end of summer rituals of Labor Day. Everything seemed to build toward perhaps Wintergreen's most popular season, fall, with its spectacular ochre, orange, yellow, and scarlet leaves painting and transforming the mountainsides. Oktoberfest was the final blowout of the year, taking

Owners and guests gather for a spring horse show at Rodes Farm stable.

place right along with the foliage trumpeting its colors. Many of these events, like tennis tournaments and a craft fair held in the Red Barn, would later move up the mountain; but at this point they took place in the Rodes Valley.

From early on Don had dreamed and advocated for a horse program at Wintergreen. After much research and discussion, Wintergreen hired Ruth Thompson, a fine horsewoman and manager, and opened the Rodes Farm Stables. Soon Ruth had the stables going with good 'school' horses year round with lessons Wednesday through Sunday.

In 1976 and '77 Nelson County 4-H and Wintergreen hosted the regional 4-H Endurance Ride at Wintergreen, as demanding and spectacular a ride as could be imagined. It was held under strict rules and vet checks, up and over Crawford Knob, along a section of trail paralleling the Appalachian Trail and

but ended up staying 16 years. Lynn is still a valued member of the Wintergreen sales team.

There were also 10 homes under construction in Laurel Ridge and the Black Rock neighborhood. As of September 1976, in the Devils Knob neighborhood near the golf course that was under construction, house sites were available for purchase. The elevation of this area was 3,700 feet and higher, and the views from it of the golf course and the mountains beyond were spectacular.

Bar Delk was pushing his men on construction of the ski area. According to Delk, who worked to clear the ski slopes in the earliest days, at first they were instructed that all the stumps had to be buried in trenches. Since the trenches were two-to-one rocks to dirt, this was an arduous job. Delk eventually burned large brush piles after a rain storm when the surrounding forest was wet and safe.

Construction of the ski lifts

back down Shamokin Gorge to the starting point at the Rodes Farm. In May the Arabian Horse Show Association held a two-day ride using the Rodes Farm Stable's facilities.

PHIL PATTERSON HAD BEEN WORKING at Big Canoe in Georgia, but in 1976 the poor economy drove him back to Sea Pines in time to be sent up to the sales office at Wintergreen along with Kyle Lynn. "In late May and June," Patterson said, "we just exploded with a burst of sales." He figured he'd stay another six months

Payne hired a company from Amherst County that hauled away the wood and brush and burned it in the valley, which was legal at the time.

Delk, who deserved a lot of credit for the ski area being up and running for the 1975–76 season, talked about lift construction incidents that might have killed someone. Delk's story of setting the towers in place is hair-raising. Here it is, in his own words.

"The lift towers on Dobie and Potato Patch ski slopes were set using a truck crane, but, because Acorn slope was so steep, it would have required probably two bulldozers to tow the crane up the slope. Since the slopes had been graded and seeded the damage would have been expensive to repair, and it was decided to use a helicopter service to set the towers on the middle section."

"The helicopter would haul the tower to the location in a vertical position so that it could be lowered into place. We would manhandle it onto 4 bolts, which were set on a slope to facilitate the tower being perpendicular to the ski slope. The pilot was being directed by a crewman on the ground with a radio. Our next task was to quickly secure the tower on the base with two large washers and nuts at least on the uphill bolts."

"Complicating this already dangerous operation was the fact that due to the heat and the high altitude, the chopper was lifting at its very maximum load limit, so much so that it was being fueled for each lift with only a few minutes worth of fuel to lighten the load."

"On one of the last towers near the top of the slope while trying to manhandle the ton and a half tower onto the anchor bolts, the threads of the bolt were damaged and we could not get the washers and nuts on in time and the chopper had to go. The chopper could not pick it back up since it was on the angle of the bolts and as he set it down it just bent the bolts over. We came back a few days later, heated the bolts, and straightened them and set the tower by chaining it to the bucket of a 977 loader."

Once all the towers had been secured, the cable was strung around the top bull wheel, around the lower drive bull wheel, back to the top and spliced. The next step was to use a very large bulldozer to put tension on the entire assembly by attaching a 16-ton counter weight at the lower lift drive building. As tension was being applied to the lift line, a steel beam pulled out of the concrete side wall, which shot the entire lower bull wheel assembly, including the electric drive motor, auxiliary gasoline drive motor as well as the drive gear box, out the front of the building in a slingshot effect! Had anyone been standing in front of it they would have been decapitated.

In a mere second, what was once resting inside the lower lift building, 10 feet above the floor on a massive steel superstructure, was now embedded in the hillside outside the front of the building! Because this was a dangerous operation, Delk had made certain that workers were standing clear of the building, so there were no injuries. Repairs were made quickly and the lift was up and running in less than a week.

NICKLAS, WHOSE JOB IT WAS to build the golf course, declared outright "It was a terrible job. It took an extra year because of what the geologists call 'armored rock.' In the crevices of this armored rock was old, rich, black mountain dirt. We had to dig it out and cover the rocks that were too big to move."

"In most areas," continued Nicklas, "we had to dig bury pits along the edge of fairways, sometimes as large as 100 feet long and 20 feet wide, to bury the tree stumps and the rocks that could be removed. The dirt that came out of those pits was then spread 6 inches to a foot deep over the surface of the fairways as a base on which dense turf grass would grow."

The greens and tees would consist of 98 percent sand, according to U.S.G.A. standards, but where were they to lay hold of 30,000 tons of the stuff? It would

Richard "Frog" Morse at the gatehouse

Mountains of sand at Woods Mill for the golf course

Wintergreen Readying Itself

By MARY BETH DONAHUE
of The Progress Staff

WINTERGREEN— On the road leading up the mountain, one could fool oneself into believing he was in the Green Mountains of New England With the stark blacks and whites of the winter landscape, and a chair lift visible through the trees, it is hard to remember one is south of the Mason-Dixon line.

Wintergreen, a new ski area in Nelson County, is a busy place. Although the grand opening is not scheduled until Jan. 6, Wintergreen opened its doors to the public on Dec. 20. 1975

Indications of the area's newness are apparent The ski racks smell of freshly cut wood and the carpenters' pencil marks still show. Men in hard hats tramp through the ski lodge, signs that construction is still going on in the nearby condominiums

"With all the things that had to be done in the last three weeks, I think it was miraculous that we were able to open when we did," said Susan Spicuzza, Director of Public Relations at Wintergreen.

So far, only the beginner and intermediate slopes are open for skiing The expert slopes do not have snow on them

There will be no charge for lift tickets until all slopes are open

"Last year Massanutten (a ski area in West Virginia) charged full price before all of their slopes were open and people were really turned off," said Spicuzza "We didn't want to make the same mistake "

All the slopes may not be open but the lodge is fully completed and the ski school is in full swing.

Wintergreen has 12 ski school instructors, readily identifiable in their bright blue and green suits surrounded by clumps of students.

The ski school is under the direction of Randy Banks and the resident ski pro is Cliff Taylor, originator of the GLM (graduated length method) of ski instruction.

Wintergreen's ski lodge, at the top of the mountain instead of the bottom, offers a large window-lined room for eating with cafeteria facilities and plenty of tables for brown-baggers. There is also the Copper Mine restaurant, a day care center for children over two and one half, a well-stocked ski shop and the ski school center.

A nearby building holds the rental equipment, all of it brand new.

Wintergreen has the most extensive snow making equipment in the Mid-Atlantic region Its 23 snow guns can produce eight inches of snow over a 10 acre area overnight

A native of Connecticut, Spicuzza had never skied on man made snow. "Until I got out there I was a little skeptical, but conditions were really excellent. The artificial snow doesn't get icy like the real thing up north," said Spicuzza

There were about 200 people skiing the first day Wintergreen opened. "We had hoped for more, said Spicuzza, disappointedly "But we did very little advance publicity. Jan 6 is the date we are concentrating on."

According to Spicuzza, things went smoothly over the weekend. "After three years of planning it is strange to actually have all these people here," said Spicuzza

Investment in the planned resort community of Wintergreen is in excess of $16 million at this date. Developed by Cabot, Cabot & Forbes, it is a year-round vacation community.

The ski facilities have six slopes on 50 acres, with 5,301 foot vertical drop at 3,400 feet elevation. The longest run is half a mile.

Fifty miles from Charlottesville, Wintergreen is in hopes of an u0 to 100 day ski season, from December into March.

WINTERGREEN WILL OFFICIALLY OPEN ON JAN. 6
Nelson County Ski Resort Is 50 Miles from Charlottesville

Progress Photo by John Atkins

---

have to be hauled up the mountain, 15 to 18 tons at a time, trucked to the sites of the greens and tees.

The depths of winter 1975 meant that construction halted briefly, and Nicklas spent that time researching where to get that much sand. Buying it would be incredibly expensive, but Nicklas knew that Hurricane Camille had changed the course of the Rockfish River, leaving quantities of sand at Woods Mill, where Route 6 meets Route 29 in Nelson County.

Sand samples taken over a 15-acre area and analyzed in the U.S.G.A. laboratory met specifications, so Nicklas got a surface mining permit and set up a processing plant. The sand had to be screened to remove anything larger than one quarter inch in diameter, so a diesel-powered screen and a front-end loader were rented, and independent truck drivers were hired.

The trucks were driven by men from Nelson County with names like Giles, Campbell, Mays, and Fitzgerald, names well known in the County. They drove from dawn to dark, Monday through Saturday. As Delk

put it, "I guess if it wasn't for Campbells from Nelson County and Sh:fifletts from Augusta County, this place would never have been built so quickly."

Nicklas reported that the scale of the job "was just overwhelming," and they couldn't meet their deadline, despite hiring another contractor from Georgia who came up to help with the clean up. The golf course took an extra year to build, and opened in the spring of 1977. At that point skiing had already had two seasons.

As of mid-September 1975, 11 holes and 15 greens on the golf course had been seeded. The men worked at a feverish pace to have all the seeds sown and germinating before cold weather set in.

BY THE FALL, the mountain pipeline bringing water from Lake Monocan to the bottom of the ski slopes was completed. Despite all odds, they had successfully met their deadline. The compressors and pumps had been installed, and they were capable of pumping two million gallons a day up the mountain to be made into snow.

Sand-screening at Woods Mill

Construction of sewage-treatment plant

GODWIN, RIGHT, CONGRATULATES SKI INSTRUCTORS
Governor Dons Ski Jacket After Watching Skiing Display

Wintergreen Ski Resort Opened by Governor

By GARVEY WINEGAR
Progress Special Writer

WINTERGREEN — Governor Mills E. Godwin formally opened Virginia's newest ski resort at Wintergreen in Nelson County Tuesday by throwing a ceremonial switch which activated a chair lift.

Gov. Godwin, standing hatless in the 26 degree weather at the top of "Potato Patch" ski slope, called the multi - million dollar resort community "a milestone in the progress of our Commonwealth."

He got cheers and applause from the 300 invited guests at this mountain - top resort when he said, "Maybe we ought to invite President Ford to see how he performs on these Virginia slopes. He dare not refuse the invitation in a year like this."

He also got laughs from the crowd when he apologized for being half an hour late by saying that he had flown in from New Hampshire with a headwind that had slowed his plane, then added:

"But I can assure you I didn't go to New Hampshire in support of any Presidential candidate," obviously referring to Ronald Reagan, who is presently campaigning in that State.

Gov. Godwin, in fact, studiously avoided politics during the time he spent at Wintergreen.

When asked by reporters after the ceremony if he cared to comment about Attorney General Andrew Miller's announcement Tuesday that he will run in the Democratic primary, the Governor declined.

"It would be premature for me to comment until I see his statement," he said.

The weather was perfect for Tuesday's ceremonies outside Wintergreen's $1.4 million Sports Center Building.

The sun was brilliant, yet the temperature stayed well below freezing so that Wintergreen officials, who were taking advantage of the sub - freezing weather to make artificial snow, had to cut their snow - making guns off until the Governor and other officials were through speaking.

Gary Green, project manager at Wintergreen, welcomed Governor and Mrs. Godwin.

"This is an exciting day for us," he said. "A development like Wintergreen isn't created overnight. This was a long time in the making."

Green said there are approximately 300 property owners at Wintergreen at present.

The resort community will eventually offer 2,750 mountain homesites, 1,475 condominiums and cluster homes, 575 homesites at the foot of the mountain, and 200 rustic cabin sites.

The Governor praised the de-

acres allotted to no development...except to nature's snowfall in its beautiful splendor."

Nearly 7,000 acres of the 13,000 will be left as a natural preserve.

G. W. Blakeley Jr. of Boston, president of Cabot, Cabot and Forbes Co., was Governor Godwin's host for the day.

After a banquet in Wintergreen's window - lined cafeteria, the Governor returned to the slopes to present trophies to the winners of the Governor's Cup Race, a special event held in his honor featuring junior racers from across Virginia.

Gary Green introduced Governor Mills Godwin at the grand opening of the ski area in December 1975.

Construction was complete on the 200,000-gallon-a-day-capacity advanced waste treatment plant, one of the most sophisticated in Virginia. The plant had both a primary and secondary treatment unit and extended aeration. The water was clean when it was expelled.

They were nearing the opening of the resort facilities at Wintergreen, and counting on welcoming the first skiers. Paving operations on Wintergreen Drive, Laurel Ridge and Black Rock roads were in full swing following the lengthy and costly installation of the underground water, sewer and electric lines. Rough grading was finished on the loop road around Devils Knob (holes 12 through 17) allowing access for salesmen and their clients as lots in that area came on the market.

The snowmaking system pipelines, compressors and pumps, along with three chairlifts, were in the final stages of completion and testing. This was not work any of these men had done before. As Delk explains, "We were being asked to build something that none of us had ever even seen except on TV.

"The chairs for the lift were assembled and painted in the parking area of the new sewage treatment plant, and then taken to the lifts. They were assembled exactly according to the blueprints, but no one understood that a chairlift could run clockwise or counter-clockwise, and we had no power to the lifts to operate it and see the direction."

They did have to change the direction, but it was a simple matter of taking out the bolts, reversing the chair hanger, and replacing the bolts, most easily done while the chairs were hanging on the cable.

The Sports Center (the building that currently houses the Copper Mine restaurant) and the rental facility for the ski area were both still under construction as fall progressed. Like the workers on the golf course above them, those in the ski area were also racing against time and working at a fevered pace.

The Sports Center was constructed entirely of wood and so was all brown. When the CC&F official sent from Boston to inspect it saw it, he declared, "I feel as if I'm in a tree!" Apparently he didn't mean this as a compliment, so Payne had some stripes of color painted on the walls in the cafeteria.

Newsletter reports make progress sound orderly, but behind the scenes everyone was scrambling to live up to deadlines. Nicklas described the finger-in-the-dike approach to running the new potable water system that first ski season. "Because we had so many frozen and burst water pipes inside houses due to the extreme cold, our crews had to read water meters three times a day to try to find leaks and turn off meters so as not to drain the water tank."

Thanks to workers, some of whom worked 80-hour weeks that fall, miracle of miracles they were making snow by December of 1975, when Governor Mills Godwin came for the grand opening. He declared Wintergreen the latest jewel in the crown of Virginia, and the ski season started. What up until that moment had been Wintergreen community was now taking on some of the characteristics of a resort.

As the old year turned into 1976, CC&F was reeling as the economy faltered and the prime-lending rate went over 20 percent. Wintergreen was not in trouble, but CC&F was over-committed, with too many projects spread across the United States. When they began to take a hard look at what they might slough off,

Wintergreen rose to the top of the list. That was because it was their only property that had no lien on it.

As if this wasn't enough of a shock, a little more than a year after the first Wintergreen Administration Building fire in 1975, just as the finishing touches were being applied to the new building in nearly the same spot, someone tried to set it ablaze. They picked the Sunday night before it was to be officially opened the next day. Fortunately, because the fire was reported early, and due to the quick response of volunteer fire departments from Rockfish, Lovingston, and Wintergreen, the blaze was contained to one upstairs wing of the new building. Restoration was completed in less than six weeks.

CC&F had been operating on a line of credit from Bankers Trust, and owed the bank $10,000,000. Bankers Trust, at that time the fifth largest bank in the United States, decided this had gone on too long, and cut off CC&F's line of credit. This forced the issue for CC&F, which ended up trading equity for debt. Bankers Trust cancelled the debt and took over the deed to Wintergreen.

Phil Patterson just happened to be in the office during ski season one evening around 6:30 p.m. when nobody else was around. In came a man in a London Fog raincoat and summer shoes, looking out of place. Patterson began to talk to him, but was cut off abruptly. He asked Patterson to have dinner with him and his wife, an invitation that of course Patterson accepted.

"The first thing he proceeded to do," remembered Patterson, "was order a round of cocktails. I was halfway through with mine and he was grilling me with questions and I said to myself, 'I don't think he's a

Phil Patterson

Herbert Merser from Bankers Trust

potential candidate to buy anything, but he's here on a mission.' Well, on the next round of cocktails, mine was full and his was full of water.

"He was going to get the salesman tipsy, so he would spill the beans on how mismanaged Wintergreen was, how everything had gone awry here. So I continued to pay attention to what he was doing, what I was doing, being very much aware. And after dinner he proceeded to cut me off again. He said, 'Would you have breakfast?' And I said, 'Sure, I'll have breakfast.' Well, that night it snowed six inches.

"So we get up, go to breakfast. We get inside the Sports Center. There's no help in there, except maybe three people. You got folks coming in the door who want something to eat. We go down the buffet line. The person who is serving the bacon says, 'Hey, I've never done this. I usually work in the kitchen and wash dishes.' You could just see the man's eyes roll back in his head.

"I proceeded to take him on a tour. Again he was grilling me with questions. But I began to pay attention to his eyes. And you could see his eyes, I mean, this he couldn't hide. You would show him something and he began to gravitate to the magic and the beauty of what Wintergreen was.

"We had gotten to the overlook. None of the roads had been plowed. There was maybe a third of the resort staff that was working. And everything that could go wrong did go wrong; it was a disaster. But you could watch his eyes and watch his facial expressions. We had less than 300 owners at that point in time, if I'm not mistaken.

"So, we stayed out maybe an hour, hour and a half. And he said 'Take me back.' So, I took him and his wife, Dee, back to their condominium. And that's when he kind of pulled the mask off and said, 'Let me tell you why I'm here. I'm Herb Merser, and I've been hired by Bankers Trust to do a report on Wintergreen.'

"He said, 'Right now, Mr. Payne's getting a phone call and Mr. Rutherford's going to join him. I can't wait to meet the resort operator.' And so, I was kind of out of the picture."

Except Patterson wasn't out of the picture, as Merser and his wife ended up buying, holding, and then selling some eight to ten properties at Wintergreen, all through Patterson.

Bill Crocker was another less secretive scout sent from Bankers Trust to evaluate Wintergreen, about

L. F. Payne and Larry Rutherford

which the bank knew almost nothing. Crocker had just been hired by Bankers Trust, but knew about Wintergreen because, in his former job, he had been the chief financial officer at Sea Pines.

Green reported that, "Crocker and that whole crowd thought they would come in and find that the management team was really crooked, and people were getting all kinds of money. He could never find any improprieties in anybody dealing with the finances of this place…. Nobody was underhanded, nobody was ripping it off."

Crocker took in the progress at Wintergreen and reported to Bankers Trust, "Stop this and you've got an asset worth nothing." Payne and Rutherford were asked to do a one-year plan to continue operating Wintergreen in 1976–77 while Bankers Trust looked into selling it.

Crocker also made it known that he felt Green was not the right person to run Wintergreen for the bank. Gary Green was recalled to Boston and told, along with others being let go, that they had six months to find other jobs, and would receive no severance packages. He was devastated, and remembered going back to his hotel in tears. He loved Wintergreen and his job.

Patterson said of Green, "I always found him to be blunt and to the point. He didn't mess around with a lot of words and theory—he wanted results and he expected you to do your part. It was his job to always push the subordinates who reported to him, and he did an outstanding job of holding them accountable.

"While he could make the room tense by asking pin-point questions, he could lighten up the room just as fast with his quick wit and inviting sense of humor. He loved a challenge, which was exemplified when it was recommended to him to bulldoze the little cottage behind the Rodes Inn. It pissed him off so much that he renovated the fallen-down structure into a charming second home for his family. Gary's other strong trait was…he could be very charming when he wanted to be. Note—wanted to be!"

Payne commented about his relationship with Green, "It wasn't a matter that Gary and I ever had any difficulty whatsoever. It was just an ugly part of the deal. We're (Bankers Trust) going to come in and take over…. You take your guys and leave everybody else."

The first L. F. Payne knew about this seismic shift in ownership was a phone call from an official at CC&F informing him "Your health insurance is no longer valid." But luckily for Payne, Bankers Trust wanted him to stay on.

Larry Rutherford had been tapped by his fellow Darden alum, Payne, and hired by CC&F to be Wintergreen's chief financial officer. He had an important role to play in Wintergreen's restructuring under the ownership of Bankers Trust. He was planning to keep working at CC&F, but the bank asked him to stay on at Wintergreen, both for his financial acumen and because he knew the place.

Payne took everybody in the sales office, half of whom worked for CC&F and the other half for Sea Pines, and made a group out of it which became Wintergreen Development. This entity was the developer working for Bankers Trust.

According to Rutherford, "It was an amazing restructure. Payne and I each owned 50 percent of Wintergreen's assets. He was president and I was executive vice president, although we were co-equals."

Bankers Trust still made the decisions, often through Ralph McDonald, a senior vice president, following a strategy to eventually sell the project at a profit. As it turned out, the top four officials of Bankers Trust were interested in keeping Wintergreen, which they did for the next eight years, because they loved to visit it!

BANKERS TRUST CHAIRMAN Charlie Sanford would come, stay in the Rodes Farm Inn, and take Jeep rides and hikes in the mountains. On one hike

The 1988 Wintergreen Real Estate sales force: (seated l. to r.) Pam Lang, Tim Hess, Nancy Hernandez, Gary Horvath, Avis Laeng. Standing (l. to r.) Tim Merrick, Dick Carroll, Bo Newell, Phil Patterson, Randy Thompson, Kyle Lynn, Peter Farley. Not pictured: Betty Sue Warring, Betsy Mennas.

Laying the pipeline

someone was shooting near them. When Payne heard about it he could just see the headline, "Chairman of Bankers Trust shot dead at Wintergreen." Had it happened, that one shot probably would have killed Wintergreen as well as Sanford.

Payne stated, "We had a great relationship with Bankers Trust. As time went on, we advised them about similar mountain properties that they ended up owning." Payne continued, "No one knew how this was going to work out. We were selling properties and the skiing, but Wintergreen was still in its infancy."

Payne and his wife were invited to the Bankers Trust Christmas party. "Susan and I went up there," Payne reminisced, "and there was this room full of people and we realized they didn't know each other. So we were introducing people who worked for Bankers Trust to each other. You know, 'you should meet so and so,' and 'you ought to meet this person,' and all of that."

The Paynes realized then that they were witnessing the downside of working in such a large organization. They knew all the individuals who would come to Wintergreen independently, but there was no reason why they would ever know each other.

Bankers Trust gave Payne and Rutherford a great deal of leeway, but there was one important rule: Don't Ask Us for Money. Their recourse was to think up some very creative financing. As Payne put it, "We did all kinds of creative things, and Larry was an important part of it. We used industrial development bonds to build ski lifts, and we built the first mixed use condominium in Virginia. It had units at the top that we sold and made enough money to pay for the other two floors. We desperately needed the profits from selling these because we didn't have any money. So we ended up using the profits to build retail which we could rent."

Rutherford pointed out that they were a twenty-eight year old and a twenty-nine-and-a-half year old playing for big stakes. He said, "I lived on marketing lots of paper, it was marketing leprosy. Banks had high interest rates and kept turning down our applications for loans."

George Nicklas, Bob Ruff, and Fred Nowak consulting on construction

"I told Payne to change [his terminology] when he went to investment people and tell them they were 'financing receivables.'" This resulted in their getting a three million dollar loan.

They had their embarrassing moments, too. The project to pump water up the mountain had required expensive steel piping. When it was finally time to turn on the Westinghouse pumps everyone was there. At the crucial moment the water was turned on and the pumps were pumping like crazy. Payne, who was inside, dashed out to Rutherford, who was outside, to celebrate. Outside it was pitch dark; the pumps had blown all the transformers!

Rutherford remembered another challenging moment when raw sewage was flowing down the entrance drive. They summoned the engineers, who scratched their heads and said, "Oh we should have buried the sewer pipes deeper!" (Because elevation brings colder temperatures). They ended up putting down heat tape to get the mess to the sewage treatment plant. The pipes had to be dug up and reburied. George

Nicklas doesn't remember it as being quite that bad.

It was not until August of 1976 that Bankers Trust took over the Wintergreen deed. The new ownership was reflected in the formation of a new company, Melba Investors Southeast. Not until this point did Nicklas have confidence that Wintergreen would survive. Fortune's Ridge and Black Rock infrastructure had been built by then, but there were very few freestanding houses built.

Delk's new assignment was to bring the utilities to the upper mountain, Devils Knob, in time for the opening of the golf course in 1977.

Nicklas took over parts of Payne's job, working closely with him on all aspects of development.

Nicklas quoted Payne, who said, "A lot of people rose to the occasion over time to make Wintergreen work." To which Nicklas added, "L. F. rose to the occasion *all* the time. There were so many times that this thing absolutely could have failed. Payne had an innate ability to grasp the big picture, and the bigger picture outside of Wintergreen."

CHAPTER NINE

Lift Off

Nicklas called the first ski season, in 1975–76, "a soft opening." Only one compressor used for making snow had arrived, only two-and-a-half slopes were open, and only 400 pairs of rental skis were available for skiers. Approximately 30,000 skiers hit the slopes in the course of the winter; respectable, but not outstanding.

Cliff Taylor, inventor of the Graduated Length Method, had been hired by Wintergreen in anticipation of making its own market out of non-skiers. A beginning skier started out on short skis, and as they improved they graduated to longer and longer skis.

Even though the first season was not a particularly good one as far as snowmaking capacity went, the rental shop ran out of skis almost immediately. Everyone wanted to try skiing, so another 400 pairs of skis were ordered. By the winter of 1978 there were 1,200 pairs of rental skis available.

Bob Ash, the mountain manager at the Beech Mountain Ski Area in North Carolina, had agreed to come manage the Wintergreen Ski Area, but in the fall of 1976, at the very last minute, he decided against taking the job. Payne was giving Nicklas a lift in his Jeep one day in October, as he worried out loud what on earth he was going to do about finding a replacement for Ash at the eleventh hour.

"I did what I was told in the Marine Corps never to do," said Nicklas, "I volunteered to run the snowmaking, slope grooming, and the lifts if Ken Grover would take charge of running the rest of the ski operation: equipment rentals, ski school, ski patrol, and marketing." Nicklas admitted, "I didn't know one end of a piece of snowmaking equipment from another. I remember having to go into a sales meeting that fall and reassure them that all six slopes would be open by ski season. That was greeted with sarcasm based on the previous year's experience."

"There were three new slopes to be opened for the 1976-77 ski season, Diamond Hill, Big Acorn and Tyro. When snowmaking began prior to Thanksgiving what we lacked in experience we made up for in sheer determination. Nighttime temperatures plummeted below zero and the daytime temperatures never made it above the freezing mark for several weeks. Working 24 hours a day with two crews working 12 hour shifts took its toll on us physically, but accelerated the learning curve, and soon all of the snowmaking crew became proficient in that 'art.'"

Larry Coates, who came to work for Nicklas that second season of skiing at Wintergreen, was the youngest snowmaker at the time. His description makes it clear why this job was not for sissies. "Snowmakers are required to work 12 hours a day, 7 days a week, Thanksgiving, Christmas, New Year's, whenever we are needed—that's 84 hours a week, 44 of which are overtime. The good part is the money. The bad part is being required to remain at work until your replacement shows up."

"Sometimes that means working a lot longer than your shift. The only reason we were able to get help to work this job is because we paid more than any other department at that time, paid time-and-a-half for overtime, and paid a bonus to anyone who lasted the entire season. We hired heavy because by Christmas we would always lose a third of our workers. This job was

and is very hard on family life."

Nicklas only had one employee, Doug McGregor, who had ever had any experience with snow guns. McGregor had to teach Nicklas and all the other snowmakers how to make snow, dragging the heavy hoses and the big-nozzle guns out on the slope, and connecting the hoses to air and water hydrants located along the edge.

Each worker had to learn how to determine the right mixture of air and water. The goal was to start out with a moist mixture to build the base, then to change to a drier mixture for the surface snow. Once they got the hang of it they could tell by looking at snow crystals on their glove to see if they had gotten the mixture right. Today it is all done by computer, but at that point it was a witch's brew!

There was pressure on Nicklas to get all six slopes open and keep them open for the entire 100-day ski season if Wintergreen was to be recognized in the market place as a great family-oriented ski resort.

Ski patrols and instructors had to practice removing skiers from lifts in case of breakdowns or accidents. Jimmy Ballowe, who started to work at Wintergreen in 1975, described his role in this training.

Staff from the Copper Mine Restaurant were asked to play skiers stuck on the lift. "I had to lower Bill from the chair," said Ballowe. "Bill hooked up the harness, slid off the chair and started down. He weighed 180 pounds and I weighed 108. I immediately started up. When I was five feet off the ground Nancy Shelhorse grabbed my feet to arrest my upward climb. I was able to lower Bill to the ground safely."

"Once I was back on the ground Nancy said it would be best if I wrapped the rope around a tree before I tried again. Bill wholeheartedly agreed!" Their training in November was put to use that second season when a tree fell over the Diamond Hill lift, and everyone on the lift had to be belayed off of it.

The winter of 1976-77 turned out to be one of the coldest in Virginia's recorded weather history. "You could have made snow with a garden hose," said Nicklas. For three nights in a row the temperature went down to 32 degrees below zero at Devils Knob.

"If you build it they will come," turned out to be true for Wintergreen. 97,000 skiers came that winter, and the question became how to handle the numbers. There was not enough parking, and state police ended up having to turn people away on days when no more skiers could be accommodated. For two weeks the temperature never got above 10 degrees, but that didn't deter many. Visitors who had traveled long distances

David Jimenez

were not pleased when they were stopped at the gate and told, "perhaps you might be interested in touring Monticello instead."

Nicklas and his men were exhausted. Work managing the lifts was a daytime job, and when night came it was time to make snow. At one period he remembers working three days straight without sleep. He said, "The top of the Big Acorn lift is the best place at Wintergreen to watch the sun come up," and he should know.

Taking the season as a whole he commented, "Everyone knew this was do or die, we *had* to

make this thing work." He added, "We ended up absolute heroes; we were able to make snow before Thanksgiving, and we had every slope covered by New Year's Day, 1977."

Sales of property skyrocketed, and people were lining up to be shown condos and lots. Every month more lights were turned on and Wintergreen began to look occupied.

Ralph McDonald and his family loved their visits to Wintergreen on behalf of Bankers Trust. One day the McDonald children were skiing, and a plain-spoken worker named Doug Thompson was manning the Potato Patch lift. When the young skiers went to get on the lift Thompson said, "Where are your tickets?" The children said, "We don't need lift tickets. Our father is Ralph McDonald."

Responded Thompson, "Who is Ralph McDonald?" They answered, "He's vice president of Bankers Trust and they own this place." "Well then by God,"

Ellis Maples and Vinnie Giles

Thompson said, "he ought to be able to afford lift tickets! Get off and walk to the top!!" George Nicklas commented, "I'm sure Ralph McDonald just howled with laughter when he heard that!"

NO SOONER HAD SKIING ENDED than the Devils Knob Golf Course opened, and another amenity started to draw those who love the sport. David Jimenez was the first golf pro, and he and Vinnie Giles, a prize-winning Virginia State amateur, worked with Ellis Maples promoting the course.

Teeing off on the Devils Knob Golf Course

It is unique in many ways. First of all it is above 3,000 feet, which keeps temperatures 10 to 15 degrees cooler than in the valley. Since Central Virginia is frequently in the 90s during the summer, this makes a big difference. Humidity is much less of a problem at that altitude as well.

According to Nicklas its topography is unique in that it occupies the northwestern slope of Devils Knob that is not particularly steep. Only the 3rd and the 16th holes can be described as steep, and in both cases the player is hitting downhill, straightaway, on a par four.

At 3,600 feet above sea level, a golf ball travels further through the air than at lower altitudes, so on these downhill tee shots, the average hitter can take away some pretty impressive drive distances to earn "bragging rights!"

It is a narrow course, which means it favors accuracy over long ball hitters; and if you slice or hook a shot it is hard to recover. It is not a lengthy course, but makes up for that by being tight. It was not built for pros, but

for ordinary golfers to have fun playing it.

The course is somewhat forgiving in that the sand traps do not fit tightly into the Devils Knob golf greens, and the fairway traps are not particularly big. Greens average over 6,000 square feet, providing a sizable target for the approach shot. The 7th and 8th and 17th are the only water holes, with ponds that come into play off the tee. Most important, although it is not a "mountain goat" course, it is the highest golf course in the Commonwealth of Virginia. The holes were very carefully designed so that fairways lay with the contours of the landscape, and only a few fairways have a very moderate side slope.

WHEN SALES OF LOTS BEGAN in the fall of 1974, it spoke well for Wintergreen's future that those who were working or investing there became among the earliest purchasers of lots in the Black Rock and Laurel Ridge subdivisions. Investors Jim Wheat and Frank Louthan bought lots, as did Jim Chaffin and Charles Fraser of

Earle and Bea Holliday

Sea Pines. Fraser, when he first visited, had not initially been excited by Wintergreen. Fraser was one of the subjects in Pulitzer prizewinner John McPhee's book, *Encounters with the Archdruid*.

Managers L. F. Payne and Gary Green bought lots, as did salesmen Peter Farley, Lee Hilbert, and Doug Deaton, and marketers Bob Evans and David Martin. Locals were also part of this. Marguerite Wade, whom Farley had talked into being the hostess at the Rodes Farm Inn, and Sam Eggleston took the opportunity to buy in as well. Influential real estate brokers like Jim Faulconer in Charlottesville also joined the bandwagon.

Bea and Earle Holliday were among the first homebuilders in 1975. Earle was an engineer with DuPont who had been transferred from Germany to Waynesboro, Virginia. While he was eating lunch one day he overheard a conversation about the four-season resort being built southeast of Waynesboro called Wintergreen.

He came to investigate, and ran into Kyle Lynn in the sales office. He and Bea bought their first lot on Gum Tree Drive, and were occupying the house they built by the summer of 1975. Later they bought a second lot on Oak Lane, and built a house for their large family, which much later became their retirement home.

Earle's uncontested claim is that he was the first skier at Wintergreen in the fall of 1975. He stepped into his skis at the top of Eagle's Swoop, skied down to the cross trail, climbed back up and did it again. Skiing for him became first an avocation, and then after his retirement

a full-time interest. He helped with , and became a certified skiing instructor in his retirement years. He volunteered with the Special Olympics and travelled all over the world with it.

Earle and Bea had many stories about bears on their porch, and one bear that got in the house! They loved the concerts held on the mountain, especially listening to Peter, Paul and Mary playing and singing on the Potato Patch ski slope in the summer. All five of their children as well as five of their grandchildren, worked or volunteered at the resort in some capacity.

Bea's interest was in birding; Earle's, after ski season was over, was in botany, and he quickly became involved in Wintergreen's transplantation program, and in the propagation of native wildflowers.

These two initiatives were brought about by Doug Coleman, someone whose influence on Wintergreen started small, and grew until today it would be hard to imagine Wintergreen without him and the nature program that he eventually founded.

COLEMAN'S FOREBEAR, DR. HAWES COLEMAN, the builder of the house in the village of Wintergreen, completed in 1802, was one of the 31 justices recorded in the formation of Nelson County in 1807. John J. Coleman, his son, inherited old Wintergreen and expanded his land holdings, finally purchasing The Big Survey in 1853.

Doug Coleman was raised on his parents' cattle farm in Albemarle County, and went to Bridgewater College in the Shenandoah Valley, where he studied field biology.

Out of college, married and working with his

The original Wintergreen Plantation House, completed in 1802

103

father, he found that environmental jobs were hard to come by. His fascination was with ecosystems, and in addition to his studies, he had roamed the forests and mountains of Central Virginia.

Coleman was professionally trained in botany in college, but before that his parents' love of nature had rubbed off on him. His uncle, who was an amateur botanist, had also influenced him as a child. Coleman continued to focus on botany, and developed expertise in understanding botanical ecosystems and plants of the Blue Ridge region.

In 1975 Coleman figured he had nothing to lose by asking Piedmont Community College if he could teach a class on spring flora in the Blue Ridge. To his delight they agreed. That class filled up and was so successful that he also taught summer and fall flora. Jackie Whalen, who ran programs at Wintergreen, heard about Coleman's class, and asked him to come teach it on the mountain.

A lady who introduced herself as Kappy Wakeham drove from Richmond to take the college class, and later became an owner at Wintergreen. A room in Trillium House, which became the home of the Wintergreen Nature Foundation more than two decades later, is named "The Wakeham Room" for a gift from her family in her memory.

Through the class Coleman met many early property owners like Ambassador Ed Martin, assistant secretary of state under John Kennedy and ambassador to Argentina under Lyndon Johnson. Martin was very knowledgable about wildflowers, and recognized Coleman's interest and knowledge on the subject, and became an early participant and supporter.

A year or so before Coleman came to teach the class, Steve Key, who was working at Wintergreen, talked Coleman, his high school buddy, into helping

Teaching the next generation, L–R: Ethan Zuckerman, Meredith Lang, and Nick Gilliam

him with surveying. Coleman was simultaneously deeply concerned and attracted to this enormous 13,000-acre tract whose developers had promised to preserve half of it. He could recognize at Wintergreen a 4,000-year-old ecosystem that had been preserved by blind neglect, and he began to think about whether or not he, with his training and his interests, could make a difference there.

The more Coleman learned about the botany on display at Wintergreen the more amazed he became by how unique it was. This awareness evolved into a sense of responsibility to protect it. The urgency imposed by the development calendar and the fact, that at this point, he didn't have an official "job" at Wintergreen, meant that he had to approach management with a new, value-added rationale.

By the time that both Nicklas and Coleman arrived at Wintergreen, most of the land studies had already been done and much of the planning footprint had been established. Both put forth herculean effort in trying to "get it right." Every construction foreman and worker on any job at Wintergreen at that time was thoroughly indoctrinated and understood that no trees were to be cut or plant material destroyed that were

Birdwatching at Spring Wildflower Symposium

Rescuing shrubs, wildflowers, and ferns from future construction site

outside of the blue flagging that marked clearing limits at all construction sites.

Nicklas worked within the restrictions he was given to uphold. "For instance," he said, "even though the road right-of-way was platted at 50 feet, clearing limits were reduced to 40 feet where possible in order to preserve as much vegetation as possible. We wanted these roads to resemble trails rather than interstates."

In the field, Nicklas often went above and beyond his orders in his concern and efforts to keep streams clear and to protect forest canopy.

Coleman, in the early years, had much less responsibility than George. His efforts and influence grew, but at that point in the late 1970s he was in what he called his "salt shaker" phase, where he simply studied sites and educated any owners, realtors, or managers who would listen. However, he was starting to focus on a much deeper ecosystem piece that involved the rare plant communities that were in the path of destruction.

An ecosystem, according to the dictionary, is a biological community of interacting organisms and their physical environment. A study of Wintergreen's flora had been suggested in the early planning stages, but it never took place because it was not required by the environmental laws of the day. Many of the botanical ecosystems Coleman found in the deep forest coves, wetlands, and cliff faces were rare and ancient.

What he and George worked on involved two different levels of conservation, and both were important. Even though everything could not be saved, there are numerous examples like Trillium Field Park, the two nature preserves and Crawford Knob wetlands where ecosystems were saved. Likewise the monitoring of all the streams that flow off the mountain still goes on today, and Wintergreen's architectural review board still pays close attention to tree removal.

The water monitoring and minimum clearing of canopy that Nicklas was focused on were an active and dynamic part of the development as it was occurring. Much of what Coleman was finding in rare plant communities involved making changes to a master plan that had already been developed. In many cases these changes were expensive to accomplish. Like it or not, it often came down to dollars and a return on investment. Coleman was convinced that saving more trees and

protecting more of what nature had given Wintergreen would make its real estate *more* sought after.

After all, the original impetus had been to turn The Big Survey into a new kind of resort, one modeled on Sea Pines, where nature had the upper hand and the built environment had been planned to disappear into it. As Fraser envisioned it in Wintergreen's case, "People need to alter their behavior to accommodate the mountain, rather than the mountain having to accommodate the people."

Between his teaching and continuing to farm, Coleman began to shift his focus, and to concentrate on what he could offer Wintergreen. As road building began in earnest in the mid-1970s, Coleman couldn't stay idle as rare native orchids, likely thousand-year-old fern beds, and wildflowers were in the way of development. He was raising consciousness about the rarity of the flora at Wintergreen, but he could go only so far without raising the ire of those responsible for turning dreams into reality.

He needed advocates, and he found them in the most unlikely of places…first of all in the sales office. The salesmen already knew that the natural world at Wintergreen held fascination for themselves and for potential clients, but they didn't know exactly of what it consisted. Coleman, a passionate and insistent man, made friends with the salesmen and took them out hiking, singly and in groups, whenever he could, impressing them with the botanical magic of the mountain so that they in turn could impress their clients.

It wasn't strictly a science class he was giving them. Some of it was useful knowledge and some of it was teasing their curiosity, such as the fact that at Wintergreen some of the flowers are older than the trees, and how and why that happened. Coleman explained only as much science as could be understood, and in doing this was successful in giving the salesmen extra credibility with their clients.

Management already knew that nature was a powerful marketing tool, and with tutoring from Coleman the salesmen were able to excite their clients with what existed at Wintergreen. Said Peter Farley of the salesmen and marketers like Bob Evans, "We felt like we were the guys carrying the banner forward. We carried the soul of Wintergreen."

Bob Evans had an instinctive genius when it came to marketing. He came up with ad after ad that often had no people in them, but caught scenes of breathtaking natural beauty. Evans was responsible for the subliminal message that made potential buyers curious about Wintergreen and propelled them to visit it in the first place.

After the salesmen, the second group Coleman influenced was made up of residents like Merle and Micky Luck, and other early homeowners who were students in his classes. The Luck Family shared Coleman's love of Wintergreen's flora, and responded enthusiastically when he asked for volunteers to help him in transplanting particularly valuable plants and flowers before development started. At first this was done on an emergency basis, but later it became a Sunday-morning mass effort. Forty or fifty people would turn out to help dig up plants like wild azalea and rhododendron, or wildflowers and ferns within designated clearing limits of construction sites. They would replant some of them where they would stay permanently, such as along the sides of the golf course, while they heeled in others to await a suitable growing space.

Residents were encouraged to transplant to their own lots. This became a popular and inexpensive form of landscaping at Wintergreen. It's estimated that over the decades somewhere between 100,000 and 200,000 plants, shrubs, wildflowers, and bushes have been moved out of harm's way. They live on, a tribute to the human effort involved, and also to the ethos of the place, and the people who chose to live there.

Coleman alerted the National Arboretum in Wahington, DC, about the ancient ecosystem of ferns. Down they came with big trucks to rescue and haul away ancient ferns for their American Native collection.

Coleman had to learn to deal with construction managers like Nicklas, whose chief worry, no matter what he was working on, was to get "it" done well and on time. "Initially I was helpless confronting Nicklas," commented Coleman, "but I finally learned to use the marketing piece."

That piece was the one the salesmen had already taken on board and were using successfully—the fact that interest in the environment nationwide was growing into a genuine movement, and that Wintergreen could distinguish itself from other resorts by its sensitivity to nature. We will see how, in the 1980s, this "piece" was vindicated by public attention on the national level, but in the 1970s Coleman had a difficult time over issues he had to approach diplomatically in order to have any effect at all. Sometimes he felt so discouraged he thought he should quit; what kept him going was the promise of the developers, carried out by the planners, that half of Wintergreen would remain wild.

Both Coleman and Nicklas had the best interests of Wintergreen uppermost in their minds, both were stubborn and had tempers, and both were physically imposing men. They could have just settled into a state of permanent disagreement. They had plenty of arguments, but they were both more interested in getting to a solution than in the problem itself.

As Nicklas put it, "I had a mission to accomplish. I'm a military man, but if you can talk to me about ways to improve things, I'll listen." The following story is proof of the truth of that statement. One problem, as Coleman discovered, was that Nicklas, looking for an out-of-the-way spot to put a stump dump which became an overlook, had put it too close to a stream, creating the danger of siltation. He challenged Nicklas over it.

Architect Bill Atwood and George Nicklas

"He blew me off at first," said Coleman, "but then he turned around and came back and said, 'all right, what are we gonna do about it?' I suggested moving the stream to a dry creek bed nearby." The problem got solved. This initial confrontation led to a mutual respect and eventually a long-lasting friendship.

In his early years around Wintergreen when he was working on a contractual basis, Coleman did what he could, nibbling around the periphery of the massive project that was Wintergreen. With his teaching and his transplanting he felt he was doing as much to implant consciousness about nature on the mountaintops as he was to rescue plants.

FROM THE VERY BEGINNING, everyone involved in Wintergreen recognized that the biggest threat to what they were creating was the danger that would be posed by a forest fire. In 1952 there had been a fire on Black Rock Mountain that was so severe it burned for a week. Because of this danger, Wintergreen committed to providing a fire department in its first registration with the US Department of Housing and Urban

Development. Young Jimmy Wheat was working at Wintergreen, and he was given the job of buying a fire truck and an ambulance, which he did through Burdett Oxygen Company in Waynesboro in 1975.

Nicklas, who was in charge of building the golf course, was asked by Green to clear a bay in the Golf Maintenance Building to temporarily house the new fire truck. Nicklas's father had been a fire chief, and Nicklas himself had served everywhere he had lived as a volunteer fire fighter. "Every day I watched that truck sit in the bay, untouched for months, collecting dust, until I couldn't take it any longer. I went down to the office, approached Gary Green and volunteered to organize and train a fire department made up primarily of employees."

Nicklas knew he could count on Bar Delk, who had volunteered at the Lovingston Fire Department. Delk became his assistant chief, and twenty or so volunteers signed up, including Payne. Nicklas contacted the Waynesboro Fire Department and professionals came to train what became the Wintergreen Fire Brigade. He also contacted Eddie Embry at the Virginia

Warren Griffin and L. F. Payne on a break

Department of Forestry to ask for help in training specifically for forest fires.

"It didn't take long," said Nicklas, "for Embry and forester Lou Southard to proclaim that a forest fire under the right conditions could destroy thousands of acres that would take years and years to reestablish. To make matters worse, there was only one way in and out of Wintergreen, so it was conceivable that people could be trapped on the mountain. So we trained and learned as much as we could about fighting forest fires."

What they needed was a helicopter equipped with a water bucket that could contain a fire on the side of a mountain until the fire fighters were able to get there. The Forest Service had access to a private helicopter owned and piloted by Jimmy Stevens, but it didn't have a fire bucket or radio communications.

"So Wintergreen bought a fire bucket and radio equipment," continued Nicklas, "and had it installed on the helicopter. We trained with the helicopter and we all learned how to work together, especially using a fire hose to recharge the bucket with 100 gallons of water while the chopper was hovering overhead!"

The first time that they put their training to use was in the Humpback Mountain fire on April 20th, 1976, when lightning struck a tree, setting the woods on fire and threatening federal land. Nicklas commented, "This one was serious enough that a joint decision of the Virginia Department of Forestry and the Blue Ridge Parkway Rangers authorized smoke jumpers to jump in. Eight professional fire fighters jumped into the very center of the burnt-out ring, and joined us on the ground to contain the fire at twenty-plus acres."

The next occasion was on November 5th of 1978, when fire broke out on the slope of Black Rock Mountain in an area called the Plunge. It had the potential to destroy the core of Wintergreen had it not been for the combined efforts of the Department of Forestry, local volunteer fire departments including Rockfish, Piney River, and Lovingston, along with the Wintergreen Fire Brigade and perhaps as many as 100 volunteers.

Milton Morris with the Virginia Department of Forestry was the "fire boss," and was well-qualified, having fought the huge Black Rock fire of 1952. Maxie Campbell led a fire crew of local folk that cut a fire line, which succeeded in stopping the fire on the southern flank, preventing a great deal of damage.

The following is a first-hand account by Peter Farley: "No one who fought that fire in 1978 will forget it. It was one of those spectacular Saturday afternoons in November. There were postcard-blue skies and temperatures chilly enough for only a light sweater. The leaves had turned from their brilliant colors and were turning brown and covering the Blue Ridge—perfect fuel. It was a great weekend for hiking and exploring the natural beauty of the mountain.

"I was driving clients around the construction at Black Rock Village and the new condos at Eagle's Court, when I saw smoke over at Black Rock, and Payne and Nicklas roared by me in the fire truck in that direction, followed by a string of cars from the valley. I turned to my clients and told them that I would have to drop them immediately at their cars in front of the Mountain Inn. It was evident that there was a potentially bad fire roaring up the face of Black Rock Mountain threatening the first few homes built near Black Rock Park.

"My clients asked if there was anything they could do to help and I said, 'Absolutely.' I told them this was going to be a long battle and we would need food, water, and supplies for the men on the front line of the fire, and that if they wanted to help they might volunteer in the kitchen making sandwiches for the fire crew, and volunteer to supply the front line. We parted with thanks and each rushed to our prospective duties.

"When I arrived at the fire truck we were just attaching the fire hoses to the pump truck and then pulling the 2 ½-inch hoses down the face of Black Rock. We stumbled down the mountain toward the Plunge with several of us carrying the hose over our shoulder. Fire was everywhere. We were surrounded by it. We had responded so quickly that everyone was still in their work clothes.

"Our legal counsel, Stuart Sadler, was dressed in an Oxford shirt, dress khakis, and Bass Weejuns, and had an 'Indian pack' [filled with water] strapped to his back. He climbed over large boulders and logs with one of the members of the sales team who had a fire rake and was pulling burning embers, foliage, and decayed leaves from under the rocks. Stuart and others with portable tanks of water used a hand pump to douse the fire and embers.

"Once the water was expended they would scramble back up to the truck at Black Rock Park to replenish the Indian pack and then head back down the mountain to repeat the process. It was done over and over because it was so steep and the fire was so widespread that the hose could only reach certain areas.

"The fire had to be fought by hand. It was totally exhausting, physically punishing, and very dangerous, given the substantial weight of the packs. The worst aspects were the imminent danger of the fire, the thought of being burned alive, the thick smoke and the inability to breathe, the poor footing and the additional risk of falling off the mountain to one's death.

"It was a miserable experience, but the fire had to be stopped at all costs. Those fearless young men and women who worked in every department at Wintergreen fought the fire all day and into the night, and even the next day until they extinguished it. In some cases the fire died only 10 or 15 feet from the decks of the newly built homes at Wintergreen in Black Rock."

Mr. and Mrs. James Solo, who lived in one of those homes, expressed their thanks to the fire fighters in the *Wintergreen Gazette* Volume 3, Number 1. "While there were many anxious moments," they wrote, "our house and those nearby were not damaged by the blaze. This was the result of a great deal of courage, quick action, and perseverance by a large number of Wintergreen people and local residents. We were extremely impressed with the effectiveness, cooperation, and determination of those involved in fighting the fire.

A 24-HOUR FIRE WATCH WAS KEPT for the next few days. Three days later, on November 8th, Nicklas was driving down the mountain in his truck when he saw a blaze at the Three Ridges Condos. He was able to alert all the local fire departments and the Wintergreen Fire Brigade. Phil Birdsong and other fire fighters moved smartly to get back out all the fire fighting equipment that had just been put away, and quickly got to the scene.

The fire was going up the outside stairs of one of the condos. Because it was caught early, they were able to knock it down before it got out of control. It turned out paint had been stored in an outdoor closet, and spontaneous combustion had followed.

This was a fortuitous save, because all of the Three Ridges Condos had been sold, and to lose them would have meant a big loss, both monetarily and in terms of timing. The salesmen, now that they could show the amenities of a ski area and a golf course, needed condos for clients to purchase.

In the CC&F days, planning had called for all the actual development and construction of condominiums to be by outside investors. Wintergreen did not want to be involved in construction, they just wanted to sell the land. This had held true for the Timbers and Dobie Condominiums.

In the spring of 1976, a developer named Howland Swift had purchased the Dobie tract at the top of the Diamond Hill ski slope, and was building the first of four phases of the Dobie Condo. Completion of the units in the first phase were advertized to be ready in time for Christmas and the ski season that winter. The salesmen were on a roll pre-selling condos, attracting lots of clients who loved the idea of the skiing being right there, and contemplated inviting their families up for the holidays.

As summer turned to fall it was evident that construction was falling hopelessly behind, and sure enough, they were not anywhere near completed when fall became winter. Salesmen had to pick up the phone, break the bad news, and tell the buyer that in fact they would not be able to be in their condo by Christmas. In some cases refunds had to be made, and the whole experience was very hard on the sales force. The first phase of Dobie didn't get finished until the summer of 1977.

The element that was missing in having outside investors/developers take on the construction was an understanding of how different building on a mountain is from building in the valley. It took a long time to get to work, and working conditions were often severe— think winter temperatures, ice, snow, sleet, and freezing rain. The sought-after cycle of putting up and closing in buildings in the good weather and then working inside them during the winter becomes untenable. Fingers froze inside gloves while work went on *inside* a closed-in structure, and roads become impassable.

As Wintergreen Development, Inc., (WDI) entered

in to this new phase of development, it became apparent that a new department was necessary to manage condominium and building construction. Andy Yowell was hired by WDI in 1979 to be the director of building construction, responsible for all aspects of condominium development. Andy was a Virginia Certified Professional Engineer who had graduated from VMI in the same class as Payne and Rutherford. So the "VMI mafia" continued to grow!

During his 15-year tenure with WDI, Andy was responsible for the development of nearly 1,120 condominium and townhouse units in addition to the Mountain Inn, Skyline Pavilion, housekeeping building, telephone PBX building, Checkerberry Cabin, Stoney Creek safety services building, and Stoney Creek Golf Clubhouse. As WDI was phasing out of condominium development, Andy continued his tenure with Wintergreen for an additional five years, serving as director of facilities for Wintergreen Partners, Inc.

During that time he was responsible for a multitude of renovations and new projects such as the new Devils Knob Golf Clubhouse, Mountain Inn renovations and upgrades, including the outdoor plaza and the Treehouse child care facility, Devils Knob indoor tennis facility, and the construction of the Tuckahoe extension of the Stoney Creek Golf Course. Andy's hard work and dedication over the years has played a major role in creating Wintergreen as we know it today.

The experience with Dobie was a leading factor in the decision by Wintergreen to take over construction going forward, instead of turning it over to outside

Jan and Andy Yowell with Bob Hunt

developers. Nicklas was put in charge of construction, working closely with Payne. Nicklas had been freed from managing snowmaking when Uel Gardner was hired away from Massanutten by Wintergreen in 1977 to be the mountain manager in charge of all ski related activities.

Moving away from using outside contractors was another of those lynchpin decisions made by Wintergreen at the right time and for the right reasons.

Farley, looking back, pointed out that Payne and Rutherford were a superb management team. Payne was quiet, smart and methodical, often described as being an excellent listener. Rutherford was a risk taker and had nerves of steel. The two got along well and complemented each other perfectly.

In 1978 one of the issues they were working on came as a result of the success of skiing. The inundation of skiers on the weekends meant that management had to find ways to improve the experience for property owners, many of whom also often came for the weekends. Skiing for the winter of 1977–78 operated for 90 days for the second consecutive season. The ski school gave 22,000 lessons and management had to limit the number of tickets sold to skiers. The number of parking places for property owners doubled, and there were hours for skiing first thing in the morning that were open only to season pass holders.

The Shamokin Room in the Sports Center, "with the warm atmosphere of a roaring fire" was set-aside for property owners as well. Family dining was possible there for the very reasonable price of $4.50 a person. A toll-free telephone reporting system was set up for property owners so that they could check which gas stations had gas, as many people lived within a gas tank's drive away, but needed another tank full to get home.

Cliff Taylor, Wintergreen's ski professional, had been elected to the National Ski Hall of Fame, and Phil Patterson was Salesman of the Year. The Copper Mine Bar had been relocated and the 100-seat expansion of the Copper Mine Restaurant was under way. Construction began in October of 1978 on the 4,000 square foot Devils Knob Golf Clubhouse.

By the winter of 1979 two more slopes, Eagle's Swoop and Acorn, were lit for night skiing, which made a total of four lighted slopes. A new expert slope,

Night shot of Diamond Hill and Dobie ski slopes

Devils Gate, had been added at the top of the Acorn lift. It was narrow, so only expert skiers were allowed on it.

Tim Harschutz was now head of the ski school, and they were still teaching the Graduated Length Method. The first lesson to learn to use GLM cost $7.00. Each subsequent lesson cost a dollar less than the one before, until the final lesson was free, and presumably you could ski on your own. Wintergreen offered ski racing clinics during the week, and ran slalom races on the weekends, leading up to the First Annual Wintergreen Open Slalom Cup on February 24th of that year.

Salesmen were hitting their stride, 950 home sites had been sold, 250 homes and 380 condos built. The average price for a home site was between $15,000 and $40,000, for a built home between $73,000 and $150,000. Ninety percent of the home sites and condos were adjacent to open spaces, whether it was mountainsides, streams, or the golf course and ski slopes. Condos were clustered in high-activity areas.

Their prices varied from $49,000 for a one-bedroom condo to $130,000 for three- and four-bedroom units.

As property owners began to think about building their homes, a number of issues confronted them that started to become a deterrent to house construction as well as property sales. Most, if not all, new property owners were not local residents, and, as an "absentee owner", had to locate an architect and builder in an unfamiliar area, as well as conform to Wintergreen's architectural review board requirements. The obvious contact that new owners had was with their sales person, so sales agents' time was being cannibalized by assisting clients with all kinds of issues associated with house construction, so much so that more time was being spent "putting out fires" with property owners than selling new property. To address this issue, WDI created a new department and hired Grayson Beale to manage Home Building Assistance. Grayson spent endless hours with new property owners helping them locate an architect and builder, shepherding them through the architectural review board process,

and getting their new home to completion. Thanks to Grayson's untiring efforts, building a home at Wintergreen was transformed from a nightmare to a dream-come-true for new property owners.

By the fall of 1979 six trails had been cleared and blazed for hikers: The Plunge, Lower Shamokin Falls, Paul's Creek Waterslide, Loggers' Alley, Sliding Rock, and the rerouted Appalachian Trail across Wintergreen. A trail map was published to make them easy to explore. The marketing emphasis at that point was on discovering what Wintergreen had to offer out-of-doors.

For someone who had arrived early at Wintergreen, life did not change much when Bankers Trust became the owner. The bank had a good relationship with Payne, and their representatives—like many before them—fell in love with the place. Life went on much as it had before.

HIkers at The Plunge

CHAPTER TEN

Freedom and Restraint

Many important things happened at Wintergreen in the 1980s, but none more important for its future than the arrival of Gunter Muller to be resort general manager.

At that point he was a young man who had grown up in Germany and attended the well-known Hotel School in Lausanne, Switzerland. In 1980 he was in his tenth year of being involved with resort management on the island of St. Maarten in the Netherlands Antilles.

Luckily for Wintergreen and for Muller, the president of the company he worked for was Herb Merser, who had retired and became a consultant to Bankers Trust on its Wintergreen holdings. Merser knew the resort was looking for a manager, and recommended Muller for the job.

Muller had the manners of a European gentleman, but that formality was erased by his natural friendliness and interest in people. He had the Swiss hotelier character trait of missing no details, and holding himself and his employees to exacting standards. At the same time he made sure that he really knew those who

Lady Bird Johnson, former first lady, dedicating a wildflower garden at Wintergreen

worked for him, supported them when problems arose in their lives, and developed a personal relationship with them.

Nicklas said of Muller, "He was a hands-on guy who lived on the job. At any hour of the day he could be outside picking up trash, in a marketing meeting, or checking on a conference group function. But he was first and foremost a host. Everyone loved Gunter."

Managing a resort on a mountain is not all that different from managing one on an island. The same challenges applied: dealing with the off season, training labor for the popular season, weather issues, and the difficulty of dealing with repairs as well as water and electrical systems. These did not daunt him, and being a skier, he liked what he saw at Wintergreen.

Said Muller, "When my wife, Joost, and I first came… I was intrigued with the mountain location, its natural beauty, and considered it almost like 'an island in the sky.' I was impressed with the vision of L. F. Payne, who described what Wintergreen was all about, and when he offered me the job I enthusiastically accepted.

"From the beginning in 1980 I found the development management group very open, enthusiastic and positive. L. F. Payne and Larry

Gunter Muller

Bob Evans   Susie Seaman

Rutherford, Bob Evans (marketing), George Nicklas (construction), Stan Hardy (finance), Stuart Sadler (attorney), Peter Farley (sales)—a very supportive group of people.

"On the operations side I also encountered a group of enthusiastic pioneers, willing to do whatever it took to make Wintergreen Resort successful. Uel Gardner (ski area manager), Jim Rankin (assistant and activities manager), Tim Hess (food and beverage), Henry Nowak (maintenance), Karen Wortman (human

Early condos

resources), Dan Schablein (accounting), Susie Seaman (administration), Doug Coleman (naturalist), Nancy Donnelly (activities and children's programs), Bob Ruff (golf superintendent), Mike Mayer, David Jimenez and Warren Griffin (golf), Michael Thomas (conference sales), Jimmy Ballowe (ski rental), Andy Yowell (facilities and project manager), and many more.

"In my opinion it was a resort in the 'evolution' phase, and the most fascinating part was the synergy between the real estate development, the sales process and the development and operation of the recreational facilities/amenities.

"For example, a lot at Stoney Creek was up for sale with the anticipation of being on a golf course, which would increase its value. However the golf course was not yet built. So part of the money generated from that sale went towards financing the golf course construction. This was how not only the golf courses got financed, but also the tennis and skiing facilities, the restaurants, and the aquatics and fitness center at the Wintergarden, as well as other capital projects."

The Mountain Inn opened in 1980, and with its completion, Wintergreen, Muller felt, finally had a building that gave a visitor "a sense of arrival" in the way that a hotel does. It provided a front desk, a small café, retail stores, conference and banquet facilities, and accommodations. The Mountain Inn had 48 units, most of which were in the rental program, meaning the accommodations were condos that could be rented when the owners were not there through the Wintergreen reservations department. The entire rental program consisted of approximately 300 units both in condos and homes all over the mountain. It gave

Herbie Fisher   Lynn Tyler

Wintergreen the opportunity to offer accommodations without the capital investment necessary to build a hotel. Whether or not to build a hotel is still an issue under discussion today.

The condos in the Mountain Inn were sought after both for the convenience of the location as well as for their potential as an investment. When they were released for sale, would-be buyers drew numbers out of a hat to establish an order for choosing.

Although now there was a front office in the Mountain Inn, the offices of management were still in a "temporary" trailer that had been around for eight years. Susie Seaman started out in the trailer and was the administrative assistant from the very beginning. The trailer did not have running water, so a trip to the rest room meant putting on coat, hat, and boots and standing in line with the skiers in the Sports Center.

One of the most amazing employees is Herbie Fisher, who joined the company in 1975 and is still at Wintergreen. Lynn Tyler described him as "the face of the Copper Mine Restaurant." He takes tremendous pride in his job, and many property owners know him from decorating the luncheon buffet. He goes well beyond the call of duty and is prepared to assist wherever help is needed.

Becky Henderson recollected the early years of transporting food from the restaurants to Checkerberry Cabin. The cabin is a small facility on the slopes that offers skiers some basic food items like hamburgers and hot dogs, hot beverages, and toilet facilities. We sold a tremendous amount of hot chocolate there. "We had to travel by snow mobile in the winter. Every day food went down on a sled attached to the snow mobile. I remember taking buckets of chili and soup down. The sled fishtailed, and there went the soup and chili, all over the slopes! Not a pretty sight."

She thought back on the freezing walk down to the parking lot when the temperature was below zero, the wind was trying to knock you down, and you had no idea whether or not your car would start.

Lynn Tyler, now the vice president of food and beverage for the resort, recalled when food and beverage at Wintergreen consisted of the original restaurant, the Copper Mine, and one small cafeteria operation generating around $600,000 in revenue annually. She has witnessed the addition of many facilities, including the Garden Terrace Restaurant, Devils Knob Golf Clubhouse, the Verandah (today Stoney Creek Bar and Grill), The Edge, Devils Grill,

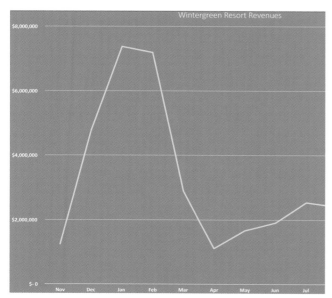

Chart showing the seasonality of resort revenues.

Gunter Muller with President Bill Clinton at Wintergreen

117

The new Mountain Inn circa 1980

and substantial conference and banquet facilities. Food and beverage revenues today are in the range of $6,000,000. She particularly enjoys working with members, organizing menus, and arrangements for celebrations like birthdays, anniversaries, weddings, golf, ski and tennis events, wine tastings, and dinners. Over the years, many members and property owners are like family and a real pleasure to work with.

Becky Henderson put to words what so many employees have tried to express, about how unique life was for workers at Wintergreen. "We worked hard and we played harder. We were one big happy family, and we took care of each other and helped out wherever needed. It has been a great ride, and I look forward to having a lot more fun."

Kate Caldwell was employed in activities and children's programs at Wintergreen in the '80s. She wrote in a recent email correspondence with Muller, "I have always referred to it as the best job I ever had.… Who could complain about figuring out where to hide the Easter eggs, or organizing the Spring Carnival and

being hit with pies…early resort activities like Maurice Williams and the Zodiacs, which we affectionately referred to as 'Mo and the Zo's.'"

In her office Kate confessed that they had a "rate-a-butt" system for the ski patrol, who ran passed their office window to emergencies; but admitted, "I'm too old to remember who had the '10' most often!"

About Muller she reiterated something many others also expressed, "I have never forgotten how you always looked for trash while walking the resort grounds… and being so impressed that you knew everyone's name and made your encounter with every employee a personal one."

The scope of Muller's job was big, and got bigger every year he was there. His responsibilities included overseeing golf, tennis, skiing, spa and aquatics, restaurants, bars and cafeterias, retailing, maintenance, landscaping, marketing, accommodation rentals, housekeeping standards, reservations, revenue management and budgeting, children's programs, and managing contractors. Keeping all these balls up in the air and dealing diplomatically with those who crossed his path seems to have been a job he had prepared for most of his adult life.

Gunter commented, "I consider myself fortunate to have had so many dedicated, committed employees who contributed to the success of the resort by dedicating a significant portion of their career to it. In some cases the third generation is now working at Wintergreen, and some of them have three or more family members employed at the resort at the same time. There are well over a hundred people who have worked at Wintergreen for over twenty years, some even for thirty and forty years."

One day Muller was working in his office when the phone rang. When he answered a woman's voice said in abrupt tones, "Did you know that geese mate for life?" She was irate because one of the golf course maintenance employees had just shot a goose. As it turned out, goose poop was a major problem for those responsible for maintaining the golf course, but problem or not, terminating with prejudice the lives of geese ended after that phone call!

One of Muller's most challenging issues was the fact that since there was no hotel, guests at Wintergreen were accommodated in rental homes and condos all over the mountain. At other meeting sites, conference attendees were used to going from their room in the morning to the Fitness Center, to breakfast, to their meetings, to cocktails, and to dinner, all without leaving the convenience of connected structures.

Arriving at Wintergreen on a rainy fall evening, the conference attendee would need, first, to check in at the Mountain Inn to find out where he was staying, and then head out with a map into the misty night to find the way to his assigned condo. In the morning he might stop in at another condo to pick up a conference attendee junior to himself, and note that this person's accommodation was superior to his own.

As they arrive at the Mountain Inn our senior attendee realizes he has left his briefcase behind. Instead of taking an elevator to his room, he must drive back to the condo to retrieve it. On a bright sunny day, in October, however, the natural beauty, the views, and the fall colors were able to overcome these negatives.

Helen Driver was living in California when she answered an ad she saw in a doctor's office magazine,

and eventually got the job working in sales and marketing where she stayed from 1983 to 2012. She had responsibility for booking corporate events.

"I booked many groups with Wintergreen that had not considered it before. Because I had faith in our staff and in delivering a great experience, I was able to bring in groups that others would have thought impossible to service, like Camp Jeep, Daimler/Chrysler, and all the biggest law firms in DC and Richmond, just to name a few. As a result of the financial impact on the area, I was awarded the 2000 Tourism Appreciation Award given by the Charlottesville Regional Tourism Council, an achievement of which I am truly proud.

"The most enjoyable part of my job was all the people I got to know and interact with through my travels for work. Those were the days of getting to know your customers and gaining their loyalty and trust. Wintergreen was a silent gem, and such an easy sale once I got people to the property to see for themselves."

Muller had to insist on a rigorous vetting of rental properties. A number of property owners had purchased condominiums planning on the rental revenue off-setting the ongoing cost of ownership. They did not appreciate being told that they had to replace the carpet, outdated furniture, or lumpy mattresses. Uniformity throughout rental properties was the key to guest satisfaction and to easier housekeeping for the staff, but there were property owners who rebelled against just that uniformity.

Renters had to be assured of comfort, not just cleanliness; and Gunter's staff had to do inspections to make sure this was the case. Consumer tastes and expectations change over time, and after a few years "This End Up" furniture was no longer acceptable. As rules got stricter and more detailed, some property owners found other rental agencies to manage their properties. This brought a whole new set of challenges for the resort.

Back to our hypothetical scenario on that same dark, misty night. A woman shepherding a youth group from a church drives up to the Mountain Inn in her van. She has already been to the house assigned to them by the valley rental agency using the map they had sent her, but did not find the key where she'd been told it would be left, on the window ledge to the right of the front

L–r, Ed Spears, L. F. Payne, Lady Bird Johnson, Doug Coleman, and Lynda Robb

L–R, Lynda Robb, Lady Bird Johnson, L. F. Payne, and Allen and Priscilla Brown

door. It is Friday at 9:00 p.m., and the agency's message machine says a rental agent will be in first thing in the morning to review messages.

At the Mountain Inn she explains her problem and asks for help. The young college student doing his weekend stint at the front desk has the unenviable job of explaining to her that Wintergreen can do nothing to help because the rental was through an outside agency.

On the other hand, for property owners there was good news in the liquidity of property at Wintergreen. L. F. Payne, in his President's Letter in the *Gazette* the summer of 1982, writes about Wintergreen's unique success story in the second home real estate market, namely the liquidity available to investors. He pointed out that despite a poor economy, in the first six months of 1982 they had completed a record number of 51 sales totaling $3,377,000. Of those, 40% were to existing property owners. "We often don't lose sellers," he pointed out, "they build again or purchase another property."

This same newsletter had an article about the creation of the Shamokin Springs Nature Preserve, made possible by repurposing land that had been on the Master Plan for development of single-family homes. Coleman had discovered that these 13 acres made up a significant high altitude spring ecosystem. It consisted of subterranean springs where cold mountain water breaks through the surface and forms networks of clear, rocky streams. The confluence of these streams created Shamokin Falls, which itself becomes the headwaters of Stoney Creek in the valley.

Coleman and his crew spent weeks carefully planning and building a trail that would allow visits without destroying the fragile ecosystem at the site. They also planned interpretive signage. Coleman gave Bob Evans a large part of the credit for helping Wintergreen management to accept the concept of a nature preserve.

Obviously, it took developable land out of the Master Plan, but Evans, as an advertising man, could see the value of a truly unique nature preserve in boosting sales. From Farley's point of view it was done for the property owners, and for Coleman it was an environmental coup. The property owners in particular were thrilled by its creation.

Moisture and altitude were responsible for the

unique plants found there. Yellow birch, which is more typically found in northern boreal forests, wild lily of the valley growing on root hummocks of the birches, winterberry, the most beautiful of deciduous hollies, beech drops, a tiny brown flowering plant that attaches itself to beech tree roots, plus shadbush, spicebush, rose azalea, and minniebush were all found there. Most luxuriant of all were the ferns and moss-covered hummocks.

In 1983 Coleman, who was part-time, had gone to Payne with his own decision that unless he could see career progress at Wintergreen and be hired, he was going to return to graduate school. Payne didn't hesitate to hire him as Wintergreen's biologist/naturalist. This may have been the first time a developer had made such a move.

Sue Ellen Lee worked with Bob Evans in the Marketing Department. Knowing that Coleman had established a wildflower garden, one day she called him and said, "Guess who is speaking on wildflowers at the Garden Symposium coming up in Williamsburg?" It turned out that Lady Bird Johnson was to be the keynote speaker. One of her main projects as First Lady was to introduce the planting of wildflowers like blue bonnets and evening primrose in the median strips of Interstate Highways in Texas, to the delight of environmentalists.

The symposium was to be a very big deal, with 600 people expected to attend. According to Coleman, Sue Ellen's pipe dream was that Coleman should attend, and while there manage to ask Mrs. Johnson if she would come to Wintergreen to officially open the new wildflower garden. Coleman's reaction was, "I may have to actually come out of my jeans and dress up for this one!"

But he took up the challenge and travelled to Williamsburg, miserable in his coat and tie, wondering to himself how in the world he was going

Many of Wintergreen's original owners greet Lady Bird Johnson.

L-R: L. F. Payne, Doug Coleman, and Tony Troy receive the National Environmental Quality Achievement Award in San Francisco.

One of Wintergreen's ancient fern communities

to manage to approach the wife of the President. He decided that his best chance would be to try to position himself after her talk so that he could approach her as she was leaving. Luck was on his side; she passed ten feet from where he stood as he said to himself, "It's now or never."

Out loud, and directly to her, he said, "Mrs. Johnson, we have a beautiful wildflower garden at Wintergreen. Please come visit." As the Secret Service jumped, she fixed him with her hawk-like look and responded, "I will." Her daughter, Lynda Robb, was with her, and knew about Wintergreen. Sue Ellen followed up and all the contacts were put together to arrange for Mrs. Johnson's visit to dedicate the wildflower garden at the Devils Knob Golf Course June 15th, 1985, again with Lynda Robb accompanying her.

On the day of the inauguration a crowd had assembled around the wildflower garden, awaiting the arrival of Mrs. Johnson. Muller was supposed to announce her arrival from the elevated balcony at the clubhouse. He was so excited when Mrs. Johnson did finally appear that he rushed to the deck from inside, going through the screen and knocking it out of its frame. This succeeded in getting everyone's attention!

Come, as she said, "to spread the gospel," she was curious about Coleman's wildflower restoration projects. Mrs. Johnson walked with Coleman in the nature preserve, and asked many questions about the concept of preservation at Wintergreen and the involvement of the property owners in the transplantation project.

She commented, "I must say the education, from what I'm hearing, is marvelous and I'm excited about the enlistment of people who have become involved." Coleman responded that what she was seeing "represents the fact we know what we have and are doing the best we can to understand and protect it."

In 1987 Muller, whom Coleman describes as "the most thoughtful and efficient person I have ever known," had a brilliant idea. He, along with Mark Glickman, urged Coleman to enter Wintergreen in the contest for the National Environmental Quality Achievement Award to be given by the American Hotel and Motel Association.

Coleman took his time and wrote detailed descriptions of the environmental projects at Wintergreen. As he put it, "They were either going to conclude I was lying, or that we've worked hard enough to win this award!"

And win they did—Wintergreen was chosen from among hundreds of contestants. According to the *Wintergreen Gazette* quoting Payne, "We won for our outdoor conservation and development program, and for an on-going outdoor program directed by Doug Coleman." Glickman put together an impressive video to be shown, and Payne, Tony Troy, and Coleman flew out to San Francisco in June of 1987 to accept the award on behalf of Wintergreen. As it turned out, the second place finisher didn't even come close to what Wintergreen had accomplished.

At this point Jim Rankin was in management as assistant to Gunter Muller, and frequently butted heads with Coleman. Rankin found Coleman difficult (the feeling was apparently mutual) and at one point said, "Coleman had a will of iron and was difficult to manage, but he had the soul of integrity and the support of L. F. Payne, which enabled him to accomplish things; but trying to manage him was like

an invitation to an ulcer!" However, after Lady Bird Johnson's visit and the National Environmental Quality Achievement award, support and respect for Coleman grew among the management team.

PAYNE STATED THAT THE PERIOD between 1976 and 1984 was the period of Wintergreen's greatest expansion through building. Also resort operations revenues increased tremendously. These were the years of Bankers Trust ownership, and although relations between Wintergreen and the bank were excellent, a change in the banking laws of New York State meant that they could no longer hold on to Wintergreen. No one had expected it to last eight years. Even so, the bank's representatives and their families were sad to call a halt to their visits.

In 1980, Payne, Rutherford and Sadler, who were managing Wintergreen for Bankers Trust through its subsidiary, Melba Investors Southeast, Inc., entered into an incentive compensation agreement with Melba. Under this arrangement, Melba agreed to a right of first refusal under which the resort and the real estate development could be purchased by the management group once it repaid the accrued debt to the bank. Wintergreen Development, Inc., (WDI) continued to act as the managing agent for the bank.

In 1982, Payne asked Faulkner to do a survey of Wintergreen property owners. Faulkner's research revealed that "a significant number of property owners are concerned with what they perceive as a significant conflict between the goals/needs of the community and of the development company....By and large, property owners interviewed are of the opinion that the company undervalues their importance to the health and profitability of the company."

Faulkner's report also found that there was growing concern among property owners and employees that the company's promotion and marketing were more and more focused on a demographic different from those to whom it was originally marketed, who were individuals committed to the protection of nature and the environment. The report also revealed that property owners were worried about the future.

"There is every expectation," Faulkner wrote, "that the ownership of Wintergreen will change in the next several years, either to the great advantage or the detriment of the community, the property owners, and the resort, including finding a way for the property owners to buy and own *all* of Wintergreen." Faulkner's survey ended with a list of 51 suggestions for how to improve the atmosphere and help property owners feel appreciated and part of the decision-making process.

While development and sales on the mountain moved ahead quickly, a lot of research and thought were given to the valley portion of the development. It became clear that a new marketing approach was needed, since the potential purchasers were expected to come from a different demographic. More people were looking for permanent residences in the valley. To clearly mark the difference between the mountain and the valley, the name "Stoney Creek at Wintergreen" was selected.

Market research suggested a product that appealed to retirement-age people looking for a back-to-the-country lifestyle. A championship golf course would be the centerpiece, complemented with a golf clubhouse offering relaxed dining, pro shop, and exercise spa,

Rees Jones   Fred Nowak

with spacious decks overlooking the 18th green. To preserve the rural Virginia image, homesites surrounding the golf course should be one-half to one acre in size. Some higher-density townhouse products should be developed near Lake Monocan. A fire station and rescue squad facility separate from the Mountain would be needed as would a medical facility. Master planning for Stoney Creek began in 1985 and incorporated most of the suggestions and recommendations of several market studies. Fred Nowak, who had joined the WDI team in 1976 as director of planning and design, worked with Rees Jones, golf course architect, to create the most efficient use of the land to incorporate an 18 hole golf course and homesites. Fred was no beginner at this process, having graduated from the University of Georgia, with a degree in Landscape Architecture. He joined Charles Fraser's organization in 1971 as director of land planning and landscape architecture, creating environmentally sensitive communities at Sea Pines Plantation, Hilton Head Plantation, Kiawah Island, Amelia Island and Brandermill in Williamsburg. Fred's influence and professional contributions have had a major impact on designing and developing Wintergreen over the years.

Another important player, who, as L. F. said, "rose to the occasion," was Bob Ruff, superintendent of the Devils Knob Golf Course. Bob, his wife Susan, and their two infant daughters had come to Wintergreen in 1978. For 7 years he had taken care of the Devils Knob Golf Course, but in 1985 his life changed when plans were laid for a new 18-hole golf course in the valley. His responsibilities expanded to include overseeing the construction and maintenance of the new, Rees Jones–designed Stoney Creek Golf Course. Once again in 1997 his responsibilities were expanded with the

Wintergreen's original boundary showing land sold to the Department of the Interior in solid green.

new Tuckahoe nine-hole addition. The golf courses at Wintergreen are a living tribute to Bob's hard work and dedication.

According to Muller, "People who were concerned about driving the mountain roads, or the added distance from shopping and medical facilities in Charlottesville and Waynesboro, felt more comfortable in the Nellysford valley location. Weather played a role as well, especially in the winter, when the mountain had colder temperatures and more snow.

"Some Stoney Creek property owners hardly ever travel up the mountain," continued Muller, "except when they have visitors and want to show them around. As a result of the growing populations both on and off the mountain, Nellysford developed into a hub of activity. There is a small shopping center, a bank, restaurants, and medical and dental offices, and businesses that already existed have prospered."

Bit by bit, WDI repaid most of the outstanding loan, and then in 1983, it was able to sell 2,700 acres of land along the Blue Ridge Parkway to the Appalachian Trail Conference. They in turn sold it to the US Department of the Interior, headed at the time by Secretary James Watt. This land was in the extreme northern portion of what had been The Big Survey, and as such shows up on the early Wintergreen development maps.

In the early stage of planning for Wintergreen, this frontal slope of Humpback Mountain that rules the landscape of the Upper Rockfish Valley, had been ruled out as a possible site for the ski area. Aerial photography and topographic map study showed the terrain unsuitable as well as lacking a potential base area.

This sale was a coup for Wintergreen for many reasons. Not only did it enable Wintergreen Development to keep its commitment to Bankers Trust, but it also lowered the possible future density on the Wintergreen master plan, and helped the resort live up to its promise to leave half of its land undeveloped. This had enormous appeal in attracting buyers.

The federal government was at that point feeling pinched and unable to add to its parklands, but Secretary Watt took the time to come down to see it, and approved the purchase. The sale brought in enough money to complete the repayment of the bank debt, and triggered the right of first refusal for the purchase of Wintergreen.

According to Payne, when Bankers Trust knew that they had to sell, "we had developed enough credibility that we said to them, 'you know, we'd like to buy it.' They said 'we know you guys and you don't have enough money to buy it.' But eventually they gave us the option. We had to move on the option by putting a deal together in 90 days or less. It was an incredible

Dedication of the new Wintergarden indoor pool and spa, completed in 1984

thing actually, one of the incredible stories about Wintergreen."

The option actually was to Payne himself, who took it in lieu of a bonus. At the time, as he put it, "What we had hoped is that we could just sell this to the Property Owners Association. However it was voluntary, and since everybody wouldn't join and you couldn't have half the people paying and half the people not…we had to abandon that idea and create a new entity."

Ed Morrissett, who had been involved with Wintergreen from the beginning, said that "When it became evident that Bankers Trust was ready to do something, I talked to the on-site management at Wintergreen about developing the idea that property owners should buy Wintergreen."

"My concept was that if any outside third party bought it, most likely they would increase the density of the development and increase the amount of people using the amenities. On the other hand if the property owners bought it, they could control to some degree the level of development and how it was marketed … and they could prevent time-sharing."

So Wintergreen Partners Inc. was born. Figuring out how it would work had to be done simultaneously with trying to sell property owners on the idea, and all this in a very short time frame. "Normally," said Payne, "this would have taken a long time, with accountants, lawyers, meetings etc., but we just didn't have the time. Bankers Trust didn't think we could pull this off, quite frankly. What they were doing was putting on hold their process because we worked well together. If I hadn't gotten it together they would have been back to selling it to someone else. I convinced them that our deal was the very best thing they could do, because if they sold it to the people they were thinking about, I thought they were going to get sued by a bunch of property owners."

It should be remembered that Bankers Trust by 1984 had faith in Payne and Rutherford. They had used Wintergreen management to advise them on failing properties in the Catskills and elsewhere. Commented Payne, "They got us to go look at lots of things and advise them on how to deal with them." The bank was also inheriting the lot loans from sales at Wintergreen.

Vice president of marketing Mark Glickman and assistant Martha Hill at the Overlook Condominiums

Another reminder: before 1984 when WPI came into existence, Payne said, "It was all about the Wintergreen Property Owners Association (WPOA)." This was established from the very beginning, and the covenants and restrictions were given to each real estate purchaser. Every property owner was committed to paying an assessment to contribute to WPOA, which handled municipal services—police, fire, and rescue, as well as road and open space maintenance.

Once a significant number of properties were sold and sufficient revenue generated, WPOA became independent, and an elected board managed its affairs. Many property owners were high-powered business people with very definite ideas, who were used to calling the shots. "It became a matter of taking all this energy and instead of fighting each other, getting them to all work together," commented Payne.

With respect to Wintergreen Partners Inc. (WPI) there were important questions to be answered, such as would the SEC look at this arrangement as a security, and would the IRS see it as taxable, since people were going to receive benefits (such as parking places close to the Mountain Inn and ski hours exclusively for WPI members). Payne took the show on the road, heading to the cities where most of the Wintergreen property owners lived: Richmond, Norfolk, Raleigh, Northern Virginia, and Washington, DC.

"The tough sell," commented Payne, "was that people would say, 'OK, has this ever been done before'?' And the answer was nowhere, ever. 'Then how do you know it's going to work?' And we didn't know.

"What I knew then but wasn't at liberty to talk about was that I knew who Bankers Trust was talking to, I knew exactly what they wanted Wintergreen for, and it was not to keep doing what we were doing. We had built a brand and things were going quite well.

"The other potential buyer was going to try to make a bunch of money quickly and then leave the place, and it would never be what it might have been if we could have continued moving it in the direction it was trying to move. One of the things we did put in place was a covenant restriction that Wintergreen could never be time shared, no matter who purchased it."

As soon as selling property owners on becoming

Outdoor pool at the Wintergarden

members of WPI became the goal, the salesmen were immediately involved, both at Wintergreen and on the road. Farley said, "Each salesman contacted the property owners to whom they had sold a condo or a lot." This time around they were making a sale of a different kind, that of membership in WPI.

Faulkner, who had done the survey for Payne in 1982, was asked by him to return in '84 to promote the WPI concept and help sell memberships. As he put it, "I went after it with all I had to give. Without a doubt it was the most challenging, difficult, and exhausting project I've ever experienced." It was a short but intense period of hectic activity for all involved, but it was ultimately successful.

Everyone's job on the road was to convince property owners that they needed to join WPI in order to control their own destiny, and that of Wintergreen the resort. This came with a price tag for each property owner of $6,000. The residents' understandable reaction was, "We've paid for our land already, why are we being asked to put more in the kitty?" The bare bones answer to that was, "So that you can keep Wintergreen the way you want it."

Said Morrissett, "The amount of heat generated in these meetings was enormous and the amount of personal abuse that management at Wintergreen took about this process was staggering…It is evident that this could not have been done in most other communities. For example, if it were undertaken in a retirement community in Florida where there were lots of doctors, lawyers, and accountants and other people who were very intelligent and not otherwise busy, they would chew over each point instead of actually getting it done. The fact that 95% of Wintergreen property owners did not live at Wintergreen made it possible to deal with it on a more objective basis, and made it more difficult for the opposition to get together and chew on it and drag out the process."

When Morrissett looked back on the governance change in 1984 from the vantage point of 1988, he wrote "One of the key elements of the process that made it successful is that once a property becomes a member that property will always be a member. It may be an active or an inactive member but it will always be a member." (This situation existed until the resort was sold to a corporation and governance changed).

Tim Merrick fly-fishing Stoney Creek

Morrissett continued, "Furthermore, Wintergreen Development agreed that each time it sold a piece of property (lot or condo) it would attach a membership to that property. Therefore the number of properties that are not members could only decrease over time." (This situation changed with the demise of WDI, Wintergreen Development Inc.) Initial ownership participation was around 65% and current (1988) ownership participation was over 80%.

Payne described one particularly heated discussion as he was explaining the facts at a meeting in Northern Virginia. "We had probably 250 property owners in one of those big ballrooms and one irate Wintergreen property owner who was both a lawyer and a developer was there. I was on stage and trying to explain all this, and all of a sudden this man storms up on the little platform that was set up. I'm holding the microphone and he tries to take it. I won't let him. I said, 'If you want to hold your meeting you can go ahead, but this is my meeting.' He was just beside himself, and it was quite a show, actually."

Longtime Wintergreen realtor Tim Merrick described the schedule for the salesmen during those 90 days. "We would hit the road Monday morning, headed for DC We'd rent a room at the Ritz Carlton and give a cocktail party for property owners. We'd do the same in Norfolk the next day, and get to Richmond on Wednesday. Thursday and Friday we'd be back selling property at Wintergreen. Monday we'd start all over again."

Tony Troy had been the Attorney General of Virginia under Governor Mills Godwin. He and his family owned a condo in the White Oak section of Wintergreen, where they could often be found on weekends and holidays. Troy and Payne were good friends. Troy was practicing law at that time with an old Richmond firm, Mays & Valentine.

At the height of the campaign to talk property owners into joining WPI, Dick Nelms, who was a property owner and also a real estate broker in Richmond, put together a protest group to fight the creation of WPI. He did not like the deal, and called Troy to ask if Mays & Valentine would represent his group in quashing the deal.

Troy responded that he would be glad to try to improve the deal, but would not be party to trying to

kill it. The legal issue was that WPI was being set up as a not-for-profit corporation, and intended to treat the $6,000 that each member would contribute as a capital contribution instead of as ordinary income. Mays & Valentine lawyers analyzed the proposed structure of WPI and determined that this would not get by the IRS.

Troy remembered a meeting at McGuire Woods, the Richmond firm representing Wintergreen, at which he and attorneys from Mays & Valentine were present. Payne, Spears, and Wheat were there as well. (Wheat still owned a house he had built at Wintergreen). Troy and the Mays & Valentine lawyers were able to convince their McGuire Woods counterparts that the deal did indeed need restructuring. Nelms agreed, and his group dropped their resistance to the creation of WPI.

Payne commented, "In the end we pulled it off, closed the deal, and then the challenge was executing. We started with Tony Troy as part of our board, and we had Phil Barger, who was probably the most respected businessperson in the area, who agreed to be our chairman. It was a diverse board in terms of geography, and had both women and men on it."

The first WPI board, under the leadership of Phil Barger, included Tony Troy, Catherine Ellyson, L. F. Payne, John Little, Ed Spears, Jim Fish, Ed Morrissett, and R. H. Tysinger.

Troy said, "I was on that first board, but missed the first meeting over Thanksgiving weekend of 1984. "I came home to find they had elected me vice chairman in my absence!" The next year he was elected chairman, and continued in that job for four years.

1,500 property owners joined WPI, which raised $9,000,000. Together with bank loans this allowed WPI to purchase the operating assets of the resort. WDI (Wintergreen Development Inc.) acquired the land still open for development. Payne pointed out, "WPI was very dependent on people being willing to step up and volunteer while not getting paid anything. They had to care enough to run a big operation that was fairly complicated in terms of all the different things that needed attention: restaurants, golf, tennis, skiing, maintenance, marketing, and sales, etc." Step up they did, eventually forming so many committees that more than 100 people were involved on one or another of 12 committees.

"I was there four more years," commented

Payne. We (WDI) actually had the contract to run Wintergreen during this period, so if you were from the outside you wouldn't have seen anything different because all the same people were doing all the same things. We just had a different governance model."

However, as time went on, Muller remembered that the main worry of the board and members of WPI was that WDI marketing was more focused on attracting potential real estate clients rather than resort business, such as overnight guests, conferences, groups, and day visitors.

When Wintergreen had a good ski season, it meant that WPI could plow that money into construction projects—more tennis courts, building a new golf clubhouse, or expanding the ski area.

The funding for the addition of these facilities was generated both through real estate sales and through additional WPI memberships. This was part of the agreement between WPI and WDI in 1984.

WPI's goal, of course, was not to generate losses, but from the earliest days a poor ski season usually meant that the resort did not meet its yearly budget projections. Conversely, a cold winter that allowed for extensive snow making and produced an extended 90- or 100-day ski season meant a balanced budget with dollars left over to plow back into capital projects.

For instance, 1984 turned out to be a bad ski season; it generated a loss of $825,626. In contrast, 1986 was a record ski season thanks to the arrival of extended cold weather and 179,000 paid skiers, helping to create a revenue windfall that year. The cyclical nature of highs and lows, such as climate, interest rates, country-wide economic realities, etc. meant that WPI tried to off-set these factors by urging their members, many of whom had contacts at big companies, to help generate conference business for Wintergreen.

The Skyline Pavilion opened in December of 1989, and a part of its 37,000 square feet that served as space for ski and locker rentals, ski school, and ski patrol could, after ski season, be transformed into conference space for large functions accommodating up to 400 people. It also provided a restaurant, and the administrative offices could finally move out of the trailer and into their new quarters. It also housed the new marketing, accounting, and human resources departments.

It was during this period that Mark Glickman was hired as public relations director for Wintergreen. He came up with some zany ideas that caught the imagination of city folk for whom Wintergreen was an easy weekend drive. Glickman and Uel Gardner, the ski area manager, plotted to take their skiing show to Richmond and Washington, DC.

Glickman, in his book, *Marketing Paradise,* described Gardner. "He was a crusty, old-school snow maker from New Hampshire who wore a cowboy hat and barked loudly at guests who walked on his snow without their skis on." Glickman persuaded Gardner to be his partner in an ambitious plan they actually pulled off.

Glickman remembered, "So my idea was to bring a portable snow gun to DuPont Circle in DC and turn a three-block stretch on 19th Street into a ski slope where we would hold races to make money for charity. I met with several hot bars and restaurants on 19th Street to get their buy-in and participation and they all loved the idea and were stoked to participate. Then I approached the city in order to get the permits that I needed to rope off three city blocks and hook our snow gun up to a fire hydrant. That also required getting approval from the DC fire department and police.

"The bars and restaurants had agreed to run specials over that weekend, and so there were events that ran the gamut from wet tee shirt contests to ski aerobics… After dinner Uel went back to his hotel room to get some rest since he wouldn't be able to make snow until 2 a.m. I had tipped off the networks to come to 19th Street for a 'live' shot for their 11 p.m. news. Some of the bars sold out of beer by 11 p.m., and a crowd of over a thousand mostly drunk patrons spilled over into the streets. The police had placed barricades to keep people off the street and away from the snow gun."

The crowd lined the streets along the barricades and started chanting loudly, 'Snow, Snow, Snow, Snow!' I received an urgent call from the chief of police to meet him on the street ASAP. He told me that I needed to turn the snow gun on immediately before a riot broke out…I knew I had to wake Uel up and get him out on the street to turn on the snow gun."

"As Uel ducked under the barricade and walked toward the snow gun… the chants grew louder. Uel was moving hoses around and putzing around with the snow gun. Five minutes went by, then ten minutes. The police chief glared at me and said 'tell him he needs to turn the damn gun on now'. So I went under the barricade and said, 'Uel, what the hell are you doing? Please turn the damn gun on already before we cause a riot'. Uel glared at me and said, 'Glickman, I'm building drama.'"

"I stared back at him and said, 'Uel, there are over a thousand snow-crazed, drunk people ready to knock down the police barricades. I think we have the drama thing covered.' So finally Uel turned the snow gun on. It shot cold water up in the air, which sprayed all over the crowd. They were so drunk, they loved it."

Glickman slept a few hours while Gardner and his employees made snow. "When I returned to 19th Street at 5 a.m. I couldn't believe the amount of snow that was covering three blocks," wrote Glickman. "The streets were not only covered with snow but so were all the trees and sidewalks. It looked like a massive snowstorm had hit the city. People were walking down the street later that morning with puzzled looks. I overheard someone say to his friend, 'When did it snow, and why did it just snow here?'"

The event raised $50,000 for the Sunshine Foundation, and coverage included all the Washington television networks, a picture in the *Washington Post*, an article in *Ski* magazine, and global coverage on CNN. Unfortunately temperatures reached record lows, the snow froze, and Monday's *Washington Post* had a front-page photo of city workers down on their knees trying to melt the snow with hair dryers on 19th Street!

Apologies abounded in Glickman's thank you notes.

Another of Glickman's crowd-pleasing coups was to talk the *Today Show* into filming a segment on the ski slopes at Wintergreen. Willard Scott rode up the chairlift

Uel Gardner at Wintergreen with the Mahre twins, gold and silver medal–winning Olympic skiers. "I don't care if you are the Mahre brothers, you will not walk on my snow with dirty shoes."

and was greeted at the top by Uel Gardner. What were the first words out of Gardner's mouth? "Contrary to popular opinion, southerners don't ski on grits!"

Probably Glickman's riskiest move was to agree to let a former Disney producer film a children's movie called *The Summer of Cubs* at Wintergreen. As Glickman wrote in his book, *Marketing Paradise*, the plot was simple. "Bad guys unknowingly steal little baby tiger cubs from a magic show along with the money, and the cubs are found by a group of kids."

The mother Siberian tiger searches for her cubs on our 11,000 acre resort, encountering bears and other wildlife along the way before being reunited with her cubs at our resort lake."

"During the final scene, the young children who had found the tiger cubs and had been taking care of them are swimming in the lake with the cubs and the mother Siberian tiger. What you don't see are the four trainers holding the tiger with a chain around its neck submerged under water. The 'stage' mothers of the children in the movie were present for every scene involving children."

One of the three children in the lake swimming with the tigers started crying hysterically. His mother, who was standing on the dock, dove into the water and started swimming toward her child…It's really never a good idea to dive into a group of tigers. Thankfully, one of the trainers who had been underwater holding the Siberian tiger surfaced when he heard the splash and carried the boy to his mother before she got any closer to the tigers.

"Hosting Siberian tigers, 'trained' bears, and other animals makes for a pretty unrelaxing several weeks. I tried to arrange the locations as far away from our guests as possible because no matter how many times a trainer tells you a tiger or a bear is trained, my attitude always is there's a first time for everything. I don't ever want to have to hear the words, 'The tiger never did that before.'"

Glickman might not have gotten much sleep while the filming went on, but it was all for the greater glory of Wintergreen. As he admitted, the whole time, "I was feeding the media great footage with images of animals and kids from our resort."

CHAPTER 11

Holding the Dream Together

After the all-out effort of putting WPI in place, things settled into a quieter phase. Muller, whom Payne said "had a special talent for getting disparate people together," (a talent Payne also possessed) concentrated as manager on the smooth running of the resort. Muller worked closely with the WPI board, attended many committee meetings and regularly reported at board meetings. He and Payne got along well together, but this easy relationship was not to last for long.

When Dan Daniels, who represented Virginia's 5th District in Congress died suddenly, Payne decided to run to replace him. He won, and was reelected in the next regular election cycle, leaving Wintergreen for Washington in 1988. Payne stayed connected to Wintergreen and maintained an office there, but appointed Ed Spears as his replacement as President of WDI. Payne was known for his skill at listening and absorbing what he had heard, and had the confidence of the locals. He was a hard act to follow.

Spears did not have Payne's people skills and those previous years of trust. He also entered at a different stage in the life of the community, and had to make some necessary business decisions that did not win him any popularity contests.

In 1984, when WPI came into existence, Payne's development company (WDI) had signed a five-year contract to manage the resort. When this ended, it was extended for a year, but the sentiment was building within WPI that Wintergreen Development (WDI) was not doing enough to enhance the Wintergreen experience for its members. As Payne put it, "There were some difficult (WPI) boards to work with at that time." In 1990 WPI voted to end the resort management agreement with WDI, and contract with a new management company.

Muller put his finger on the inherent tension at Wintergreen and at many other resorts. "As the resort is promoted to day visitors and rental guests, facility use can become an issue. On the one hand, 'outsiders' are needed to generate revenue, on the other hand property owners, and especially members, are not happy when they are unable to get a golf tee time on Saturday morning, or when the ski slopes are very crowded and the lift lines are long. It is essential that the balance does not tip too much towards revenue

The Paragon management team and their spouses: L–R: Dave and Elizabeth Zunker, Jack and Sharon Bickart, Dan and Cynthia Schablein, Mignon and Dana Percival, Joost and Gunter Muller, Bruce and Lynn Tyler, and Liz and Mark Glickman

generation rather than member satisfaction."

Finding this balance between underutilization (lack of revenue) and overutilization (unpleasant crowding) is essential, and is done through targeted marketing, sales restrictions, pricing, and policies, such as advantages for members in booking golf tee times. In the hospitality business it's all about service. Muller, reminded of the old joke, said "The sales people sell the dream; operations delivers the nightmare!"

When this tension caused WPI to drop WDI as manager of the resort, Payne, knowing how much value Muller brought to Wintergreen, suggested to him that he form his own management company, with the same cast of characters that had been working with

Ed Spears

him smoothly ever since he came to Wintergreen ten years before. Muller took Payne up on his idea, formed Paragon Management Group Inc. and reapplied for the job. In 1990, in this new guise, he and his team, again got the job of managing Wintergreen with a five-year contract! WDI continued to develop

and sell its remaining parcels of land.

Meanwhile, after the triumphs of the Lady Bird Johnson visit, numerous articles in magazines about Wintergreen's environmental initiatives, not to mention the American Hotel and Motel National Environmental Quality Achievement Award, there was a growing awareness in the late 1980s and early '90s that the values that Coleman brought to Wintergreen needed a home. A nature program would be the logical extension of the projects, initiatives, and education that many property owners felt was at the heart of the Wintergreen experience. It would also be a way for them to extend their exercise of stewardship over an extraordinary landscape.

The question was: how do we get a building, and how do we pay for it? After the award in 1987 Coleman and Payne had discussions about it, but the resort could not afford to build it. WPI wanted to find a way, as did WPOA, the Wintergreen Property Owners Association. WPOA, according to Coleman, "had always been very supportive of our programs," and as it turned out, a huge groundswell of approval for the idea by the property owners themselves caused WPOA to hire an attorney to help set up a non-profit foundation.

At the recommendation of the Forward Planning

Committee of WPOA, The Wintergreen Nature Foundation committee was established, prompted in part by a letter from Ken Gladstone, a committee appointee, to WPOA board president, Paul Greeley. Their initial work, along with other committee members, resulted in the incorporation of The Wintergreen Nature Foundation in time to announce it at the 1989 Annual Meeting.

WPOA also voted to turn over 15 acres at the Overlook (today's Founders Vision Overlook) as a location for the home of the Nature Foundation. Approximately $40,000 was spent planning a modern building that would hang off the rocks at the Overlook, and Coleman and faithful committee member Ed Buynacek traveled all over the region visiting sites where similar facilities had been built. Just as this option was looking hard to achieve and too expensive, a better opportunity arose.

Ed and Betty Dinwiddie were close friends of the Nature Foundation and supporters of its mission. In 1986, with the approval of WPI they had built and run a mountaintop bed and breakfast inn named Trillium House. By the late 1990s they were planning to retire. Because it had been built as an inn, it lent itself to being renovated into offices for the Nature Foundation.

The subject arose between Coleman and Ray Ashton's wife, Ann, in their condo one day while waiting for Ray Ashton, who at the time was board president of the Nature Foundation. They agreed that Trillium House presented an easy solution to the location issue. This was achieved, and with a lead gift from Jim and Gana Dunlop and others who contributed, Coleman and his growing staff enabled Trillium House to quickly become the environmental heart of Wintergreen.

WPOA had a big influence on this project and on life in general at Wintergreen. Russell Otis was running the association at this point, and looking back on it stated, "I want to acknowledge how proud the board of directors of WPOA were at being able to move the discussion regarding the Nature Foundation to its actual incorporation."

Russell Otis's name has come to be synonymous with WPOA, but in late summer 1988 he was the county administrator for Nelson. The county was preparing to buy the Wintergreen Utility Company,

Ed and Betty Dinwiddie, the original owners of Trillium House

The Wakeham Room, the Nature Foundation's native plant propagation room at Trillium House.

PERSONALITIES

Russell Otis: 'the mayor of Wintergreen'

Russell Otis

and it was Otis's job to set up the Nelson County Service Authority to take over running it. In this capacity he worked with two WPOA board members, C. Warren Crandall and Niles Hysell, who had been appointed to the board of the Nelson County Service Authority.

They were also looking for a manager to run WPOA, and asked Otis if he would help a committee of the board working to draft a job description. He arrived with a fairly detailed description of the job already written out. This so impressed Crandall, Hyssel, and Charles Chewning, who was president of the WPOA advisory board, that after the meeting Crandall asked Otis if he would be interested in the job.

His immediate reaction was no. However, driving back to Lovingston to his office he thought about the endless night meetings that his current job entailed, about wanting to start a family and have more time with his wife. As he put it, "I thought, are you kidding me, of course I am interested!" He called Crandall and said he had reconsidered. Otis has been at the helm of WPOA ever since.

Nelson County approached Wintergreen Development, Inc., manager of the resort, with a proposal to purchase the Wintergreen Utility Company in 1988. Nelson wanted the additional Utility Customers so its service authority would become large enough to allow efficiencies of scale. All the water and sewer system components of the mountain community except the raw water system were included in the sale. Nelson County had the utility company appraised by Langley, McDonald and Overman for about $6,000,000; however Wintergreen Development

personnel reviewed the appraisal and suggested that a more realistic value would be $4,000,000 as they felt that an excessive sales price would have resulted in excessively high utility bills for owners. WPI used the proceeds for capital improvements.

When Otis started work at Wintergreen in January of 1989, it was to begin the independent management and operation of WPOA without direct input from Wintergreen Development. Said Otis, "When I came on board, WPOA had in its employment 14 police officers and dispatchers, two firefighters and one EMT. Any other work for which WPOA was responsible was performed by contractors that we hired."

At the time of this writing, Otis has 60 full-time employees on his maintenance staff alone. The fire and rescue departments are among the best in the Commonwealth. The chief benefit of this large crew is that it makes it easier to maintain quality control. When Otis came, the yearly assessment that every property owner had to pay was $500. For 2016 it is $1,600 but, said Otis, "It is still considered a good value by many property owners."

In 1990 WPOA bought the landscaping operations from WPI, and because WPOA didn't have a profit motive they were able to reduce rates by 14 percent.

As its responsibilities mounted, WPOA bought the Community Office Building, which was renovated for office use. Otis commented, "The major building addition provided much-needed office space and a wonderful conference room, which sees much use."

In the early 1990s Coleman had done a survey on the prevalence of the gypsy moth, and had reported that unless spraying was done, whole sides of the mountains would be defoliated. WPOA agreed that spraying had to be done, at a cost of $50,000 for coverage of 5,000 acres. Since then the gypsy moth threat has been regularly assessed by the Nature Foundation, and, if recommended, spraying is carried out by WPOA.

When deer populations soared, the same mutually dependent relationship between WPOA and the Nature Foundation helped to deal with it. Coleman's staff studied the need for culling the herd each year, and WPOA carried out their recommendations. Over the years 1,700 deer have been culled, with the approval of the Virginia Department of Game and

Fire chief Curtis Sheets with volunteer firefighter Frank Ott

Dobie Fish with Don Fitzgerald

Early Wintergreen fire chief Don Fitzgerald

Current fire chief Curtis Sheets

Bill Taylor, Wintergreen's first chief of police

Top: Current chief of police Stan Olah, Greg Turner, Todd Cook, Bill Jackson
Bottom: Richard (Frog) Moore, Julie Froesh, Lawrence Martin

Inland Fisheries, since overpopulation was a threat to their survival. The processed meat was donated to Hunters for the Hungry.

Otis declared 1992 The Year of the Skunk. There were so many that he turned the trapping of them over to his assistant, Jim Kneas. When Jim asked him how he could do this without being sprayed, Otis explained to him that if the trap was short enough the skunk could not raise his tail, and so could not spray.

Otis admitted, "After Jim had successfully trapped and relocated over a dozen skunks, he asked me how I knew about such things. I confided that I really didn't, but appreciated his faith in me!"

THERE ARE MANY "TIGHT" COMMUNITIES under the Wintergreen umbrella, but few that perform a more vital function than the Ski Patrol. They make sure the slopes are set up safely in the early morning, and monitor the operation throughout the day. They bring skiers who have had accidents to the patrol room, which is set up like an emergency room, and assist the Rescue Squad when needed. They "sweep" the slopes at the end of the day to make sure everyone is off the slopes, and are trained in how to rescue guests stuck on a non-functioning lift.

Many are volunteers, and they come from the ranks of doctors, dentists, lawyers, judges, professors, and business people. Muller stated "They make up one of the finest groups of people we assembled at Wintergreen." Judge Morgan Armstrong has served on the patrol for thirty years, is on the National Ski Patrol board, and is a homeowner at Wintergreen. Richard Chaddick joined when Wintergreen first opened its ski slopes in 1975, and is still actively involved after 40 years.

The Ski Patrol is also an incubator for romance. Muller told the following story. "Dr. John Dobson first came to Wintergreen in January of 1976, when the road from the valley up to the resort was unpaved. Weary at the end of the day, he and his family became one of the first condominium renters at Wintergreen. They inquired about renting a condo that night at the Sports Center, which at the time was the front desk, and a hub of activity. The individual at the desk confirmed availability, but did not know 'the rental procedures.'

Gypsy moth intervention

"After checking with others in the complex, the employee was able to rent them a two-bedroom condo on Eagle's Swoop! Very impressed with Wintergreen, John was the first person to purchase a lot in the Pedlar's Edge Section in 1979. Soon after that he built a home there.

"Dr. Nici Singletary, while a student at UVa in 1976, was employed at Wintergreen as a ski instructor with Cliff Taylor, using the Graduated Length Method of teaching. She joined the Wintergreen Ski Patrol in 1978, began medical school the following year, and continued to be an active patroller and instructor following her eventual residency in emergency medicine.

"Nici was also an EMT with the Wintergreen Rescue Squad beginning in 1976, and recalls transporting injured skiers to the UVa Hospital in the old hearse-style ambulance driven by former golf pro/EMS director Warren Griffin. During her thirty years on the patrol, she served as medical advisor, and wrote much of the medical protocol for the resort patrol.

"In 1979, Nici met John Dobson in the Wintergreen Tennis Pro Shop. Nici was cramming for an upcoming med school anatomy exam while her friend, Tim Carwyle, was trying on tennis shoes. John noticed her anatomy textbook and asked her where she went to medical school. Nici had come up to Wintergreen from Eastern Virginia Medical School the day before, and had intentionally skipped her Friday classes. John, who had taught the med school lecture she skipped, questioned her about the class she missed.

"He finally introduced himself to her as 'Dr. John Dobson. I'm the orthopedist who taught the lecture you skipped yesterday!' Several years later, after Dodson was divorced, they began to see each other socially. In 1984, Nici brought John to the Wintergreen Ski Patrol fall refresher, and soon after he joined the patrol as well. They were married three years later, and would not be together today except for Wintergreen."

Wintergreen was fortunate to have such highly skilled physicians on their team. Nici and John contributed a great deal to the patrol, helping Wintergreen to win the 'Outstanding Alpine Ski Patrol in the Nation Award' in 1987. Their hard work on behalf of the resort Patrol was rewarded in 2006, when they both received the highest recognition in the National Ski Patrol—the Distinguished Service Award.

On March 12, 1993, what was referred to as "the Storm of the Century" dropped between 24 and 36 inches of snow on the mountain and up to 20 inches in the valley, accompanied by winds that often reached hurricane strength. Wintergreen's machinery was overwhelmed in the removal of snow, so heavy equipment was brought in. Over the years Wintergreen has had more than its share of big weather events, and each time it puts a strain on budgets, and sometimes causes an assessment to finance the clean up.

Another "Storm of the Century" came along before three years of the so-called century were up. In 1996 the board had just allocated a $20,000 line item for unforeseen expenses when two early January snowstorms hit. Otis's mantra has always been "If you can get to Wintergreen you can get to your home."

"As a rule of thumb," he continued, "when you see large yellow vehicles on the roads, somebody's adding

Wintergreen's first ski patrol

machine is very busy. The cost differential between storms our equipment can handle and those that require heavy outside equipment is exponential." The final tab for those two storms equaled the entire snow removal budget for 1996.

Everyone in a position of responsibility had to constantly deal with unknowns over which they had no control. On the positive side, in 1991 *Golf Digest* magazine selected Stoney Creek as the best new resort course in the continental United States, and *Golf Magazine* gave Wintergreen the silver medal as the top golf resort in the country. This had the happy result of increasing golf revenue by 32 percent over 1990.

The unknowns were more often in the negative category. The next year a national recession hit. Muller, who had been working so hard with the marketers to bring more conference business to Wintergreen, saw group business drop by more than 21 percent, despite the fact that the Skyline Room had been converted to conference space. The Stoney Creek Golf Clubhouse was undergoing renovations amid sluggish sales. Wintergreen needed to look its best for the Stage Finish

The "Storm of the Century," March 1993

of the Tour DuPont Bike Race. This was another Mark Glickman accomplishment and resulted in tremendous media exposure throughout the country

Nineteen ninety-four marked the ten-year anniversary of the establishment of WPI, which now had 2,500 members. Their aggressive ski marketing program and a colder than normal winter helped them complete the $3,700,000 renovation of the Mountain Inn and courtyard, and an expansion of the snowmaking system.

But then the very next winter the month of January was the second warmest in the 20th century, causing an $814,000 loss. Paragon was informed by WPI that their contract to manage Wintergreen would not be renewed in the spring of 1995. That year WPOA oversaw the installation of the new 911 compatible road signs, and the activation of a new phone system as well as the emergency identification of properties that came with it.

The seesaw didn't stop. Nineteen ninety-six was the best year in the history of WPI, leading to an agreement to develop a nine-hole addition to the Stoney Creek Golf Course, plans to enlarge the Devils Knob Golf Clubhouse, and to increase water storage capacity in the valley by enlarging Lake Monocan and adding ponds.

In the period when Paragon had managed Wintergreen, Wintergreen Development had been able to focus again fulltime on real estate sales. WDI was developing and selling land, mostly in the valley. In the early stages of Wintergreen, before the golf course was built, the valley consisted only of Rodes Farm, with its separate entrance off of Route 151.

Rodes Farm was made up of the inn and restaurant, barns, the riding stable and ring, and a nucleus of tobacco barn style houses that could be rented. It also had a swimming pool and tennis courts.

This had served as a little outpost, with its Jeep trails used as a staging point for sales on what was then the empty mountain.

AS HAD HAPPENED SO OFTEN at Wintergreen, an able, competitive, and financially astute man, Michael Donovan, appeared on the scene. In fact he had made his initial appearance much earlier as part of Herb Merser's family. (Merser had been the "secret agent" for Bankers Trust, previously described by Phil Patterson.)

Stoney Creek Golf Course

WINTERGREEN ADAPTIVE SPORTS

W.A.S. had its beginnings in 1984, when adult amputee Vince Fiore took a ski lesson from Michael Zuckerman. Inspired by Fiore, Zuckerman attended a skiing clinic on meeting the needs of those with disabilities.

In 1995, Wintergreen allowed "sit down" skiers, which led to the creation of a volunteer instructors group. In 1996 W.A.S. achieved non-profit status, and began raising funds.

Zuckerman, who taught high school, quickly sensed the potential for students, age 14 or above, to act as Junior Instructors. This has been an incredibly successful program. Both they and the Senior Instructors help people of all ages enjoy the outdoors, teaching skiing and snowboarding in the winter, and kayaking, canoeing and riding in the summer.

Many of the Senior Instructors bring their professional training in orthopedics, psychology, therapy, teaching, carpentry, and neurology into their volunteer work. The Juniors do demanding work like "tethering," which involves holding back a disabled skier in a sled so that they go down the slope at a manageable speed. They also make friends with the disabled young people with their informality, humor, and empathy. Both Junior and Senior Instructors find the work deeply fulfilling.

In 2005 the Wounded Warrior Program was started. The over 2000 people that have been served so far have suffered from amputations, autism, cerebral palsy, M.S., traumatic brain injury, spinal injury, and hearing and sight impairment.

Michael was an engineer but pursued a very successful business career in New York City.

Romance often struck like lightning at Wintergreen, and on a visit south Michael met Linda Ramsey, who was working in Sales. Lightning did strike, and they were soon married. Linda moved to New York City with Michael, but when she was expecting their daughter, Logan, they decided to build a house in Stoney Creek and become more involved in Wintergreen.

Logan arrived in 1991and they returned to Wintergreen. Linda pointed out that Michael was a busy, energetic man, and that she encouraged him to run for election to the WPI board. He was elected in 1991 and reelected in 1994 for a second term. In 1994 he became vice president of the WPI board and chairman of the strategic planning committee. Said Donovan, "I'm an engineer. I had a vision, and planning just suited me."

AFTER THE STONEY CREEK GOLF COURSE was built to encourage real estate sales, Donovan proposed doing three things he called 'the package':

First of all, redoing both golf clubhouses, at Devils Knob and in Stoney Creek. Second, building an indoor tennis facility on the mountain. Third, buying the land from WDI to build the aforementioned Tuckahoe Nine to make a total of 27 holes of golf in the valley. Donovan was able to get WPI board approval for these projects. On the promise of this, WDI sold the lots adjacent to the Tuckahoe Nine, and more private homes were built.

Donovan reminisced, "It would have made the economics of the resort much better if, when WPI was created, everyone had had to join. Dues would not have had to go up as much, they would have taken in more money, and it would have been easier for the resort to carry itself."

Legal issues, such as the difficulty of changing the WPOA covenants, made it highly unlikely that a super majority of owners would have subjected themselves to the potential liability and additional assessments necessary to run the resort.

In the deal with Bankers Trust, the original $6,000 paid by those who joined WPI was considered an initiation fee and a property right of membership. This fee gradually went to $15,000 for those who chose to join later on. Resort revenue tripled between 1985 and 1998, from seven million to twenty-one million dollars. Owners' equity did almost as well, rising from seven million to twenty million in the same time period.

Even though Paragon was no longer managing the resort, Muller and his Paragon management team were reabsorbed into WPI. For Muller this lasted until the summer of 1998, when Bob Ashton became the new general manager. Muller went on to a series of interesting jobs in England and California before returning to Wintergreen in 2012.

In 1998 the WPI board engaged in a strategic planning process to implement a long-range capital improvement program. They hired "The Design Workshop" to put together a master plan, calling for approximately $35,000,000 of improvements, to be implemented over several phases in future years. It included new facilities as well as improvements to and remodeling of existing facilities on the mountain and at Stoney Creek. The hope was to have most of the capital improvements completed by 2007.

WPI also hired Hillier and Associates to launch a new membership program under the banner of "Enhancing Wintergreen for All Generations," and in 2001 the amended bylaws provided for a Premiere Equity Membership. For additional capital contributions these Premiere Equity Members were entitled to a more extensive benefit package and voting rights. Going forward the club had two classes of members.

Throughout the first decade of the 21st century this new membership program generated a substantial amount of capital contributions. The annual dues paid by the membership contributed to the funding for the operation of the resort. Capital contributions increased over the years, and various dues options were considered. As a result of a member survey, the WPI board appointed a committee to make recommendations in response to member input and suggestions.

The master plan envisioned the development of a hotel, and the board of directors started exploring the feasibility. The board stated, "If such a project is undertaken, it will likely be developed and owned by a third party." Elaborate color brochures, describing the proposed master plan, were distributed to potential members, and meetings were held in various parts of Virginia, DC, and North Carolina, to provide opportunities for WPI members to have their questions answered.

ACCORDING TO STUART SADLER, legal counsel to Wintergreen, Ashton's mistake may have been in spending large sums of money on outside consultants to do studies, and planning for a hotel that never became a reality. Said Sadler, "Since the hotel was not built, it was investing a whole lot of money in something with no return. You can't spend that kind of money on this small a business." After all the serious consideration and study, in the end the decision was that a hotel was not economically justifiable.

WPI attempted to pay the debt incurred during this process by attracting more premier memberships. The membership perks that had been given to those who joined WPI in 1984 when it purchased the resort had been structured to make them all feel special. Everyone paid the same amount and was able to use any of the facilities on the mountain or in Stoney Creek. To property owners that became members, it signaled that they were privileged.

According to Sadler, most were happy with it and considered these privileges relatively inexpensive. However, as Wintergreen grew, and the financial situation ebbed and flowed according to how good the ski season was, the WPI board had to come up with more money. The premier memberships did not bring in the hoped for numbers of new members, and only furthered the level of tension between WPI members and those who chose not to upgrade, not to mention those who had not joined WPI in the first place.

Premier members had the privilege of weekend early skiing hours, separate member ski lift lines, special parking privileges, and during golf season, access to preferential golf tee times on weekends.

"At first," said Sadler, the fees were reasonable, but then administrative costs kept going up. In part it was a club and in part it was a business. Members were asked for additional investment and some resented it. Plus, the more people have spent on exclusive memberships for themselves, the less likely they are to ease the restrictions for others."

WE HAVE ALREADY DEALT WITH a major forest fire at Wintergreen, but a bizarre house fire in 1999 was an extreme justification for the steady increase of personnel and training on the part of the Wintergreen Fire Department. The following account of this fire was told by salesman Kyle Lynn.

"A doctor and his wife bought two building lots in 1991 and built a large home which they used and enjoyed with their children. In October 1999 their daughter, her husband, and their infant daughter were using the home with friends. At the end of the weekend they were cleaning the house and preparing to leave and return home. The husband, thinking the ashes were cold, cleaned the fireplace and placed the ashes in a paper bag, which he took outside and placed by the car to dispose of later.

"The couple were vacuuming the lower level when they heard an explosion which blew in the front door. They raced up the stairs to find the front of the house in flames and two cars burning in the driveway. The ashes had enough heat remaining to light the paper bag and the leaves in the driveway. The leaves had been burning under the car when it exploded and covered the front of the house and the other car in flaming gasoline. The couple grabbed their baby, escaped through the back of the house, and called the fire department from a neighbor's home.

"Another salesman, Tim Merrick, was driving clients by and witnessed the fire department fighting the fire. He took his clients back to their condominium and returned later. Both of the cars, an SUV and a BMW, were still burning and the fire department had called in a helicopter to bring buckets of water from a pond on the golf course to add to the water they could produce from the hydrant near the house. At that time of year there were lots of leaves, and the fear was the fire would spread and create a real disaster. The fire was extinguished with some effort, but not until the house was a total loss. The WPOA fire department did an excellent job, and avoided what could have been a disaster of far larger proportions."

AS ITS PROPERTY WAS SOLD OFF, Wintergreen Development entered the home stretch of its lifespan at Wintergreen. This is an inevitable moment in the maturity of any resort development. When this happens, often the developer will simply take on other projects elsewhere, or reinvent itself to take a smaller role.

As Wintergreen Development wound down, its real estate company also fragmented. Bo Newell, a bright, forceful person and a co-sales manager with Peter Farley, left to start Mountain Area Realty. This became competition for the original Wintergreen Real Estate Company for which Newell had previously worked. Farley said of Newell, "He was a great guy, but that was a period of time when everybody had a plan B."

For all of the resort's history Multiple Listings (known to many as a mixed blessing) had existed in the real estate world, but Wintergreen's sales force had managed to capture their clients through direct marketing, phone calls, and referrals. Their sales persons were expert at getting a client to Wintergreen, and then spending as long as necessary driving them around while telling them the history of the place, and showcasing many of the unique spots of preserved beauty.

Now there were agents from other areas visiting with their clients. They knew nothing about the Wintergreen community and all its complex and interrelated workings. To many of Wintergreen's original dedicated realtors this threatened the cohesiveness that comes from sharing a common vision and it was hard on morale.

Wintergreen Development, had taken the initial risks and had built most of the original resort infrastructure and understood the "dream."

For years the sales force had sold the dream and found their way through to articulating it to potential clients. If outsiders came and sold property to buyers, how would these new owners learn about and want to maintain the special ethos that was Wintergreen? Why would they know or care about the concept of the built environment blending into the beauty of the landscape, rather than standing out from it?

That new residents know these things was important not just to Coleman, but also to the sales force, and all the managers who had worked hard over many years to make Wintergreen what it was. If they didn't know about it, it meant the message was no longer controlled and unified and for the benefit of the community as a whole.

Coming at the issue from the other perspective, as more property owners were putting their properties on the resale market, they presumed that the Multiple Listing Service would be an advantage, since properties would get more exposure and visibility. Many of them welcomed the competition, as it meant the potential for more properties and memberships to be sold.

ONE OF THE TOUGHEST REAL ESTATE ISSUES WDI faced involved the development of the mid-rise condominiums along Blue Ridge Drive. These mid-rise condos were thought by many, including Don Faulkner, to be a breach of Wintergreen's original concept of keeping all structures below canopy height. The tough truth was not easy to swallow: that without them Wintergreen Development may have been forced into serious financial difficulty early on. From the inside looking out, the view from the condos was stunning, the opposite of the view they created looking up at them. Likely they could not be built today, but at the time neither Wintergreen's covenants nor local ordinances prohibited them.

Coleman was not fond of the breach of the ridgeline, but being a biologist, latched on to the density concept that preserved more open space in other areas. He and property owners moved more than a hundred thousand azaleas, ferns, and other unique plants off the site before development occurred.

"There was little choice other than to work within the framework we had," commented Coleman, "and saving elements of the biota on the site became more important than the visual impact of the condos. The density that the condos represented allowed me to focus on the preservation of Crawford Knob and the rest of Wintergreen's forest. I knew that Wintergreen was ultimately bound by density and the cluster concept, which would preserve more of its pristine woodlands, wetlands, and ancient natural gardens."

Unlike all the other architecture at Wintergreen, the mid-rise condos don't pretend to fit into the landscape. They stand out like teeth on the ridgeline. This was the first time that Wintergreen had broken the $100,000 condominium sales barrier. The bottom line was that the sale of these condos some considered unsightly paid for many of the environmental assets agreed to over the years by Wintergreen.

As Payne had realized early on, there had to be some concentrations of people in mid-rise condos in order to fund the water supply and water treatment, the roads, and the other infrastructure. These were the indispensable utilities that served everyone on the mountain, whether condo owners, private house owners, or guests.

THIS DIFFICULT ISSUE would re-surface as High Country Associates attempted to develop the Summit House site.

In 1993, the site of the Trillium Field, home to four acres of an over 2000-year-old ecosystem of 20,000 trillium plants, had been scheduled for development. A wild lily, trillium produces a showy pink or white bloom in late May. Remembered Coleman, "The site was so well known by owners for its spring displays that Payne met with me and suggested that in order to save it we should get it appraised. His company, WDI, owned it."

Payne was willing to donate one third of the value of the land if WPI and WPOA would pick up the other two thirds. A half-million dollars worth of developable land was taken off the planning table to establish the Trillium Field preserve. WDI kicked off the initiative, and both WPI and WPOA came in behind it.

According to Coleman, "There was a special assessment done and for a small amount per person the park was saved. It was dedicated in May 1993. Special guests included Peter Mazzeo, botanist from the US National Arboretum, and Fred Case, who at the time

was the nation's foremost authority on trillium."

As Russell Otis put it, "everyone was behind it, no one balked at the cost," an example of how much the property owners valued the natural attributes of Wintergreen. As Otis further pointed out, "decisions were made in favor of the environment long after the blue print had been set." Hindsight has shown that these decisions have proven to be of enormous value to Wintergreen, but in the moment that value is hard to quantify. At the time those decisions were made on faith, and required strong leadership. In this case, it also had the enthusiastic backing of the property owners.

Coleman lost some arguments with Bob Ashton, the resort manager who had replaced Muller. Snow tubing had become a popular sport, and a tubing park was being built. Coleman knew from Bartholomew's exhaustive geological studies done for the master plan that the construction for the tubing park was going right along an ancient fault line. The engineers had apparently not looked at Bartholomew's work. He took Ashton to the site to show him what was at issue. No changes were made, and a serious erosion problem did arise that was expensive to correct. Vice president of resort operations Jay Roberts was a key personnel component in correcting some of the engineering mishaps and enhancing the tubing park and ski facilities from that point forward. The good news was that the difficulties caused Ashton to authorize a stormwater management plan for the resort. Coleman admitted that from his perspective, the decade of the '80s represented one of the high points of community unity and environmental sensitivity at Wintergreen.

IN 1997 AN UNFORTUNATE LAWSUIT spelled the end of Wintergreen Development. An engineer-designed home's foundation and its attached garage separated approximately three inches in a month of heavy rains. The resulting lawsuit against Wintergreen Development and Wintergreen Real Estate was long and drawn out and in a trial by jury ultimately the developer lost.

A judgment lien prohibited Wintergreen from selling additional lots until the judgment was paid. As a result sales came to a halt, and Wintergreen Development was in foreclosure.

Trillium Field Park in May

Jay Roberts, vice president of ski operations

The bank appointed WDI attorney Sadler to manage its Wintergreen/WDI assets. Sadler summed up the lawsuit by commenting, "It was a prime example of how things can go wrong without anyone intentionally misbehaving."

LOOKING BACK AT THE FORECLOSURE of Wintergreen Development, some saw it as a non-resort issue, but it was connected by the "umbrella" of the Wintergreen Community as a whole and those who founded it.

Those in the Wintergreen Real Estate Company knew better than anyone how important it was to keep a unified approach to Wintergreen's future.

As the result of the foreclosure of WDI, Tim Hess went to see former WPI board member Michael Donovan to see whether he would be willing to provide some financing, to allow a group of Wintergreen Real Estate sales executives to acquire remaining assets of WDI. Donovan who was also worried about the situation, agreed to lend Hess, Farley, Lynn, and Carroll the money to buy the specified WDI assets. They formed High Country Associates with each of them, including Donovan, holding 20 percent.

Wintergreen Development had been a closely held corporation, with L. F. Payne and Ed Spears holding most of the stock, and Stuart Sadler, George Nicklas, Stan Hardy (WDI's accountant), Phil Patterson, and Gunter Muller holding smaller percentages. Payne, Spears, Sadler, Nicklas, and Hardy each had to assume a substantial guarantee on the development loan, which was called when the development company was foreclosed.

Wintergreen Development Inc. was now called High Country Associates, LLC, and their original real estate company remained Wintergreen Real Estate Company. As it turned out, High Country Associates had made a brilliant investment. Said Sadler, "The boys got it at the perfect time, and they got it at a very good price." The bank had been holding it a long time. To have the necessary management expertise, they hired Stan Hardy, WDI's traditional accountant, to be the manager.

In order not to be accused of profiteering, Donovan gave his profits to a non-profit foundation he created, which then distributed it to Wintergreen-related non-profits, such as Wintergreen Adaptive Skiing, Wintergreen Performing Arts, and the Nature Foundation. This made High Country Associates more palatable to the community. "More important," said Coleman, "it helped keep alive the original vision of Wintergreen by keeping the early realtors who knew the history engaged. Their relationship had been endangered by the developer's foreclosure and now they were able to continue to do business as Wintergreen Real Estate Company."

Within three years, Donovan had been paid back all the money he had lent his associates.

WINTERGREEN PERFORMING ARTS

Wintergreen Performing Arts began on a Saturday morning in June 1995 when Sarah McCracken brought together a group of mountain and valley residents who shared a love of music. Its first concert was held that November at the mountain home of Joan and Erwin Berry, and featured local Wintergreen baritone George McKinney and pianist Dr. Arnold Popkin.

From these modest beginnings an organization emerged that has garnered national attention. The keystone activity is the Wintergreen Summer Music Festival which takes place every July. With a focus on classical music, other offerings have included dance (*Appalachian Spring*); film (Chaplin's *The Tramp* featuring a world premier score by Daron Hagen); and the many well-attended morning educational seminars that give special meaning to lifetime learning. Favorite themes have been "Vienna," featuring the works of Mozart, Haydn and Beethoven, and "Appalachian Roots," highlighting the musical legacy of Wintergreen's Blue Ridge Mountain home.

Over the years programming has expanded to include an annual Christmas holiday concert by the Virginia Consort and the Blue Ridge Mountain Music Fest in August.

WPA also runs a Summer Music Academy every July for talented students from across the nation and abroad. The students, who are competitively selected, interact regularly with the Festival Orchestra and showcase their skills in special performances. Additionally, WPA provides music opportunities for local schools.

WPA is a happy mixture of outstanding professionals and a broad-based, enthusiastic volunteer group that arranges housing, food, and transportation for the artists and students.

In twenty years, WPA has grown from one concert in one home to an organization that is an integral part of Wintergreen and draws audiences from the East Coast and beyond.

The Evans Center

An outdoor performance on the Devils Knob Overlook.

George and Mickey McKinney perform.

CHAPTER 12

Between a Rock and a Hard Place

From 1973 till 1984 the Wintergreen Dream had been under the developer's control. It had been a relationship of calculated risk, trust, and success built upon successful development and real estate sales. While many other resorts that been developed at the same time went through some form of insolvency, Wintergreen Development under Payne's leadership managed to stay solvent during the economic downturns. From 1984 until 2012, the property owners who chose to become WPI members, through their board of directors, continued to control successfully the resort's destiny in spite of weather and an economy that sometimes brought unforeseen losses.

While the last decade of the twentieth century brought an economic downturn with too much real estate inventory and lower prices, the first eight years of the new millennium turned positive. Sales were brisk and prices high. High Country Associates, reminisced Sadler, were flying high. "They had no debt except to Donovan," he said, "and people would buy anything HCA put together."

But then in 2008 the bubble burst, bringing a recession for the whole country with significant negative impact on Wintergreen. A considerable amount of real estate went on the market at the same time, and the bottom dropped out of prices. Despite the lower prices, sales were depressed.

The Wintergreen Property Owners Association, however, was on a solid financial footing, and WPOA kept providing services—police, fire and rescue, road maintenance etc.—in their usual first-class fashion. The commercial resort facilities, however, were not so fortunate. WPI had previously sold 1,400 premier memberships (offering a higher level of benefits) and this had raised approximately $8,500,000.

That capital had allowed WPI to take on several major improvements, including a computerized and expanded snowmaking system, the Grassy Ridge bridge, a high speed detachable lift known as the Highlands Express Lift on the Highlands ski slopes, and a similar improvement on the Dobie ski slopes.

The bridge on Grassy Ridge Drive now allowed year-round access to the area defined as Discovery Ridge. Previously Grassy Ridge Drive was not accessible during the winter, since the ski slopes crossed the road.

L-R: back row, Tony Troy, Hank Thiess, John Coy, Brent Douglass, Tom Smith (Director of Virginia Division of Natural Heritage), Dr. Dennis Whigham (senior scientist, Smithsonian Environmental Research Center), middle Row, Zoe Smith (post-doc Smithsonian), Judy Juergens (president of the Nature Foundation board), front row, Doug Coleman, Don Faulkner, Preston Bryant (Virginia Secretary of Natural Resources)

Preston Bryant signs the deed of dedication for the Crawford Knob Natural Area Preserve. L-r: Dr. Dennis Whigham, Doug Coleman, Tom Smith, and Brent Douglass

Brent Douglass, accompanied by his wife, Carter, receiving an award from Doug Coleman for his work on the Crawford Knob easement

Doug Coleman talks with Governor Tim Kaine in celebration of the Crawford Knob easement.

154

The slopes now pass under the bridge. The Plunge Tubing Park was built, as well as facilities for food and beverage and children's programs, a zip line, and additional parking. New irrigation for the golf courses was also accomplished.

The plan was that the increased capital raised through premier memberships would drive expanded and more attractive amenities, thereby increasing income from resort guests and day skiers.

What was not accomplished was fixing Wintergreen's business model, which often did not provide the operating profits for long-term sustainability. The WPI board and resort leadership under CEO Bob Ashton believed a key component for sustaining profitability was better conference facilities, including meeting space and attractive lodging. Early in the twenty-first century, four-season resorts in the west, New England, Canada, and as close to home as Snowshoe in West Virginia had developed resort villages around conference hotel facilities. Following this trend the surge toward building a hotel and associated resort village again surfaced.

The board formed Wintergreen Hospitality Partners, LLC, in early 2005 to again study the feasibility of the project and to begin design work. Several million dollars were spent on planning for a mountain village concept to surround the new facility.

As an avenue to pay down debt and partially finance the project, Brent Douglass (WPI vice president of development and facilities) and Doug Coleman began work to place the 1,422 acres owned by the resort on Crawford Knob under a conservation easement, thereby generating tax credits that could be monetized. Simultaneously two additional projects were begun: a major expansion of the Wintergreen Spa, and the construction of the Blue Ridge Commons, an employee-housing complex.

Meanwhile WPI continued to accumulate debt on the basis of a good or bad ski season. In the minds of the leadership they were gearing up Wintergreen's infrastructure for the day when a hotel would be built. The staff also was expanded.

According to Dan Schablein, "Wintergreen relies on December for significant revenues. Warm weather leading up to Christmas week can reduce that revenue by up to $2,000,000, resulting in financial challenges."

L–R: Des Gourley, Gana Dunlop, and Jim Dunlop.

WPI, unlike WPOA, could not assess their membership. There were limited ways of raising money: sell additional memberships, raise member dues, or market more aggressively to attract more guest business. As it happened, borrowing became the solution of last resort.

With the onset of the economic downturn in 2008, the hotel project was again abandoned, but the debt from the increased related infrastructure remained. This added to WPI's vulnerability, which came home to roost when the recession hit late in the first decade of the new century. WPI had never missed, or even been late, on any loan payments, but dwindling financial reserves and rising debt placed them in violation of loan covenants, which gave Bank of America the right to call the notes and ultimately take possession of the resort. In this instance the bank demanded a large payment in a relatively short time frame.

THE PROCESS OF CREATING the Crawford Knob conservation easement had continued and been completed. The deed of easement was recorded in November 2008 and the tax credits had been granted. These were sold to individual investors, and by this means $3,000,000 was paid to the bank to reduce the outstanding debt.

Central to the value of the tax credits was the appraisal of the donation value of the Crawford Knob conservation easement. Two values had to be established. First was the value of the property as a single family home development, its "highest and best use." Determining the value of the property as restricted by the terms of the easement was the second task. The difference between these two values was the "donation value"—the amount eligible for tax credits.

Determining the value of a fully-developed Crawford Knob had been a long and complicated process. First, a detailed land plan, including all roads and infrastructure necessary to support the development, was created. In order to make the value credible, the development plan had to be approved by Nelson County, another complex and controversial process. Finally, comparable properties that had been sold were identified to support the value of the land under both scenarios. At the conclusion of the process the proposed Crawford Knob development was approved by Nelson County. It included 142 residential lots, 89 of which were "view lots", and were valued at $95,000 per unit (lot). In 2007 and 2008 similar view lots on Devils Knob (fully developed with infrastructure) sold for more than three times that amount. The Crawford Knob parcel was appraised for $13.5 million under its highest and best use scenario.

The value of the land under a conservation easement scenario was no less complicated to determine. There were no comparable sales of similar properties under easement anywhere. After researching many properties under easement, a value of $2 million was set for the property under the conservation easement scenario. The donation value was determined to be $11.5 million.

THE SIGNIFICANCE of what Brent Douglass and Coleman had accomplished also fulfilled the goal of protecting the wetlands and forests of Crawford Knob. Since the land was a habitat for rare plant species and globally ranked ecosystems, the Virginia Division of Natural Heritage was persuaded to hold the easement if the Nature Foundation was willing to co-hold it and manage the property. The Wintergreen Nature Foundation and the Commonwealth became the easement holders and The Nature Foundation was named the designated manager of the property under the terms of easement.

This was a significant conservation accomplishment and a major step in fulfilling the 40-year promise of preserving the majority of Wintergreen's land in its natural state. It also bought WPI some time to put its financial house in order, but did not end its loan vulnerability with the bank.

Specifically, to overcome this vulnerability, WPI embarked on a private placement offering to raise funds from existing WPI members to eliminate their remaining bank debt. What followed again showed the community's depth of commitment to Wintergreen. Even though there was considerable risk and individual commitment involved, and no clear picture as to how the monies would be repaid, $7,500,000 was ultimately raised from WPI Members through this offering, and the bank loans were paid in full in 2009.

Two good ski seasons followed, and WPI was able to pay down $500,000 of the private placement ahead of schedule. The future appeared more positive than it had for some time. Much of the increased operating costs, added to accommodate planning the hotel project, had been reduced under the leadership of Hank Thiess, the new general manager, who had been brought in to orchestrate a general downsizing. Relations between the board of directors of WPI and the members were greatly improved. Confidence was growing, and things were looking up.

THEN, DOWN CAME THE GUILLOTINE. In November of 2011 the Virginia Department of Taxation took exception to the appraisal that was the basis of the tax credits issued for the Crawford Knob conservation easement. The department's position was that the appraisal was seriously overstated.

The timing of the appraisal, completed in the fall of 2008, was in part associated with the precipitous drop in real estate values the following year as the recession deepened. The commonwealth's review of the appraisal was arguable because of the fall in real estate prices, most of which was realized after the appraisal was completed. It was, however, within the state's right to audit the conservation easement value within three years of granting it, and during that three years, the market dropped significantly.

A number of Wintergreen managers and legal experts thought that the state's challenge was wrong and that the 2008 appraisal was correct. It had originally passed muster almost three years prior with the Attorney General's office, the State Division of Natural Heritage, and the boards and management of both WPI and the Nature Foundation. This was based on the peak real estate values when the appraisal background work was being done in 2006–08.

Although the audit was conducted in 2011, the commonwealth was authenticating an appraised value as of 2008. Nelson County real estate values remained high in 2008, and although the number of parcels that were sold declined as the economic downturn worsened, neither the average purchase price, nor the county assessment of single family home lots on the mountain fell to the level of the commonwealth's revised appraisal.

"From the beginning of the process," Douglass maintained, "we were very aware of the importance of an accurate, credible appraisal. This easement was under a great deal of scrutiny from the outset because it was one of the largest tracts of land placed under easement in Virginia at that time."

Negotiations with the commonwealth continued for several months. Ultimately, due to the timing of the commonwealth's audit, and the significant legal expense that would have been involved, Wintergreen's attempt to challenge the commonwealth's case was short lived. A now struggling WPI feared potential lawsuits from individuals who had purchased the tax credits.

December of the 2011–12 ski season also delivered the worst financial results in many years. Although WPI now had no outstanding loans with Bank of America, in early January of 2012 the bank informed WPI that it wished to sever ties with Wintergreen. This left WPI without a line of credit, and under the circumstances without the option to secure one. WPI would run out of cash by the end of the summer, and was forced to prepare for the worst: Chapter 11 bankruptcy, or the sale of the resort.

The membership was informed of the seriousness of the situation, and once again stepped forward. In February and March a large percentage of members agreed to pay dues and fees for the membership year that wouldn't even begin for several months. These payments provided a lifeline that allowed for an orderly transition.

Settlement was reached with the commonwealth on the tax credits, creating a $2,500,000 liability, and the commonwealth agreed to a late payment schedule in recognition of the situation, considering also the

importance of Wintergreen as the economic engine of the local economy. As WPI moved through the spring of 2012, available cash continued to dwindle, and efforts to sell the resort or file Chapter 11 moved forward. Few outside investors were interested in buying Wintergreen when bankruptcy and a bottom dollar acquisition price seemed imminent.

At the eleventh hour, the James C. Justice Companies made an offer to purchase Wintergreen Resort, and to do so without the need to file Chapter 11. As part of the purchase, they agreed to pay the liability to the commonwealth, to pay all interest and principle on the remaining $7,000,000 in outstanding private placement notes, to offer partial payments to the equity owners of WPI, and to accept all other obligations of WPI. Equity members did not receive the full value of their equity, but were offered the opportunity to rejoin the club at a substantially reduced rate.

The Justice purchase converted WPI from a non-stock membership corporation to a privately held corporation wholly owned by the James C. Justice

Jack Daly and David Juergens

Companies, Inc. To some, Justice arrived just in time to save the resort. To others, this was one more instance in Wintergreen's history of not having enough time to figure out how to keep the resort owned by the membership. The following stories relate the struggle within the community and how hard it was to make the decision.

Jack Daly and his wife, Gloria, fell in love with Wintergreen and bought a condo in 1984, coming down for weekends from their home in the Maryland suburbs of Washington, DC. Eventually they sold their condo and moved to a house on the first green of the Devils Knob Golf Course.

Jack thrives on activity, and he's served on nearly every board that has to do with Wintergreen since he and his wife, Gloria, retired and became full-time residents in 1999. Some of his favorite volunteer work was with the rescue squad.

Daly also served on the WPI board from 2000 to 2006, and was serving on the WPOA board when major decisions were being made concerning the sale of the resort. He described his tenure on the WPI board as, "a board that was constantly going through challenges, but we always seemed to be able to reach the next year. When the ski season was good, we made money and spent it. When we had a bad season, we borrowed money and spent it!" When he first acquainted himself with WPI's budgeting process, he was amazed to find that there was no provision for unexpected expenses in the form of a rainy-day fund.

Daly had also served on the board of the Nature Foundation and currently chairs the Sara Ott Golf Tournament. Coleman good-naturedly said of his tenure, "If Jack is on your board, you can expect to have things shaken up pretty regularly in a good way." Daly said of himself, "I can't stand people who complain about things but won't do anything. I complain, but I'm willing to work on solving the problem."

Like others before him, Daly thinks that it would have been easier and more equitable if all property owners had been required to be members of WPI. This might have resolved the entire debt issue by spreading it out over many more individuals instead of just the subset that became WPI, but it was a legally complicated issue.

This question has been asked many times over the years and there is not an easy answer. While we often try to interpret yesterday's history by today's standards (20/20 hindsight), we must look at the original by-laws of the Wintergreen Property Owners Association (WPOA). The structure of the bylaws did not anticipate a need to purchase or operate commercial resort facilities on a large scale, and changing them required a super majority vote.

Motivating that majority to vote themselves a significant financial responsibility was probably correctly judged as an unlikely scenario when Wintergreen Partners was formed. The original WPI membership purchase of the resort became essentially a volunteer effort by a subset of owners.

As implied in a previous chapter, had Payne had more time in negotiating with Bankers Trust instead of the ninety days they gave him, he might have worked out just such an arrangement. Many Wintergreen Development personnel and realtors remember what a tough job it was to sell enough original rights of membership to pay off Bankers Trust. As it was, Payne considered it a miracle to have pulled off the purchase of the resort by a volunteer subset of the property owners, something that had not been attempted before.

During the recent years as it became apparent that the resort might be sold, the WPI members were asked for a vote of support for the sale and Jack felt he was asked to go along with the potential sale without knowing enough about it. He was one of the very few WPI members who voted against it. He would have preferred filing Chapter 11 to get time to resolve the issue and keep the WPI owners in control.

John Coy is also a Wintergreen resident, but he had a very different view of the events that led up to the sale of Wintergreen. He was elected to the WPI board in 2006, and served until 2012. He was vice chairman from 2007–08. John agrees that previous boards may have oversold the hotel plan and associated capital investments, which led to some of Wintergreen's debt.

By 2007, Coy said, "It was clear the existing leadership was not going to take us into the future and the WPI board elected a new chairman and Hank Thiess was hired as general manager. Thiess came from Durango, Colorado, and had a long history in the resort business. His role was to "right size" resort operations.

Coy also humorously agrees that hindsight tends to be more accurate only after an unpredictably bad ski season. The resort was heavily leveraged on the basis of ski season profits, and plans were carried out as if the building of a hotel was a given.

Coleman remembered, "When the bank called the notes, and everyone was working past midnight to get the private offering going, John was the key to making it happen. People trusted him."

Fortune's Ridge

They easily raised $3,500,000, but many were not signing on because the notes were not secured. Everything depended on whether or not Bank of America would allow Stoney Creek resort amenities to be used as collateral. The bank was waffling, so Coy called the bank manager at home.

The bank manager happened to be just leaving the house on the way to the hospital because he had such severe back pain. Coy admitted, "It was one of the rudest moments of my life. I said 'I don't care; I need your email allowing Stoney Creek amenities as collateral to move this note forward.'" And he got it! Ultimately $7,500,000 was raised, as people were happy with the healthy 7 percent annual interest rate that was offered.

The tax credits revenue and the private placement offering that John had worked on, along with several good ski seasons, paid off Bank of America entirely—the remaining debt was the private placement of seven million plus interest (debt to owners) and the state tax credit liability, but Bank of America still refused WPI a line of credit based on its perception of WPI's precarious financial position

Unfortunately the winter of 2010–11 was particularly bad, and then notice came from the commonwealth that the Crawford Knob easement had been audited and revalued, leaving WPI with a $2.5 million settlement liability. The WPI board found itself between a rock and a hard place. In Coy's view a sale was infinitely preferable to filing for Chapter 11.

Wintergreen Resort from the beginning operated the commercial facilities under one umbrella. This provided the opportunity to market and promote the entire resort in a consistent, cohesive manner, and to operate the facilities as one entity.

When Wintergreen Resort was offered for sale, concern was expressed that it might be broken up into pieces and sold to various owners as a stand-alone ski area, separate golf courses, a tennis operation, and restaurants. This would have resulted in conflicted visions and strategies by the various owners.

The resort would have lost the ability to promote itself as a total four-season resort where business agreements could be reached by dealing with one entity. This might also have spelled the end of the environmental umbrella that meant so much to Wintergreen's property owners, employees, and others who loved the place.

Consultants were brought in, and they came to the conclusion that Wintergreen should be sold. There were only a few groups interested in buying it. Coy was still on the board, and on the transition committee. When Justice appeared with his lawyer, they were interested in learning the asking price.

Coy commented, "I said $16,500,000. Within a very short period of time, Justice's lawyer delivered a *hand-written* check for $1,000,000 to ensure that Wintergreen cease negotiations with any other interested buyers.

For Coy, what made the deal with Justice a lifesaver was Justice's willingness to pay off not just the state, but the operational liabilities and the member note holders as well. He also agreed to reimburse WPI members for some portion of their membership equity.

"What Justice did," said Coy, "was swayed by both business interest and sentiment. He had played golf with his father on the Devils Knob course, and that turned out to be his father's last golf game. He had every intent of making a longer-term relationship with Wintergreen, but it turned out he couldn't give it his attention."

As part of the purchase agreement with the Justice organization, a five-million-gallon water holding tank was constructed under an agreement with the Nelson County Service Authority. All agreed that this was

a much-needed capital investment. Moreover, with the additional pumping capacity, it also effectively doubled the amount of water available for snowmaking and increased the supply for potable water and fire protection in case of emergency.

The Justice organization further built a very attractive extension to the terrace at the Devils Grill Restaurant and refurbished the conference facilities at the Mountain Inn. Part of this investment was financed with the money raised through membership initiation fees and dues.

Those who decided not to join no longer had access to facilities on Devils Knob including the golf course, tennis courts, aquatics and fitness center, and the Devils Grill Restaurant. The same rules applied to the Stoney Creek Pool, and the Tennis and Fitness Center. The ski facilities, Stoney Creek Golf Course, children's facilities, and the other restaurants remained open to the general public as well as to the property owners. Obviously not everyone was happy with the exclusivity of this arrangement.

There were two schools of thought on the issue of which is more financially sustainable: the complete exclusivity of the membership or the inclusion of all with an option to pay a daily user fee. If the residents could use these facilities while paying daily fees, community good will would result. Which arrangement is better for the revenue stream is a debatable question.

Coy's view had always been that the exclusivity created by WPI for facilities and club use under the Justice Corporations became necessary in order to make membership attractive, and to have residents take the concept seriously.

In the short term, the sale seemed a perfect match, as Justice also owned The Greenbrier Hotel, a luxury resort and spa at White Sulphur Springs in the mountains of West Virginia. The end game, commented Coleman, "was punctuated by random pieces of unfortunate timing." Coy summed it up with this statement: "The years 2000–2012 were times of optimism, success,…and disappointment." The result was that the commercial part of the Wintergreen community entered another era in another century as a for-profit corporation.

Keeping the Promise

Is ecologically sensitive development an oxymoron, or is Wintergreen part of the proof that it can be done? Here's what George Nicklas, whose name is synonymous with construction at Wintergreen, had to say about it. He was speaking at a series of three Nelson County community events featuring those who had a hand in making Wintergreen the place it is today.

"I've told you tonight what we built in the early days of Wintergreen, but now let me tell you what we did not build. We didn't build the yellow lady slippers that bloom out here at the old sawmill site in Chestnut Springs. We didn't build the rocks that have become known as The Plunge. We didn't build the stately oaks that have stood as sentinels atop Devils Knob for decades. We certainly did not build the inspirational sunrises that can be seen from the Wintergreen Drive Overlook, or the majestic sunsets that can be witnessed from the Three Ridges Overlook."

We have referred to the importance of Charles Fraser in championing the idea of making nature the star and the built environment subservient to it in his development of Sea Pines Plantation on Hilton Head.

Jim Chaffin, a preeminent salesman and marketer, pointed out that a whole generation of planners, sales people, and architects cut their teeth working for Fraser.

It became difficult for developers to differentiate themselves from other developers, Chaffin felt. All resorts provided the amenities expected of them by potential buyers; they had the promised swimming pools, tennis courts and golf courses. They had the same "hardscape," a certain generic resort look.

Muller was able to obtain a transcript of a presentation at an industry conference where Chaffin urged his listeners to differentiate the developments they were working on by emphasizing the "softscape" that could make their development unique. This could be a tangible asset, like the preservation of natural areas. It could also be intangible assets—property owners who have been persuaded to consider themselves stewards of the land, or a feeling among residents that they lived in a cohesive, friendly community.

Commented Chaffin, "I have been in the South Carolina woods for a long time with rich people, and

they don't always act according to what they tell you."

He also warned that 60% of Americans think of themselves as environmentalists, which he calls "baloney,." They just want to be thought of that way. It takes strong leaders to actually turn them into conservationists.

His point was to remember that people are lazy.

They will verbally support volunteer initiatives but then fail to show up when the time comes. It takes true leaders to inculcate a vision and to initiate programs that build this sense of stewardship and belonging.

The Big Survey was lucky enough to have Don Faulkner determined to find its highest and best use, and to go on to develop a vision that Jim Wheat

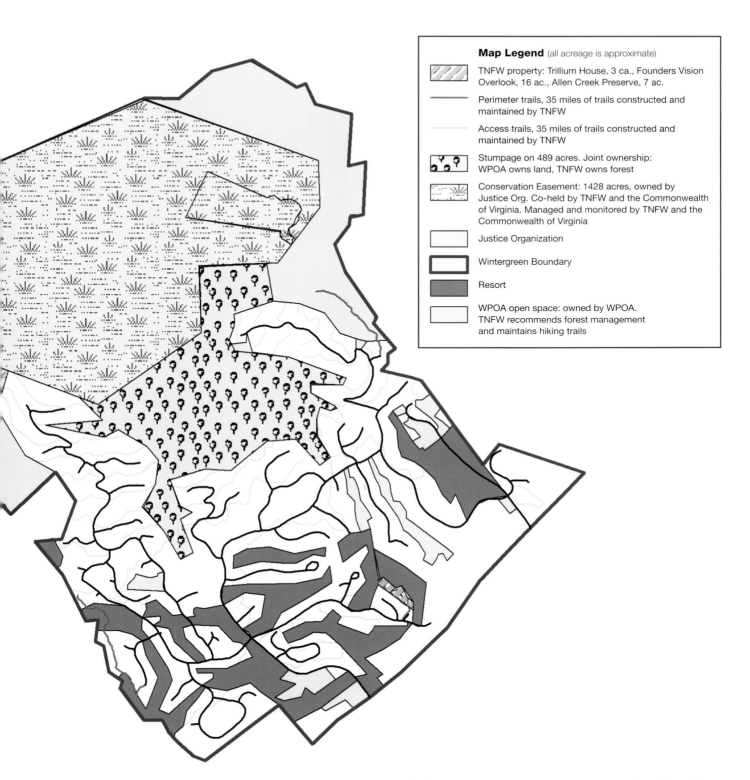

Map Legend (all acreage is approximate)

TNFW property: Trillium House, 3 ca., Founders Vision Overlook, 16 ac., Allen Creek Preserve, 7 ac.

Perimeter trails, 35 miles of trails constructed and maintained by TNFW

Access trails, 35 miles of trails constructed and maintained by TNFW

Stumpage on 489 acres. Joint ownership: WPOA owns land, TNFW owns forest

Conservation Easement: 1428 acres, owned by Justice Org. Co-held by TNFW and the Commonwealth of Virginia. Managed and monitored by TNFW and the Commonwealth of Virginia

Justice Organization

Wintergreen Boundary

Resort

WPOA open space: owned by WPOA. TNFW recommends forest management and maintains hiking trails

could see in his mind's eye, even though he was blind. Because it was such a massive, bold, almost unthinkably difficult project, it attracted scores of professional consultants and workers, many of whom gave the whole of their working lives to it, and felt an enormous pride in what they accomplished.

Timing was on Wintergreen's side when the idea of a four-seasons resort community was first floated; it was after the economic and physical devastation wrought by Hurricane Camille. The county was on its knees, so a plan that would drastically enlarge both the tax base and the number of jobs available was immediately looked at with favor by county planners and supervisors.

Timing also played a part in the hiring done to manage Wintergreen. Just when they were needed, the "VMI mafia" appeared, and the Darden Business School at UVa graduated the likes of L. F. Payne and Larry Rutherford. What older, wiser heads would have called unacceptable risk, these young men called opportunity.

Timing was also of the utmost importance as Cabot, Cabot and Forbes was making the switch to a new interest in resort community development. The youthful consultants at RTKL and Gladstone Associates had earned the confidence of CC&F.

CC&F sent Gary Green to be manager. He promptly fell in love with the place. Green hired L. F. Payne with whom he got along well, and the two of them hired George Nicklas to build the Devils Knob Golf Course. After the golf course project, Nicklas moved into other construction on the mountain, ending up in charge of development at Wintergreen.

Doug Coleman, awestruck by what he saw of ancient ecosystems at Wintergreen, caught the vision so clearly that he was patient enough in the beginning to do what he could around the edges to alert everyone to the beauty and unique qualities of the Wintergreen landscape. Finally the time came when his message was so central to Wintergreen that he went on the staff as resident biologist, and oversaw the creation of the nature program at Wintergreen.

Coleman's gig was education, which harks back to the adage: "You preserve what you care about, you care about what you know, you know what someone taught you." He had the common sense to translate his scientific knowledge into language anyone could understand, and the passion to pass it on to the sales people, who used it with huge effect in motivating buyers. These buyers became property owners who caught the bug and took a proprietary interest in furthering the vision.

Chaffin talked about turning beneficiaries into benefactors. Property owners whom Coleman won over to help in his transplantation projects often went on to become volunteers, trip leaders, and board members of the Nature Foundation and other organizations at Wintergreen, as well as hugely generous benefactors to the Nature Foundation and its initiatives.

When the bugaboos of warm winters and economic recessions hit, Bankers Trust stepped in where CC&F had failed. When New York banking laws caused Bankers Trust to have to step aside, the great experiment of ownership of the resort by property owners through Wintergreen Partners Inc. took over. When the judge's ruling in the lawsuit stymied WDI, Donovan and the salesmen scrambled and came up with High Country Associates. When debts caused WPI to fold, John Coy and others raced against time to avoid bankruptcy and find a buyer.

In each instance time was of the essence; with more time, better solutions might have been reachable. However, what is remarkable is that in each case, what Coleman calls "Renaissance men" stepped forward to save Wintergreen, its landscape, and its culture.

There has also been an on-going phenomenon of quiet generosity. Wintergreen workers who have simultaneously worked on a college degree have gotten help when they needed it. There have been many instances of Wintergreen members willing to step forward sacrificially with both money and effort at precarious times.

And then there are quiet philanthropists who routinely give whether times are precarious or not. Gordon and Mary Beth Smyth have given generously for years to scholarship funds for Nelson County students. Gordon has died, but Mary Beth's generosity continues to focus on educational issues in the county, to the benefit of both teachers and students.

Donovan is an active and well-loved philanthropist who has helped many causes in Nelson County, including Habitat for Humanity and the schools. He has also worked on many county development issues. He has a great love for Wintergreen, and has made significant contributions to Wintergreen's non-profits, including the Nature Foundation, Wintergreen Performing Arts, and Wintergreen Adaptive Sports.

Work at Wintergreen held a great deal of allure for young people, Jim Rankin made clear. Employees could ski free at night, and "The mix of local, valley, and mountain people made for a strong employee base." Romance thrived to such an extent that it took on elements of a soap opera, with new developments weekly. As Rankin put it, "The gossipers coined the resort 'As the Mountain Turns.' Many hearts were broken and many marriages made."

Jim Chaffin felt strongly that what is needed in

creating an environmentally sensitive development is more humility in the face of nature. "Think more," he cautioned, "about how to help people enjoy it, and less about how to change it."

Yet the tension is always present—weighing the effort to remain humble in the face of nature, even when styles change and clients want bigger and bigger houses with more and more amenities. There is no point in preserving nature but then losing the resort to bankruptcy. Nor is there any point in adopting a laissez-faire approach to architecture that in a decade or two will destroy the goose that laid the golden egg.

So the answer, the only answer, is to maintain a balance between the two extremes. To quote Byron Cooper, again, "All of us recognize that preservation of the natural environment of the mountainous interior of The Big Survey is an absolute requirement, and represents an inescapable restraint on its use."

Does this "inescapable restraint" still exist forty years later? Will it continue to guide future owners and managers of Wintergreen? That will depend on its residents' love of the land, and their commitment to maintaining that restraint. It will also depend on the vigilance of future generations to whom the Wintergreen ethos has been passed down.

They need to be willing to take on the stewardship of the land. To quote Peter Farley, again, "It's not a theme, it's a religion, a commitment." Hopefully its owners will continue to understand that the "nature piece" is a huge part of Wintergreen's draw. It is a monumental asset that qualifies as both tangible and intangible.

To understand its importance, you need to be with a new buyer, as Farley was recently when he sold the home of a couple that had cherished Wintergreen and worked hard to conserve its beauty. The new owners knew nothing yet about the history of Wintergreen, but had been overwhelmed by the magnificence around them. They were joyous over their purchase and full of hope. Perhaps they sensed that it is on them and their ilk that the future of Wintergreen will depend.

In the sixteenth year of the new century, what we are asking them to do is to help keep the promise. The promise, which guided the Wintergreen master plan, was to preserve and protect well over half of the undisturbed nature and ecology of Wintergreen from development.

Those who have figured in this book have kept the promise. Of the original 13,000 acres, significantly more than half is in open space. This includes Crawford Knob (1,400 acres), the sale of Humpback Mountain to the Park Service (2,700 acres), the 5,000–6,000 acres of common open space owned and managed by the Property Owners Association and protected by covenants, and over 2,000 acres owned or managed by The Nature Foundation at Wintergreen.

In the Prologue, Coleman pointed out, "While we cannot live in the past, a vision of what it took to create Wintergreen should set a precedent for the future." Our hope for this book is that it enlarges understanding of what an audacious vision it was, and how difficult it was to bring to reality. Keeping the promise is a debt we need to pay to those who refused to accept that it couldn't be done.

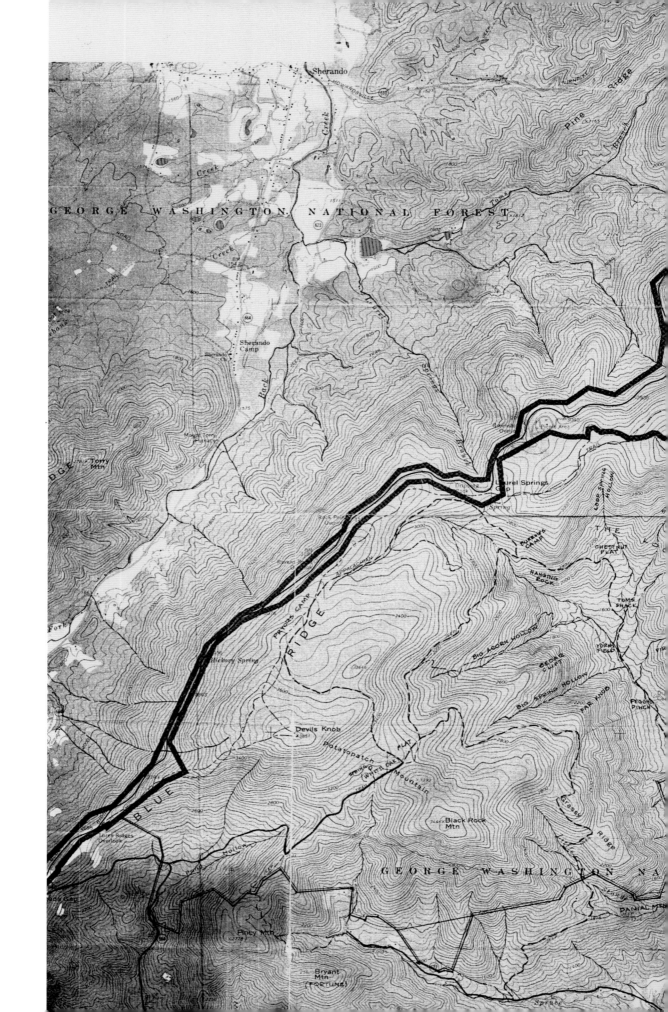

Topographic
map of The Big
Survey

Truslow's, AKA "The Bullet Burger"

The Wintergreen Family Album

T. L. Baldwin "holding court 'til the expert gets there"

Emma Fitzgerald enduring another day with George Nicklas

John Taggert with the latest telecommunications equipment.

Mike Thomas, welcome to Wintergreen

Warren Griffin and Jim Kneas in the good old days

Phyllis Fortune planning
her next prank

Hi, I'm Nancy Donnelly

Courtney Pfister—
always up

Kate Caldwell

Gordon and Helen Bormann and Janet St. Pierre

Henry Nowak

Gary Horvath, early salesman

Jimmy Ballowe and Shari Wilbur

John, Cecelia, and Gavin Soscia, Don Faulkner's family

Warren Griffin demonstrating the jaws of life

Don Fitzgerald in a happy moment

Nature Foundation forester Josh Palumbo at work tapping a sugar maple tree at Wintergreen

Smithsonian scientist Dr. Dennis Whigham and long-term Nature Foundation staff member Liz Salas Fravel

Dobie Fish and faithful companion, Ember

Mickey Graves

Brenda Coffey

Donna Hughes

Gunter and Joost Muller confer with Betsy Dunkerton.

Ski Area Manager John Kirchner

James Jackson

Accounting staff: Back Row: Linda Ward, Phyllis Fortune. Larry Delizia, Janet St. Pierre
Front Row: Pat Burton, Melanie Harris, Kathy Hughes, Dan Schablein, Teresa Robertson

Uel Gardner, Frank Armentrout, and Tony Waddell

Ronny Ponton, Dean Hostetter, and Bob Ruff having too much fun

Miss Russia and Gunter Muller

Susie Seaman and Gunter Muller. The buck stops here.

Dan Schablein and Linda Ward, accounting

Jack Bickart, Mark Glickman, and Dan Schablein share a happy moment.

John Givens, conference sales

Dana Percival, assistant resort manager

Mark Glickman describing his next marketing scheme to Gunter Muller

Nancy Donnelly, Nancy Coppage, and Avis Gianini

The women of Wintergreen—tough, competent, and capable resort staff. Front row, l-r: Marie Dennis, meeting speaker, ?, Melissa ?, Melissa Robinson, Anne Marie Nock, Jennifer Hughes, Linda Armentrout. Row 2: Helen Driver, Betty Fitzgerald, Debra Sheffer, Becky Henderson, Cynthia Wilkerson, April Lockatel?, Kristi Reynolds, Peggy Olson, ?. Row 3: Margaret Seaman, Linda Ward, Cheryl Miller, Elizabeth Patterson, Heidi Ferris, Kathie Johnson, ?, Betsy Dunkerton, ?, Robbie Keep, La Donna Kurpel, Page Bowman, Mrs. Popkin, Nancy Donnelly, Darlene Aldridge, conference facilitators.

Deborah Sheffer, Dave Zunker, Gunter and Joost Muller

Lynn Tyler, food and beverage director

Sara and Frank Ott, founders of the Sara Ott Golf Tournament

Fred Biggers, golf superintendent

L–R: Russell Otis, Mickey Graves, and Brenda Southall

Frank Ott

L–R: Mary Beth Smyth, Iantha Peterson, and Brian Koster

L–R: Marj Gourley, Des Gourley, Ruth Wales (front), Maurice Wood

L–R: Gordon Smyth and Henry Weems

L–R: Chip Morgan, Rosalind Rowe, Corin Rowe, and Dahne Morgan

L–R: Gerry Sarich, Jan Fitch, and Jim Dunlop

L–R: Pam Gallery, Claire Owen, Marion Butler, and Iantha Peterson

ACKNOWLEDGEMENTS

Wintergreen has been blessed over the years by the contributions of many, many exemplary employees and contractors. While the list below is an attempt to recognize those non-seasonal long term employees and others whose timely contributions may have meant the difference between success and failure, we know that there are those we missed.

For all of you who were inadvertently missed, please know that we are grateful for your efforts in making Wintergreen a special place and also know that we are all connected in the ownership and legacy of its success.

WINTERGREEN EMPLOYEES

Jerry Acheson	Clarkie Campbell	Bill Earp	Don Gordon	Alfred Hudson
Phyliss Ammons	Cameron Carroll	Bob Evans	Kathy Gordon	Kathy Hughes
Stephen Anderson	Dick Carroll	Kenneth Falls	Barbara Gormes	Robert Hunt
Sheila Anderson	Leslie Carter	Ray Falls	Billy Gormes	Melissa Hutchinson
Gene Angle	Alfred Carter, Sr	Peter Farley	Rick Gould	Dercilla Jackson
Frank Armentrout	Michael Cash	Don Faulkner	Mickey Graves	Tom Jackson
Morgan Armstrong	Keith Cassidy	Frank Feeney	Gary Green	Bill Jackson
Hilda Ashley	Richard Chaddick	Emily Ferguson	Betty Green	James Jackson, Jr
Tommy Ashley	Pat Ciavola	Ricky Fields	Warren Griffin	Jen Jenkins
Cindy Ashley	Larry Coates	Dobie Fish	Ken Grover	Elaine Johnson
Bob Ashton	Cindy Cobb	Herbert Fisher	Judy Gumm	Vance Johnson
T.L. Baldwin	Bumpy Coffee	Alfred Fisher	Laverne Hale	Tommy Johnson
Pete Balin	Brenda Allen Coffey	Jean Fitzgerald	Edward Hamner	Ronald Kemp
Jimmy Ballowe	Robert Cole	Becky Fitzgerald	Nick-Edward Hamner	Jeff Kessler
Debbie Ballowe	Doug Coleman	Roger Fitzgerald	Stan Hardy	Joe Kincaid
Dorothy Ballowe	Paxton Collins	Emma Fitzgerald	Melanie Harris	John Kirchner
Randy Banks	Todd Cook	Toby Fitzgerald	Kathy Harris	Steve Kiser
Mikie Banks	Nancy Coppage	Warren Fitzgerald	Theresa Harris	Jim Kneas
Mitchell Barker	Gary Cornwell	Harvie Fitzgerald	Tim Harschutz	Lorrie Knies
Grayson Beale	Laura Covert	Don Fitzgerald	Richard Hatch	Liane Kolaski
Jack Bickart	Tucker Crolius	Fuzzy Fitzgerald	Gene Haus	Avis Laeng
Fred Biggers	Mike Davidson	Betty Fitzgerald	Becky Henderson	Pam Lang
Phil Birdsong	Joe Davis	Jane Fitzgerald	Leigh-Ann Hensley	Len LaSala
Sharon Bloom	Joyce Davis	Jean Fitzgerald	Nancy Hernan-	Doug Lawhorne
Helen Bormann	Doug Deaton	Raymond Fitzgerald	dez-Newell	Sue Ellen Lee
Gordon Bormann	Bar Delk	Phyllis Fortune	Tim Hess	Eva Lowe
Page Bowman	John Dobson, M.D.	Liz Fravel	Lester Hibbs	Reed Lunsford
Deane Brandon Jr	Wanda Dodd	Barbara Frazier	Andy Hickman	Sid Lyda
Dondi Brandon	Nancy Donnelly	Julie Froesh	Lee Hilbert	Kyle Lynn
Bob Brent	Linda Ramsey Don-	Uel Gardner	Martha Hill	Shirley Marshall
Richard Buckingham	ovan	Sandy Gardner	Earle Holliday	Diane Martin
Jim Butler	Brent Douglass	David Garwood	Susan Holliday	Don Martin
Lilly Butler	Andy Dow	Avis Gianini	Tommy Holliday	Lawrence Martin
Kate Caldwell	Peggy Dowgwilla	Dave Gilbert	Dima Holmes	Cub Massie
Kay Campbell	Helen Driver	Ed Gilliam	Chuck Hopkinson	Mike Mayer
Clark Campbell	Betsy Dunkerton	John Givens	Gary Horvath	Kimberly Mays
Bruce Campbell	Roberta Holly Duncan	Diane Givens	Dean Hostetter	Sterling McCann
Steve Campbell	Kate Durkee	Mark Glickman	Wes Hubbard	Doug McGregor

180

Dave McLucas
Tim Merrick
Robin Meyer
Michael Miles
Karen Miller
Doug Molineaux
Chris Monteleon
Richard Moore
French More III
Gunter Muller
Nancy Newell
Bo Newell
Roger Newport
George Nicklas
Rita Nicklas
Henry Nowak
Fred Nowak
Stan Olah
Karen Osborne
Russell Otis
Josh Palumbo
Gary Parker
Billy Parrish
Phil Patterson
L.F. Payne
Bill Peacher
Charlie Peake
Janis Pendleton
Dana Percival

Courtney Pfister
Eric Pfister
Ronnie Ponton
Ruth Prevette
Stephanie Quigley
Randy Randal
Jim Rankin
Kristi Reynolds
Jay Roberts
Dennis Roberts
Clay Robinson
Charlie Rowe
Leslie Rowe
Rosalind Rowe
Bob Ruff
Larry Rutherford
Don Rutledge
Stuart Sadler
Paul St. Pierre
Janet St. Pierre
Dan Schablein
Jonathan Schilling
Susie Seaman
Bud Shaw
Jessie Shaw
Curtis Sheets
Debra Sheffer
Nici Singletary, MD
Wayne Sites

Bob Smith
Stephen Smith
Ron Smith
Ray Snably
Debi Snyder
Jim Snyder
Debra Snyder
Melinda Souder
Brenda Southall
Ed Spears
Earling Speer
Wilma Stevens
Lelia Stevens
John Taggart
Bill Taylor
Janet Taylor
Jerry Terry
Hank Thiess
Connie Thomas
Michael Thomas
Randy Thompson
Melissa Thompson
Charlie Thompson
Cindy Thompson
Geoff Truslow
Judy Truslow
Greg Truslow
Greg Turner
Lynn Tyler

Ty Tyler
George Vest
Tony Waddell
Betty Wade
Marguerite Wade
Jack Wade
O.J. Wade
Millie Wade
Betty Walker
Linda Ward
Helen Warring
Rebecca Watkins
Jackie Whalen
Jimmy Wheat
Fred Wilbur
Shari Wilbur
Mac Wilcox
Robert Steve Wilson
Charlie Wineberg
Nina Wood
Val Wood
Robbie Wood
Karen Wortman
Jimmy Wright
Andy Yowell
Jan Yowell
Dave Zunker

CONTRACTORS, CONSULTANTS, ARCHITECTS, ENGINEERS, OTHERS

Bill Attwood
Fred Bainbridge
Jerry Bartholomew
Mike Boggs
Brock & Davis Construction
Hank Brown
Byron Cooper
Jay Dagliesh
Floyd Dean
Jerry Dixon
Dufresne-Henry Engineering
Dunbar, Milbey, Associates, Structural
    Engineering
E. O. Gooch, Geologist
Eggleston & Thelen
Ellis Maples & Son Golf Architects
Environmental Systems Service

Frank Black Construction
Gloeckner, Lincoln & Osborne
Gordon Larew, Geotechnical Enginer
Gregg, Wood & Brown
Warren Griffin
H & F Construction
Halley, Chisholm & Morris Const.
Sel Hannah
Ivy Construction
J. E. Jamerson & Sons
J.M. Turner Construction
James Harris & Sons Const.
Jerry Saunders & Sons Const.
Gerald Johnson
Mathews Soil Consultants
Moss Construction
Joel Myers

Neilsen Construction
Rees Jones Golf Architects
Fred Rogers
RTKL Associates
S. L. Key Surveying
Saunders Construction
Sayre & Southerland
Sno-Engineering
Talley, Erwin Associates
Ciff Taylor
Torrence Construction
Margaret Wade
Jack Wade
O.J. Wade
Wiley & Wilson Engineers
Charlie Winnenberg

Index